TIGER IN THE COURT

TIGER IN THE COURT

Herbert J. Stern:
The U.S. Attorney who prosecuted
8 Mayors, 2 Secretaries of State,
2 State Treasurers, 2 powerful political
bosses, 1 U.S. Congressman...
and 64 other public officials

Paul Hoffman

A PLAYBOY PRESS BOOK

CONTENTS

1. The Congressman Cops Out 1
2. The Making of a Prosecutor 15
3. Introduction to Justice . . . and Jersey 33
4. A New Team Takes Over 59
5. A Tale of Two Tapes 73
6. The Unmaking of Mayor Addonizio 101
7. Memoirs of Hudson County 139
8. The Senator Advises, The President Consents 174
9. Sons of Hudson County 190
10. Stranded in the Sludge 210
11. Stern's "French Connection" 221
12. Rattling Republican Skeletons 241
13. A Prosecutor's Philosophy 264
    Appendix: Herbert Stern's Who's Who of
       New Jersey Politics 274
    Notes 287

PREFACE

This is the story of slightly more than three years in the history of a prosecutor's office—that of the U.S. attorney for the district of New Jersey. To say that those years were typical would be absurd, for few—perhaps no—prosecutors in American history have compiled so sensational a record in so short a time span as have Frederick Lacey and Herbert Stern.

I have tried to put the story in perspective, to relate it to what has gone before and to what is going on elsewhere. The story is not complete. It would require a multivolume encyclopedia to give a full account of even the 45 months since September 2, 1969. In so short a space one can only skim the cream.

Nor is the story finished. As I write, the office has launched another major investigation into payola and dope-dealing in the pop-record industry, an inquiry that promises more headlines and which has already caused the ouster of the president of Columbia Records. And the office's investigations of political corruption continue unabated.

I have chosen to tell the story through Herbert Stern—in part because his career spans the entire time sequence; in part because I have had a personal relationship with him going back more than a decade. But the story is equally that of Fred Lacey, who built the office; of Senator Clifford Case, who was determined that it would be and would stay independent; and of the men and women—some known to me, some not—who made it function. This book is dedicated to all of them.

Paul Hoffman
June 16, 1973

TIGER IN THE COURT

1
THE CONGRESSMAN COPS OUT

Until six months before, he had been a United States Congressman, the ranking Democrat on the House Foreign Affairs Committee, widely recognized as an expert on the Far East and hailed by many as a champion of civil liberties. Nine years before, Lyndon Johnson had considered him as a possible vice-presidential running mate.

At 53, his yellow hair showed streaks of white, but his pink face still had the cherubic look of an altar boy. But it was not the deed of an altar boy that had brought him before the bar of justice. Cornelius E. Gallagher had pleaded guilty to evading $78,000 in income taxes and stood before Federal District Judge Leonard I. Garth not as a member of a co-equal branch of government, but as a supplicant pleading for mercy.

He peered through metal-rimmed glasses at the notes he'd scrawled on sheets of a yellow legal pad and reviewed his life aloud—starting with his boyhood days as a bootblack on the streets of Bayonne to working his way through college and law school, to combat service in World War II and recall to active duty during Korea to his rise in politics from Hudson County freeholder to state highway commissioner to seven terms in Congress, and finally to the first disclosure by *Life* magazine that all was not legitimate in the career of Cornelius E. Gallagher and the years of investigation by the Internal Revenue Service.

"I was a prisoner without chains for nearly six years," he insisted.

For an hour and 17 minutes he ran on, rambling, repeating, at times almost lapsing into incoherence, except perhaps to those thoroughly familiar with the minute details of his case.

Though he pleaded for mercy, he never truly admitted his guilt, and he again denounced those who had brought him to his present crisis.

"I appeal to this court for leniency in sentence and ask for an opportunity to put my life back together without being put in an institution," he said. He begged Judge Garth for a "second chance" and, removing his glasses, turned toward his wife and four daughters seated in the rear of the tiny courtroom, his voice choking on a sob as he concluded: "I ask . . . that I be allowed a period of redemption and renewal."

Judge Garth was not impressed. He said that his review of the record showed that a "custodial sentence" was indicated. He sentenced Gallagher to two years in prison and fined him $10,000. The sentence was relatively light; the fine was the maximum possible. He also found the Congressman in contempt of court for a letter he had written in violation of a court order and fined him an additional $500.

It was Friday afternoon. The defense attorney asked that the sentence be stayed so Gallagher could spend a last weekend with his family. Judge Garth was reluctant: "If you have an abscessed tooth, the best thing is to get it out fast." But he relented and gave Gallagher his freedom until 9:30 Monday morning.

The Congressman showed up at the appointed hour, and was led off to prison in handcuffs.

That sort of scene occurs in New Jersey these days with refreshing or depressing frequency—depending on whether one is heartened at the sight of corrupt officials going to jail or saddened at the thought that there are so many of them.

"New Jersey," as Terence J. Flanigan recently noted on the Op Ed page of the *New York Times*, "is a small state on the eastern seaboard halfway between Honest John Lindsay and the Liberty Bell. It is best known for its turnpike, Atlantic City, Imamu Baraka, Newark Airport and the *Morro Castle* disaster. Most of its leaders are in jail for stealing money. . . .

"New York and Philadelphia TV channels—the only ones around—rarely mention New Jersey, and then only at the end of the weather report: 'Meanwhile,' the announcer smiles, 'over in the Garden State . . .' and then we are shown another of our leaders entering prison."

Most of them are in prison because of Herbert Stern, the 36-year-old U.S. attorney for the district of New Jersey. Since September 3, 1969—first as chief assistant to Frederick B. Lacey, then as his successor—he has compiled a record of corruption indictments and prosecutions unmatched in the annals of modern law enforcement. The toll is greater than that of the Seabury investigation of the early 1930s, which brought down (but never nailed) New York City Mayor James J. Walker; greater than the "racket-busting" that skyrocketed Thomas E. Dewey to Albany's Governor's Mansion and two shots at the White House; greater even than the 30-year total of Stern's old boss, Manhattan District Attorney Frank Hogan. Indeed, one would have to go back to the breakup of the Tweed Ring a century ago to find a prosecutory parallel.

In the past three and a half years, a total of 79 federal, state and local officials have been indicted by the U.S. attorney's office in New Jersey.* Only a handful of those who've gone to trial have escaped conviction and only a few of those convicted escaped stiff prison sentences. In addition to Congressman Gallagher, the roster includes two successive secretaries of state, two successive state treasurers, a former speaker of the state assembly, a state senator, two commissioners of the Port of New York Authority, the executive director of the Garden State Parkway, plus the mayors and a significant part of the municipal administrations of New Jersey's two largest cities— Newark and Jersey City—its most famous resort—Atlantic City—and a half-dozen lesser communities, a handful of judges, the state's most powerful Democratic "boss" and its most influential Republican party leader.

In the process, the office developed a technique—now being

* For the list, see Appendix.

copied by prosecutors around the country—of going into a community "cold," without a shred of evidence or even a lead where to look, subpoenaing the books and records and combing through them for traces of graft and corruption.

The beneficiaries of the office's techniques include James Thompson, the U.S. Attorney for Chicago, who utilized similar methods in his investigations of Court of Appeals Judge (and former Illinois Governor) Otto Kerner and of various henchmen of Mayor Daley's machine; Whitney North Seymour Jr., the federal prosecutor in Manhattan, who publicly thanked Stern for his help in preparing the indictments of former Attorney General John Mitchell and former Commerce Secretary Maurice Stans in the Vesco case; and George Beall, the U.S. Attorney for Maryland, who met with Stern to learn his methods before launching his investigation of Vice President Agnew.

Given New Jersey's political climate, more often than not, Stern's investigations uncovered evidence of corruption wherever they looked. The problem was not where to look, but where to start. "You'd have to be deaf, dumb and blind not to know the situation was rotten," Stern says. The result, according to *Time* magazine, is that New Jersey now has the unenviable distinction of leading the nation in "discovered corruption."

But justice, in the hands of Lacey and Stern, *was* blind. Unlike most prosecutors, they proved bipartisan in picking their targets, impartially indicting both Democrats and Republicans. As Stern once put it: "The fact remains that there is nobody—absolutely nobody—who has violated the law in New Jersey who is protected by my office."

No target was too big. To the consternation of the State Department, Stern indicted the head of the French secret service on charges of conspiring to smuggle $12 million worth of heroin into the United States.

The office also sent away one of the state's most powerful Mafiosi—Angelo (Gyp) DeCarlo—helped the Organized Crime Strike Force nail another—Simone (Sam the Plumber) DeCavalcante—while a third—Anthony (Tony Boy) Boiardo —escaped probable conviction only by suffering a massive heart attack in midtrial. In prosecuting these overlords of the underworld, the federal prosecutors also spread on the record the shocking documentation of the links between organized crime and the political process in New Jersey—a pattern of illegal alliances previously the province of rumor, fantasy or fiction.

If no target was too big, none was too small either. The roster of public officials nailed by Stern includes the manager of the General Services Administration store in the lobby of Newark's federal building—five floors below the U.S. attorney's office—on charges of fraudulently padding his sales records.

"I suppose next you'll get the shoeshine boy?" an interviewer asked Stern.

"No," the prosecutor replied. "The IRS got him."

Nor have the cases always involved crime and corruption. Stern successfully intervened on behalf of an Elizabeth, New Jersey, family whose rent was hiked $16-a-month beyond the limits of the federal wage-price freeze. And when police on the Palisades Parkway staged an overtime-pay protest by flagging down every car on the road for an on-the-spot inspection, Stern got traffic flowing again by threatening to indict the cops for obstructing interstate commerce.

In conjunction with the federal prosecutors from New York and Brooklyn, he filed the most sweeping environmental action in the nation—against a dozen New Jersey municipalities and municipal agencies and their officers, as well as New York City and Mayor Lindsay, for polluting the Hudson River. On his own ground, Stern obtained an injunction forcing 19 Jersey Shore communities to stop dumping sludge into the Atlantic Ocean—an act that won him rare kudos from consumer crusader Ralph Nader and an award from the Sierra Club.

Yet, these accomplishments have gone relatively unheralded.

"If this were happening in New York," said Jerome Wilson, the political editor of WCBS-TV News, "the media barons would be beside themselves. Who is the man responsible? Who is the chief prosecutor? Get his name. Run him for governor. Run him for president. It is Tom Dewey reincarnate. But the scene is not New York. It's New Jersey and . . . as for running him for high office, the only thing Jersey party regulars talk about running him for is out of state."

One ingenious way was joined in by *both* Stern's supporters and his enemies. Led by politicians of both parties, a group collected 10,000 signatures on a petition to have Stern appointed special prosecutor in the Watergate case. But the new attorney general, Elliott Richardson, chose Harvard law professor Archibald Cox.

Needless to say, such relentless prosecutions of political corruption have left a wake of recriminations. Leaders of both parties in New Jersey have occasionally mounted high horses to denounce first Lacey then Stern not as a reincarnation of Tom Dewey, but of the Inquisition or the Gestapo. And needless to say, those yelling the loudest were usually those closest to indictment.

A few months after he assumed office, when Stern was fielding flak for one investigation, Lacey—by then on the federal bench—sent his successor a note of encouragement: *"Oderint, dum metuant."* (Let them hate, provided that they fear.— Cicero.) It's not a bad motto for a prosecutor.

It's fortunate for Stern that he's something of a loner. "I'm not the most popular man in New Jersey," he acknowledges. It may be the understatement of the year. While the political leaders connived at ways to run the federal prosecutors out of state (or at least out of office), the Mafia bosses and union thugs considered more direct methods of eliminating them. Throughout most of his 17-month tenure as U.S. attorney, Lacey and his family lived under a round-the-clock guard because of threats against them. And on three separate occasions, federal marshals were detailed to protect Stern because of threats from those he'd put behind bars.

However, a few in New Jersey have a different view. Newspaper editorials have sung paeans of praise to the prosecutors and so have some of the attorneys Lacey and Stern bested in court.

"I regard the Lacey-Stern administration as the best thing that's happened to New Jersey in my time—if not ever," said defense attorney Donald Robinson. "The only way we're going to be able to attract honest business and industry is to clean out the corrupt city halls and state capital. I admire the completely unpolitical indictments of those two guys. They're a great breath of fresh air."

And some who stopped to scorn returned to praise. One public official gave a speech denouncing Stern's investigations. A few weeks later he came to the prosecutor with a problem: His electoral opponents were spreading the word that he was about to be indicted.

"What do you want me to do about it?" Stern asked.

The politician didn't know.

But Stern did. He picked up the phone, called the editor of the local paper and squelched the rumor.

The politician—who won reelection—sent Stern a note of thanks, along with a sheet of yellow legal paper on which he'd written 50 times: "I am so sorry I gave 'that' speech on Law Day, 5-1-72."

Occasionally, some "crank" fires off a letter-to-the-editor suggesting that Stern run for governor, or senator or something—without even knowing where he stands on the issues. But Stern himself professes no political ambitions and says his only aspiration is to remain a trial lawyer—in the prosecutor's office or out.

He won't comment on political questions—as a federal employee, he's "Hatched." But he does have some strong views on the issues he confronts in the courtroom: He's against the death penalty—except as a possible deterrent to a lifer's killing a prison guard in an escape attempt, or for "crimes against humanity" like those of Himmler or Eichmann. He thinks that wiretapping is a waste of investigative manpower and, worse, an unwarranted invasion of privacy; he favors it only for surveillance of foreign agents or in investigating crimes like gambling, where the telephone itself is an instrument of the crime. He does *not* believe that marijuana smoking leads to heroin addiction; he favors a scientific study of the weed and, if the study shows that it is not debilitating, would urge the removal of criminal sanctions against its use.

Most important, he feels that political graft and corporate corruption—"crime in the suites," in Ralph Nader's phrase—pose greater threats to society than crime in the streets.

As he put it in a recent speech: "Is it not more important by far that one bank president he deterred from embezzling ten million dollars, as in the case of the [ex-] president of the Eatontown National Bank, than that one bank robber be deterred from stealing ten thousand dollars? Is it not absolutely vital that we insure that those men who make our laws, who administer our laws, who enforce our laws, that these are honest men, or, at the very least, men deterred from dishonesty?"

Strange sentiments indeed for an appointee of the Nixon administration!

But then Stern was no more popular among the wizards of Watergate than he was among the political powers of New Jersey. Attorney General John Mitchell sat on his appointment for more than a year. He became U.S. attorney not *because of* the Nixon administration, but *despite* it. He got the job not through political pull, but through his own demonstrated ability and the luck of being in the right place at the right time.

It's just one of several anomalies in his career as a federal prosecutor. When he was named Lacey's chief assistant, he wasn't a resident of New Jersey. When he became U.S. attorney, he wasn't even a member of the state bar. And for an office that's normally regarded as a patronage plum, he had no political credentials whatsoever; he wasn't a member of a political club, he wasn't even a registered Republican.

In the flesh, Herbert Stern stands six-feet even and weighs 165 pounds, but his slim build makes him appear smaller than he actually is—especially when contrasted with his predecessor Lacey, who has the physique of a football tackle. He also looks younger than his 36 years. A few years back, he was turned away from a Los Angeles nightclub because he couldn't produce proof that he was over 21 and the bouncer wouldn't accept his Justice Department credentials.

To see the slim Stern of today, it's hard to believe that he once weighed a puffy 220. "I went on a crash program to reduce," he says. "Like everything else I do, I did it to excess. I got down to one-forty and found I couldn't function at that weight. So I had to build myself up again." He kept in trim by working out regularly at a gym and, for a while, he even took to toting a bottle of low-calorie salad dressing around with him when he went out to eat.

At 36, Stern is the oldest attorney in the office. The average age of his assistants—Stern paternally likes to call them his "kids"—is 29. He keeps an open-door policy with the staff; any assistant is free to wander into his office to discuss a case. Although Stern's attempts at lighthearted banter usually seem forced, there's a genial camaraderie between the prosecutor and his staff. But he expects his assistants to work as hard as he does and he likes them to be lean, hungry and aggressive.

Though the accent is on youth, there's nothing "mod" about Stern's style. It's pure organization man. His suits are dark and narrow-lapelled; his ties thin and somber-striped. In recent months, he's let his curly brown hair grow a little longer on top and his sideburns have inched down, but he keeps closely cropped around the ears and neck. His only concession to sartorial flamboyance is monogrammed white-on-white shirts with French cuffs that extend three inches beyond his coat sleeves.

Similarly, inside the courtroom there's nothing flamboyant about Stern's style—no headline-hunting, jury-swinging histrionics, no dramatic gestures, just a patient, plodding piling of fact on fact. An observer at one of Stern's summations would be hard put to find a phrase that sticks in the mind.

But he's a tiger in the court, possessing a prosecutor's instinct for the jugular. The story is apocryphal, but apt. During a recess in one case, Stern was walking rapidly down the courthouse corridor. A few feet ahead, a defendant dropped his briefcase. Without stopping or breaking stride, Stern stepped on it.

As a prosecutor, his chief forte is a computerlike memory for detail—an essential in the complex corruption cases he tries. It's not a natural gift, but a talent developed by dogged determination and laborious study. Stern estimates that ten hours' preparation is required for every hour in court.

Yet he has mastered some subtler tricks of the trade. He cultivates a jury as carefully as a florist does his delicate orchids, nodding individually to each juror as he enters the box. When opposing witnesses are on the stand, Stern will glance at the jury box, indicating with a grimace, snicker or an arched eyebrow a message like, "Do you really believe that?"

He has also developed the knack of making himself and his cause appear the embodiment of all virtue. Without bantering patriotic slogans, he manages to enfold himself in the flag. It's never "the prosecution rests," or "the government rests," but always "the United States rests."

Though some courthouse observers labeled him "Herbert the Hawk," some defense attorneys—and their clients—sneer at him as a "boy scout." The attitude even infects the bench. During the Hudson County trial—in which Stern successfully prosecuted seven of Jersey City's ranking political figures—Judge Robert Shaw once snapped at him: "Sit down, Mr. Stern! I'm getting just a little tired of your boy scout antics." At such rebukes, Stern is likely to fall back into his chair with a look of injured innocence—"Who me?"

Yet even those he's bested—and he's yet to lose a case he's personally tried—admit a grudging admiration for his ability. Bernard Hellring, who defended Newark's Mayor Hugh Addonizio—and who continues to protest Addonizio's innocence—summed up the reasons why he lost the case: "The extraordinary performance of Lacey and Stern, their courtroom strategy, thinking on their feet, making the most of their material."

Pressed for details, he elaborated: "I'd say it was Lacey's summation; Stern's development of the Rigo testimony, his ability to break into my cross-examination with advantage at just the right moment; his handling of discovery, making it appear that we got everything when in reality we got nothing; the ability to bring in things like the Kantor testimony and the FBI accounting charts to create an atmosphere in which everything was conceivable—masterful; the volume of preparation, its intensity and enormity."

Trial attorneys have egos as big as Brooklyn—perhaps larger than those of prima donnas and politicians—and like to see them massaged. Stern is no exception. At idle moments, he's apt to turn to a newsman covering him and ask, "Tell me truthfully. Do you know of a better prosecutor's office in the country?"

Stern's critics seldom fail to cite what they call his manipulation of the media. Though his office has no PR man, Stern has managed to cultivate the best possible image for himself. Staying strictly within the bounds of legal ethics, he orchestrates his announcements with the increasing intensity of Ravel's *Bolero* and times them carefully in order to make the six o'clock news.

But then, as Jerry Wilson noted, "Who ever heard of a public prosecutor who wasn't insane for press coverage? In fact, compared with Bronx District Attorney Burton Roberts, Stern is positively retiring when it comes to the instinct for public attention. Nor would Stern ever resort to anything as crude as trying to peddle preindictment exclusives to *Life* magazine, as Whitney North Seymour, Jr., his Southern District of New York counterpart, recently contracted to do."

Especially, Stern has never been guilty of some of the crudities of his superiors at the Justice Department. And unlike them, he calls the Fourth Estate "the best friends we have." Another strange sentiment for a Nixon appointee!

Whether they like him or not, no one depreciates Stern's dedication to duty. For him, it means an endless cycle of ten- and twelve-hour days, six days a week—even more if a major trial is in progress or a major investigation under way.

"He has no hobbies," said Harold Borg, a defense lawyer who has known Stern for a decade. "His work is entirely a pleasure for him. He thrives on it."

Such dedication tends to make him a one-dimensional figure. Though he's well versed in current events, Stern's intellectual horizons are narrow. When he was invited to judge Yale Law School's mock-trial program, he pored through the briefs blissfully unaware that the names of all the characters in the freedom-of-the-press case—from *New York Examiner* editor Jebediah Leland to political boss James W. Gettys—had been taken from the movie *Citizen Kane.*

Stern may thrive on work, but it also leaves him drained and exhausted at the end of a day. After a session in court, he has only time and energy enough for a drink and dinner, then a cigar and back to the motel to sleep—so he can be up the next morning hours before the session starts to review the testimony and prepare his questions. Even after a routine day at the office, there's an hour's drive to his home in rural Bloomingdale, a late-night dinner with his wife, Sandy—and then to bed, so he can be back at his desk at nine the next morning.

"It's right off a lake," Stern says of his home. "You can swim off the front porch in summer and ice skate in winter."

But he has little time for that. When he can get away, he likes to break away completely—not for an hour or a day, but for a week or a month. He enjoys traveling and he likes to go first-class. He pursues his pleasures with the same zest he shows for work. The end of a day on vacation will leave him as exhausted as a day on trial.

He could give it all up now, enter private practice and probably pull down three times his present salary. But he won't. "The work—it's great," he explains.

True, there's a sense of purpose. But one also gets the feeling that he relishes his position of power, keeping people on the hook, wondering where he'll strike next, then plunging in the needle and watching them squirm and wiggle.

"I am here," he says, "and as long as I am here I'm going to do the job I am supposed to do."

Largely as a result of his office's activities, New Jersey now leads the nation in "discovered corruption." But, somewhat surprisingly, Stern does not feel that it is necessarily more corrupt than any other state. Almost any competent prosecutor, anywhere from New Hampshire to New Mexico, he believes, could do what he and Fred Lacey have done.

But they don't. The first impediment is that prosecutors are usually political persons, all too often obligated to the very people they should be investigating.

But, "There's another reason why and that goes to the heart, and it's more difficult to understand. There's very little in it [investigations of political corruption] for a prosecutor. When you indict a Cornelius Gallagher or a John V. Kenny or a Paul Sherwin, you are risking as a prosecutor almost as much as they are as defendants. You won't go to jail if you lose, but you may ruin your career, destroy your credibility. You'll be regarded as a fool, an incompetent, a headline-hunter. And if you win, you won't have many friends."

The problem, according to Stern, is that most prosecutory posts are way-stations for their occupants, a stopping place on the trek to political advancement, a career on the bench or a more lucrative law practice. One wrong move and the path upward may be blocked.

"No man can be a really good prosecutor," says Stern, "if he's worried about his personal future. The only way to do this type of job is to pretend that it's the only job he's ever going to have. Friends—you'll have few. Enemies—you'll have many."

2
THE MAKING OF A PROSECUTOR

Herbert Jay Stern was born on November 8, 1936, the only child of Samuel and Sophie Stern. His first home was in a six-story elevator building at 15th Street and Avenue C on Manhattan's teeming East Side. The neighborhood was then known as "the Gas House"; today it's the massive Stuyvesant Town development.

In those Depression years the Sterns were better off than most of their Gas House neighbors. Samuel Stern, the son of Hungarian Jewish immigrants, was a lawyer and, like many of his profession, active in politics. Unlike most East Side Jews, he was a Republican. When Herbert was born, Samuel Stern was in private practice. A few years later, he joined the staff of the New York City Corporation Counsel. In 1943, after the GOP regained control of the state administration, he became an assistant attorney general, eventually rising to head the Employment Security office. He retired in 1971.

Sophie Stern, who died when Herbert was 16, kept a kosher home and young Herbert went to an orthodox *shul* (synagogue) on Friday night and to *cheder* (Hebrew school) after his regular classes. Stern's childhood was devoid of dramatic detail. He was a bookish youth who would rather go home and read than play stickball in the streets. "He read every book that was ever given to him," said one friend.

Herbert's parents wanted him to become a dentist, but, like millions of other kids, he dreamt of becoming a fireman. Then, when he was about ten years old, he discovered a stack of papers stashed in a closet and started reading them. They were transcripts of cases from his father's private practice.

"It was fascinating," he recalls, "especially some of the murder cases. The cases were interesting, of course, but what was more interesting to me was the functioning of a courtroom—how the facts were brought out. It was a different world and it wasn't too long before I forgot all about wanting to be a fireman. I wanted to be a trial lawyer."

Still his father tried to dissuade him. "He told me being a trial lawyer was the most demanding work—both physically and mentally—known to man. And he was right."

Herbert started his formal education at the experimental school run by Hunter College. When he reached the fourth grade, the Sterns had to move because the neighborhood was being razed to make way for Stuyvesant Town. While his parents resettled, Herbert was packed off for a year to Pennington, a boarding school in New Jersey. He finished the fifth and sixth grades at P.S. 102 in the Parkchester section of the Bronx, where his parents took up temporary residence.

When he was 12, the Sterns moved into an apartment in Stuyvesant Town that stood on virtually the same ground as their old apartment. It would remain Herbert's home until he struck off on his own. He finished his elementary education at P.S. 60, a junior high school, and went on to Stuyvesant, one of New York City's "elite" public high schools.

In 1954, it came time to start college. "I wanted to find a school that was fairly small, one that was far enough away so I'd be away from home, yet near enough so I could get back on weekends and holidays." Hobart College in upstate Geneva fit the bill. As the crow flies, the campus is about 190 miles from Manhattan. At that time, Hobart had an enrollment of about 600 men and about half that number of women in its sister school, William Smith College.

Again, Stern's college years were devoid of dramatics. Apart from studies, his chief student activity was an attempt to establish a nondiscriminatory fraternity at Hobart, a relatively radical move during those complacent years before the civil-rights revolution. The plan was approved by the school's student council and student body, but vetoed by Hobart's board of trustees.

Stern took a liberal-arts course, writing his senior honors thesis on Machiavelli. He remained unwavering in his ambition to become a trial lawyer. He was accepted at Harvard Law School, but the University of Chicago offered him a scholarship that covered full tuition for three years—then worth about $3000. So Stern set off for the Midwest and the Midway. Like most departments at the University of Chicago, the law school is academically oriented, more concerned with turning out legal scholars than with producing trial lawyers—scarcely the grounding Stern sought. As a student, he helped set up the school's first mock-trial program.

Between his junior and senior years of law school, Stern got his first taste of the prosecutory life, working as a summer intern in the U.S. attorney's office in New York. That September, just before he returned to classes, he married Lorena Feidt. Like many romances that flower on campus, it faded after graduation. The Sterns split the following year and the marriage was formally annulled in 1962.*

Stern returned to New York after graduation and took the state bar examination in July, 1961. But he had one more hurdle before he could embark on his chosen career as a trial lawyer—the military. After several years of student deferments, at age 24 he was 1-A draft bait. He escaped a two-year hitch in uniform by enlisting in the National Guard—in New York's famed 42d (Rainbow) Division.

In August, he was packed off for six months' Army training at Fort Dix, New Jersey. He was out on bivouac when the bar-examination results were announced. "They wouldn't let me in to get the newspapers, so I didn't know whether I'd passed or failed," he recalls. "I came in on Saturday and ran around like—I ran around trying to find an edition of the *New York Times* that had the results. I finally found one and found I'd passed."

After eight weeks of basic training, Private Stern drew his permanent MOS—military occupational specialty. It was a

* Until 1967, adultery was the only ground for divorce in New York State.

perfect example of the military mind at work. The Army authorities reviewed his record, studied his academic credentials, noted his law degree—and made him a truck driver! Stern served out his stint wheeling a two and a half ton truck around the base.

Upon his discharge from active duty, he started his career as a prosecutor. The initial lure was not so much law enforcement as the trial experience. "I wanted the court work. You weren't going to get very much experience in the private area." So in February, 1962, he was sworn in as an assistant district attorney of New York County—at $5500 a year.

His boss was Frank S. Hogan, a living legend in law enforcement. He is the personification of "Mr. District Attorney," the model of a modern prosecutor. For more than 30 years he has held absolute sway over what many consider the second most powerful office in New York City, his integrity unquestioned, his prerogatives unchallenged. Through eight successive elections he received multiparty endorsement and was returned to office without opposition (save for an American Labor party candidate in 1949).

Hogan professionalized and institutionalized his office. He transformed it into a full-fledged investigative agency, rather than one merely content to press the cases brought by the police. He took it out of patronage and partisan politics, recruiting his assistants from the law schools rather than the clubhouses. He insisted that they be full-time prosecutors—no outside law practice, not one cent in outside income—and extracted a four-year commitment from them.

Though his personality pervaded the office, Hogan's person did not. He hadn't tried a case since 1943, hadn't conducted a grand-jury investigation since 1945. He remained closeted in his eighth-floor office in the Criminal Courts building. Aside from casual encounters in the elevator or at office parties,

Stern saw Hogan only three times during his nearly four years on the staff—when he was hired, when he inquired about a raise and when he quit.

In recent years, Hogan's halo has slipped. His image has become tarnished and the once-inviolate prosecutor has become the target of increasing criticism—and electoral opposition. Worse, the office has lost several major cases, a thing unheard-of in past decades.

But in 1962, when Stern joined the staff, Hogan and "Hogan's office" were at the peak of their glory. Just behind them were some far-reaching investigations—Jack Molinas and the basketball fixes; Charles Van Doren and the rigged quiz shows; Mickey Jelke and his call-girl rings; Hulan Jack and the municipal building scandals. Within a few months, it would break the biggest investigation in its history—into the rampant bribery of the State Liquor Authority.

These were matters miles removed from Stern. Like all new assistants, he started at the bottom of the ladder—in the Complaint Bureau, listening to the problems of those who "came in off the street." Some were kooks—like the lady whose radio emitted "death rays." Some had cause for civil, not criminal, actions. Others had legitimate grievances in other jurisdictions; Hogan's authority extends only through the island of Manhattan.

Occasionally, though, a complaint materialized into a criminal case. In his first few weeks on the job Stern fielded one that hit the headlines.

Charles Kingsley was a 24-year-old Canadian con man with no visible assets, but one viable talent—an operatic tenor with which he warbled his way into New York's musical circles. He became friendly with Nell Rankin, the Metropolitan Opera soprano, telling her he was heir to a $200-million fortune. He promised her and her husband, Dr. Hugh Davidson, $105,-000 each "to further her career," provided they'd pay him the $3200 "gift tax." Miss Rankin wrote a check, but her husband became suspicious, stopped payment on it and called the DA's office. The call was referred to Stern. He checked into the case and discovered that Kingsley had also fleeced his voice teacher of $6400. He ordered Kingsley's arrest. When detectives picked him up, he was carrying a plane ticket for Brazil. The arrest ended Stern's involvement in the case; Kingsley was later tried and convicted.

After a few months of fielding complaints, Stern was promoted one rung up the ladder—to the Indictment Bureau. His job was presenting felony cases to the grand jury. Most of them were cut-and-dried—assaults, thefts, robberies, the routine of police work—and the presentations seldom took more than ten minutes. A few months of this and Stern was promoted again—to the Criminal Courts Bureau. For the first time he would actually be in a courtroom trying cases.

The New York City Criminal Court was empowered to try all offenses and misdemeanors—crimes carrying penalties of up to a year in jail—and to hold pretrial hearings on felony arrests. There were no juries; trials were held before a judge or, in some misdemeanors, a three-judge panel. The atmosphere was hardly conducive to the administration of justice. Calendars were jammed with as many as a hundred or more cases a day. There was hardly time to arraign the defendants, much less hear and weigh the evidence against them. Courtrooms were crowded and noisy; often testimony could not be heard above the din. Only a minuscule percentage of the cases actually went to trial; most were disposed of by plea bargaining, with defendants "copping a plea" to a lesser charge. The trials that were held seldom lasted longer than an hour, with impatient judges shouting out verdicts as soon as the defense rested.

During his first months in the bureau, Stern worked in a trial part, fielding whatever cases came his way. Harold

Borg, now in private practice in Queens, served as Stern's "opposite number" for the Legal Aid Society. Although they were bitter rivals in the courtroom, they became close friends outside.

"Herb never had any sympathy for defendants," Borg said. "He always made it a personal thing. All defendants that came before him he treated with the same ferocity."

Soon Stern was assigned a specialty of sorts—obscenity prosecutions. Hogan's record on censorship is one of the least enviable aspects of his office. Twenty-five years ago, it prosecuted Edmund Wilson's *Memoirs of Hecate County*, which is still legally banned in New York State. Two decades later, it convicted comedian Lenny Bruce.

For nearly a year, Stern spent his working hours pressing cases against Times Square book dealers, photographers of homosexual orgies, or ordinary citizens who happened to get caught with a few reels of "stag movies." Under recent U.S. Supreme Court rulings, many of the cases he prosecuted then could not be brought today.

It's not a period of his career of which he's particularly proud, but he does not apologize for it: "I don't think it really matters what my personal feelings are. I think it only matters as to whether or not it's a crime. One thing ought to be stressed —you shouldn't be bludgeoning prosecutors because they enforce the laws that the democratic processes have put on the books. God knows, if they did anything other than that, if they substituted their own judgments of good laws and bad laws, if they arrogated unto themselves an authority to nullify or emasculate a law because they didn't like it, we wouldn't have a democracy."

During this time, Stern also had occasion to wind up in Criminal Court other than as a prosecutor. One evening, he was on the Times Square subway platform waiting for a train to take him uptown to his apartment on West 76th Street when he saw a sneak thief lifting a wallet from the purse of a woman boarding a train. Stern followed the thief through the station, looking desperately for a policeman. "As always seems the case when you're looking for a cop in New York, there was none around." So he made a citizen's arrest and marched his prisoner several blocks through Times Square until he finally found a policeman and turned over the thief. The man subsequently pleaded guilty.

In 1964, it came time for Stern to be promoted to one of the office's senior bureaus—Supreme Court,* Homicide, Rackets, Frauds or Appeals. His preference was for either Supreme Court or Homicide—"the two bureaus where you get the most trial work." He got Homicide.

The Homicide Bureau took charge of a murder case from the moment a suspect was taken into custody until sentence was imposed. "You learned not only how to try a case," says Stern, "but how to investigate and prepare it—which is what most of trial work is."

The bureau was headed by Alexander Herman, a career prosecutor who, according to Stern, "probably tried more capital cases than anybody in the entire country." By then he had developed a throat ailment and had given up trial work. The bureau's star trial lawyer was another career man, Vincent Dermody, who would soon succeed Herman as bureau chief.

"For my money, he [Dermody] was probably the finest prosecutor I've ever seen," Stern says. "He was completely simple—nothing grand, nothing flamboyant. His only technique was to be himself, to be honest and completely sincere to the jury. And he was devastatingly effective."

---

* In New York State, the Supreme Court is the court of general jurisdiction, equivalent to other states' circuit or superior courts.

If anyone has served as Stern's model and mentor in the courtroom, it's Vince Dermody.

Dermody got the tough trials, the headline cases. Routine murder prosecutions went to a half-dozen assistants only slightly junior to him. Like the others at the bottom of the totem pole, Stern got the legwork. About once every ten days, each junior assistant in the bureau pulled "duty" for 24 hours. As soon as the police picked up a murder suspect for any Manhattan homicide, they had to call the assistant on duty to take charge of the investigation and interrogation. Until the case went to trial, it was "his."

"In eighty percent of the cases," Stern recalls, "these things would happen at two o'clock in the morning. You'd stagger out of bed and go running to some dismal station house in the dead of night. There you'd be confronted by some man or woman who shot or stabbed a relative in a brawl. The majority of these homicides were family disputes or fights among friends."

Not all the cases involved death. The assistant had to go out on any assault likely to result in a death. Stern had so many such cases that he soon formed the theory that the difference between freedom and imprisonment isn't a question of law and evidence, but a matter of millimeters. If the bullet pierced the brain or the knife severed an artery, the victim died—and the culprit went away for 20 years. If the bullet missed or the knife thrust fell short, the victim lived—often to forgive the errant spouse or lover and not press charges.

Most of the cases Stern handled tend to blur together in his memory. But a handful stand out.

First was the case of Joseph Donohue. "Crazy Joe," as he was known, was a hired killer whom the authorities had never been able to convict. Stern was assigned the thankless task of reviewing the evidence against him.

"From all the available intelligence and evidence, Donohue

had killed five people," he recalls. "The authorities could prove that Donohue and a good friend of his named Raymond Tobin had gone into the Castillian Room [a bar on East 75th Street] and that there came a time when there were only four people in the bar—Donohue, his friend Tobin, the hat-check girl and Robert Hannigan, the owner. We could prove that a string of shots rang out about four o'clock in the morning and that Donohue and Tobin walked out of the bar and that the remaining two were dead. Hannigan was found dead under the pay phone with a dime in his hand. The girl was on the floor.

"It was obvious from the background of these people that Donohue was a murderer. The problem was, Tobin wouldn't talk. When he was brought down to the district attorney's office, he took the Fifth Amendment. Then they told him they would put him before the grand jury.

" 'I'll take the Fifth Amendment there.'

"He was told that he'd be given immunity and forced to testify.

" 'What'll you do if I testify that I shot them?'

"That scared them off from even putting him before the grand jury."

Tobin reportedly was also an eyewitness to the slaying of Presley Wilkes in a Harlem bar and had information linking Donohue to a second double murder in the Bronx.

Stern decided to call Tobin's bluff. He haled him before a grand jury and had him held in $100,000 bond as a material witnesss. The idea was to hint that Tobin *was* talking and thus make him so scared of Donohue's revenge that he'd have to cooperate for his own safety . . . except it didn't work.

While all this was going on, Donohue struck again. The victim was a petty crook named Lawrence Krebs. He was shot to death in a stolen car in Central Park—by the driver of the moving vehicle. The car crashed into a wall, the driver walked away and tossed his gun into a clump of hedges on Fifth Avenue. Donohue's fingerprint was found behind the mirror of the car, and a woman who had seen the driver from a passing taxi identified him from a photo as Donohue.

"The problem was to give her an opportunity to view Donohue," Stern says. "But he was already a fugitive. The FBI would not enter the search unless we had a warrant, and we didn't want to get a warrant until we gave her a chance to view him.

"An old homicide detective by the name of Walter Curtain found out that Donohue had jumped bail on an assault charge in New Jersey. We didn't even know about it. Based on that case, we got a warrant and then asked the FBI to help."

The FBI found Donohue holed up in Boston. When he was searched, a master handcuff key was found sewn in his underwear and another secreted in his shoe. Stern went to Boston and arranged a lineup. As soon as Donohue realized what it was, he fell to the floor. Two policemen picked him up and a third held his head so his face was visible. But Donohue so contorted his features that a woman who had seen the killer throw away the gun failed to identify him. The woman from the taxi later viewed Donohue in a court anteroom and identified him. Stern brought the prisoner to New York and obtained an indictment against him for Krebs's murder.

Stern assisted John Keenan in the preparation and trial of the case. "All we had was a fingerprint behind the mirror and the identification of the woman who had seen the driver walk by at night," he notes. But Keenan secured a second-degree murder conviction and Donohue was sent away for 35 years to life.

Stern was not around for the conclusion of the case. Midway through the trial, on Sunday, February 21, 1965, he drew "duty." That afternoon he was in a midtown restaurant when a man rushed in and yelled out the news:

"Malcolm X has been shot!"

Stern grabbed the man. "Was he killed?"

"Yes."

"Did they catch anybody?"

"Yes, they caught somebody."

"When you're on homicide duty," Stern notes, "you don't have to sit by a phone. You call in every couple of hours. It was a couple of hours since I'd called in and I realized they must be looking for me. So I called Manhattan Homicide North. They were in a panic. All the top police brass were there at the station house and of course they couldn't proceed without an assistant."

Stern speeded to Harlem and took charge of the case.

El-Hajj Malik El-Shabbazz, born Malcolm Little, better known as Malcolm X, was, perhaps next to Martin Luther King, Jr., the most dynamic figure of the black revolution. A thief, dope peddler and pimp, he converted to Elijah Muhammad's Lost-Found Nation of Islam while in prison. After his release, he rose to become the most potent of Muhammad's ministers and a rival to Muhammad himself. In 1963, after he described President Kennedy's assassination as a case of "the chickens coming home to roost," Muhammad suspended him. It was a ploy in the pair's power struggle. Malcolm X soon broke entirely with the Black Muslims and formed his own Organization of Afro-American Unity. He started to move away from the Black Muslims' policy of strict separation of the races.

He believed himself marked for death for his apostasy. A few days before his murder, his home in Queens was fire-bombed. On the fatal day, he addressed a rally of about 400 people at the Audubon Ballroom on Harlem's West 166th Street. There is a tape recording of his last moments:

"Asalaikum, brothers and sisters!" he said.

"Asalaikum, Salaam!" the audience replied.

Suddenly a scuffle broke out in the audience. A man could be heard shouting, "Take your hand out of my pocket!"

"Hold it! Hold it!" Malcolm X said. "Don't get excited. Let's cool it, brother——"

At that point, the tape went dead. A bullet had pierced the microphone.

In the confusion, three men had stepped to the foot of the stage and opened fire at close range. Malcolm X was hit with slugs from a Luger and a Colt .45 and with pellets from a shotgun. He died en route to the hospital.

Malcolm X's bodyguard wounded one of the assassins, who was taken into custody by police outside. A partially used .45 caliber cartridge clip was found in his pocket. The other two assassins and their accomplices, if any, escaped.

Rather than a paucity of evidence, as in the Donohue case, there was a superabundance of it.

"The problem," Stern says, "was to try to piece together from this confusing mass of detail what had actually occurred. The murder took place in front of perhaps 200 witnesses and, as you know, no two people ever see the same thing the same way.

"The second problem was that the prospective witnesses were people who were not partial to the authorities. The one saving grace was that, by and large, the people in the ballroom were absolutely devoted to Malcolm X. We received quite a lot of cooperation from his followers, who were sincerely interested in finding out who had killed him and bringing those responsible to justice."

Stern and the police patiently pieced together the accounts. The man caught at the scene was identified as Talmadge Hayer. Within a week, two more were arrested—Norman 3X Butler and Thomas 15X Johnson. All three were Black Muslims.

"From the evidence," Stern continues, "Butler was the

fellow who ran out through the audience, colliding with the wooden folding chairs, tripping and stumbling over them as he made his escape. So I ordered the police to take nude photographs of his body. They show that he had bruises on his thighs and shins."

Stern presented the case to the grand jury and obtained a first-degree murder indictment against the trio. The following year, after Stern had left the office, they were prosecuted by Dermody, convicted and sentenced to life imprisonment.

But the trial and conviction did not completely clear up the mystery of the murder of Malcolm X. First, the motive.

"I think the motive was fairly clear," Stern says. "All three of the people convicted were Muslims in good standing and in fairly good positions in the Muslim organization. Malcolm X was on the outs with the Muslims. Indeed, he was a competitor to the Muslims and he had been making personal charges against their leader. The motive of the three men seems to me to be rather obvious."

But it was never proved. Nor was it ever proved who had ordered the killing or if the killers had accomplices.

"I've said from the beginning," Stern continues, "that there were other people involved—not only at the scene, but, I'm quite certain, behind the scenes. But under our system of laws, we could not compel any of these three men to tell us who had sent them in to do this homicide. I think it was a fine piece of police work that we were able to establish—out of the morass of people with very antithetical feelings toward police and prosecutors—the three people who were wielding the three guns in the ballroom that day."

Each Friday afternoon, the members of the Homicide Bureau—except for those on trial—gathered in Herman's office to discuss current investigations. The assistant in charge of each case would review the evidence and the others would question him or comment on it. Sometimes he would be sent back to gather more data, but if the case was ready for presentation to a grand jury, the assistants would vote on what charge to seek. Since New York had a mandatory death penalty for first-degree and felony murder, it was literally a life-and-death judgment.*

The system wasn't always foolproof. In April, 1964, assistant Peter Koste took a 61-page confession from a young Brooklyn black named George Whitmore. The youth admitted the sensational "career-girl" murders of Janice Wylie and Emily Hofert the year before. Whitmore was indicted and, by all accounts, could have been convicted and sent to the electric chair . . . except months later it was proved that he was in Wildwood, New Jersey—miles from the scene—on the day of the murder. Another youth was subsequently arrested, indicted and convicted of the double slaying.

The case was in the back of Stern's mind on April 7, 1965, when he took a statement from a Harlem youth admitting a brutal murder. The victim was the elderly wife of George Georgious, a Harlem grocer. She was found in her apartment, bound with three different cords, sexually molested and stabbed to death. A television set was missing.

The youth, who worked in Georgious's store, had a key that opened the apartment door. Under questioning by the police, he confessed the crime. Stern was called in to record the official statement.

"These cases are quite troublesome," he says. "By and large, unless you get a confession either directly to the police or an admission to somebody else, it's awfully tough to convict in an unwitnessed homicide.

"But there are people in our society who will confess to any-

---

* In 1965, New York abolished the death penalty except for the murder of a policeman or prison guard.

thing. And there are times when the police exceed the scope of their proper performance. The way to tell if a confession is valid is, if the subject has the kind of intimate knowledge which only the culprit could know. You have to be careful that you're not insinuating into his mind the details that you want to hear."

Stern questioned the youth. "He had a very modest education and very modest intelligence. It seemed that he was almost pathetically trying to please me. He told his story in a robotlike manner. He left the impression on me that he was repeating it by rote. I decided to test this, so I stopped him. 'Excuse me, I didn't quite hear what you said. Would you mind saying it again?' I stopped him three or four times at various points and made him go back to the beginning. He would begin at the beginning and repeat exactly the same words each time."

Under questioning, the youth changed his story and denied killing Mrs. Georgious. He said the key was to a friend's lodging—and, sure enough, it fit that door, too. Nor could the TV set be found where he'd said he'd left it. Subsequent investigation neither confirmed his guilt nor established his innocence. The Homicide Bureau voted not to seek an indictment, and the grand jury dismissed the charge against him.

"It was possible, even probable that he'd done it," Stern says. "But I, as a prosecutor, couldn't be morally certain that he did. The troublesome thing is, I don't know to this day whether the boy killed the woman. All I know is that his confession was worthless."

Nor was the bureau's system of review, Stern found, always fair.

Two days after Christmas, 1964, Patrolman Patrick Crowe was directing traffic at Madison Avenue and 35th Street. He flagged down a car for a traffic violation. The driver stopped and Crowe stepped over to the vehicle. The auto sped off, dragging Crowe several yards. Crowe whipped out his gun, fired two warning shots in the air, then aimed two more at the speeding car. Neither hit the vehicle or its occupants. But Julius Ofsie, a businessman who had just stepped out of a doorway on Madison Avenue, was struck in the head and was DOA at Bellevue Hospital.

Like any other homicide, Ofsie's death had to be investigated by the DA's office. But rarely was a policeman who had killed in the line of duty hit with criminal charges, no matter how outrageous the circumstances.

Stern drew the "duty." He checked out police training procedures and read the police manuals. He determined in his own mind that Crowe *had* used excessive force in firing his gun to stop a traffic violator. And he felt that Crowe had acted without proper regard for the safety of innocent bystanders—or even the innocent passengers in the fleeing car. He suggested a manslaughter indictment. But only one other assistant in the bureau agreed, and Crowe was exonerated. The case left a bitter aftertaste with Stern.

He also felt frustrated in his desire to try cases. Since joining the bureau, he'd tried only two cases—brief narcotics trials, among those farmed out to Homicide assistants to give them practice in arguing before a jury. In a year or two, he might be assigned a routine murder or manslaughter trial, one that offered no real challenge. Before he could try a major murder case, he'd have to have 10 or 12 years' seniority. He was unwilling to wait.

"I had tried literally hundreds of cases in the Criminal Court, I had presented thousands of matters to scores of grand juries, I had done investigations," he explains. "I felt that I had gained everything from the office that I could. I didn't think there was much more for me there in terms of personal growth."

In the spring of 1965 he started looking for another position. He was determined to stay in law enforcement, in an office that was, like Hogan's, essentially professional and nonpolitical—a requirement that drastically limited his choices. Through a colleague, he was introduced to John Sprizzo, an assistant U.S. attorney who had previously worked in the Justice Department's Organized Crime and Racketeering Section. Sprizzo suggested that he try there.

Stern fired off a letter of application, was interviewed by Henry Peterson, then deputy chief of the section, and was hired pending security clearance. It didn't come through until September. During October, Stern moved to Washington, relocating in an apartment in Capitol Park, a 20-minute walk from the Justice Department's buildings on Constitution Avenue. On November 1, 1965, he started work as a special attorney for the Department of Justice.

3
INTRODUCTION TO JUSTICE ... AND JERSEY

The Organized Crime and Racketeering Section of the Criminal Division of the Department of Justice was created by Attorney General Herbert Brownell during the Eisenhower administration. Initially, it was little more than a publicity stunt, never allotted more than 16 lawyers, never convicting a major Mafioso. In fact, J. Edgar Hoover and his FBI—the investigative arm of Justice—steadfastly denied the existence of the Mafia or an organized crime syndicate.

All this changed in 1961 when Robert F. Kennedy became attorney general. His experience as counsel to the McClellan Subcommittee in the late 1950s had convinced him that organized crime *was* a powerful and pernicious force in the nation. He came into office determined to do something about it. His chief weapon was the Organized Crime and Racketeering Section.

The unit became Kennedy's pet and its members the department's elite. Its size was more than quadrupled, to 69 attorneys. But it remained loose, informal, unstructured; its attorneys young, eager, fired by an esprit de corps other agencies lacked. When Stern joined it, Organized Crime was headed by William Hundley, an Eisenhower administration holdover who had successfully prosecuted Mafioso "Tony Ducks" Corallo and Brooklyn Supreme Court Justice J. Vincent Keogh for attempting to fix a bankruptcy fraud case.

Stern's first assignment was to a labor unit. He shared an office with two attorneys fresh out of law school. One was Jonathan L. Goldstein, whose future career would be closely intertwined with Stern's.

"They gave me a file," Stern recalls. "But before I tied into that, I wanted to get the feel of federal practice. I wanted to spend some time just as though I were a young inexperienced lawyer coming in, reviewing the FBI reports and the prosecutive opinions. I had no direct experience with federal statutes and wanted an opportunity to bone up on them. At the same time I was boning up on the statutes, I was masticating on this rather huge file they had given me."

It involved labor racketeering. The case had been building slowly since 1961, when investigators in the Detroit office of the Department of Labor got wind of wholesale embezzlements of union funds in the pipeline-construction industry. As a pipeline inched its way across the land, workers on the project would move from the jurisdiction of one local into that of another. While they worked in "foreign" territory, they had to pay temporary dues—called "dobies"—to the appropriate locals. All too often, the dobies wound up in the pockets of the union leaders, not the union treasuries.

Investigators Louis Woiwode (pronounced "Why, would he?") and Edwin Dooley started checking into specific cases. Their inquiry soon narrowed to the Colonial Pipeline—the largest pipeline project in history, the so-called Big Inch, a three-foot-wide conduit carrying fuel oil 1600 miles from Houston, Texas, to Linden, New Jersey. As they probed deeper, the investigators focused on a single segment of the line—the 90-mile stretch across New Jersey from the Delaware River to New York Harbor—and the role of Peter W. Weber, president of Local 825, International Union of Operating Engineers, AFL–CIO.

Weber was a giant—both in person and in the labor movement. Then 56 years old, he stood six-foot-two and weighed 234 pounds. A former prizefighter, he had been bodyguard to Joey Faye, a labor racketeer convicted by District Attorney Hogan in the 1940s. He headed a 7500-man local with jurisdiction over heavy-construction-equipment workers in New Jersey and five New York counties.

"The man had his fingers wrapped around the neck of the construction industry in New Jersey," Stern says. "He was known to be a labor racketeer in the department, he was known to be a labor racketeer in the labor movement, he was known to be a labor racketeer in the construction industry."

Weber had tangled with both John and Robert Kennedy during the McClellan hearings. Indeed, at the time of the Labor Department investigation, he was already under indictment on a charge arising from them—of being a secret partner in a construction firm whose employees he represented. But the charge was only a misdemeanor and under the Landrum-Griffin Act, conviction would not have barred him from holding union office.

Woiwode and Dooley started receiving reports that Weber was taking kickbacks from contractors, that he was forcing contracts to favored companies, that he was padding payrolls with idle employees at fantastic rates of pay. On one job, shop stewards were paid for a succession of 21-hour days, six days a week, most of it at double- and triple-time rates. Since these were matters outside Labor's jurisdiction, the case was turned over to Justice. The file filtered through the bureaucratic ladder until it landed on Stern's desk.

"There was nothing concrete in the file," he recalls. "It was gossip and rumors. The problem of investigating this kind of case was that—literally—the prospective witnesses were scattered all over the United States. So I spent about three weeks just analyzing, indexing and cross-indexing the file. Then I wrote a very long memo suggesting a course of action."

The first step was to empanel a grand jury. There were three choices for the location—in Atlanta, headquarters of the Colonial Pipeline Company; in San Francisco, headquarters of the Bechtel Corporation, which had been the prime contractor on the Jersey leg of the line; or in New Jersey, where the job was done. Stern opted for New Jersey.

Shortly after New Year's Day, 1966, Stern and his colleague on the case, Philip White, flew to Newark and conferred with U.S. Attorney David M. Satz, Jr. "He was very helpful," Stern recalls. Satz's quarters in the old post office building were cramped, but he squeezed out space for the two attorneys from Washington and provided them with a secretary. On February 14, he empaneled a special grand jury for them.

"Little did we know that when we arranged for that special grand jury," Stern says, "that all the work that was to follow, all the thousands and thousands of miles of travel and all the hundreds and hundreds of man-hours of work, and one of the most exciting and difficult criminal trials—that all of that would be wiped out by the fact that the grand jury was empaneled unconstitutionally."

But that realization was four years away. Meanwhile, White and Stern went to work, corralling an investigative staff. From the FBI, they borrowed five accountants under the direction of special agent Ray Leffler. They flew to Detroit, conferred with Woiwode and borrowed some fifteen Labor Department investigators, headed by "chief honcho" Anthony Cosolo. From time to time, they also borrowed personnel from the Internal Revenue Service.

"This really was the first Strike Force," Stern notes. "It really began here in New Jersey—agents from different departments working together under one command, using a common file system. Buffalo is usually thought of as the first Strike Force, but Buffalo was not established until after we brought our first indictment."

There were four main allegations the grand jury planned to probe: that Weber had forced Colonial to cancel a contract with the Osage Company of Tulsa, Oklahoma, and award it to a local construction firm, the Napp-Grecco Company; that he had taken kickbacks from H.C. Price & Company of Bartlesville, Oklahoma; that he had forced Bechtel to award a subcontract to the Joyce Pipeline Company of Andover, New York; and that he had taken kickbacks from Joyce.

Stern decided to confront the potential witnesses on their home grounds and persuade them to testify. It was a difficult task—"which was not surprising," Stern says, "considering that if they told the truth, they feared labor difficulties all over the United States."

First stop was Tulsa. The Osage officials cooperated, but could provide no evidence linking Weber to the canceled contract. From Tulsa, they drove 90 miles north to Bartlesville —to the modern tower Frank Lloyd Wright had designed for H.C. Price & Company—and met with the firm's chairman, Harold C. Price, Jr.

"He was very nervous, very upset," Stern recalls. "He made it clear to us that he was absolutely terrified of Weber."

The investigators got nowhere with Price.

"I gave Cosolo instructions to go through all the expense accounts and everything else in the firm," Stern continues. "I was going to have a complete audit done on all the books and records. If there was cash coming out of the firm, I was going to find it."

White and Stern flew to San Francisco for an appointment with Bechtel's officials and checked into a hotel. Early the next morning, Cosolo woke them with word that Price wanted to talk to him again: He'd admitted that he'd authorized payoffs to Weber.

"How much?" Stern asked.

"Fourteen thousand," Cosolo replied.

"We were very excited about it," Stern recalls. "We canceled all our appointments. This was the first break that had ever occurred with Weber."

What had changed Price's mind? "I decided to stop lying," he said later. "I started to feel that these people were serious in cleaning up this mess."

White and Stern hopped an afternoon flight to Dallas and

connected with a night flight to Tulsa. Cosolo met them at the airport and drove them back to Bartlesville. Tired, haggard, rumpled and unshaven, they filed into Price Tower again.

Price produced the man who had physically handled the transactions—a veteran employee named Roy Burgess. The money had been paid in four installments of $3500 each. But Burgess's memory was faulty: He couldn't remember when and where he'd actually passed the cash to Weber.

"We had a big bucket of nothing," Stern says. "We had a man who was willing to testify that he had done this thing, but he was in no position to give out any details. And we were in no position to go before a jury."

But Burgess had one saving grace: He was an assiduous record-keeper. He had recorded all his outlays in a series of small spiral notebooks, and the pages had been preserved, carefully stapled to the carbon copies of his expense accounts. Stern spent a week with him, going through the notations one by one for ten hours a day.

"By his reliving day-by-day from his notes, he was able to pinpoint the exact time and place he paid Weber each time."

They now had enough for a case against Weber. "But we knew there was so much more," Stern notes. "If he was as corrupt as everybody said, there *had* to be much more."

So they set to work tidying up the cases involving Colonial, Bechtel and Joyce, hopscotching the country, subpoenaing books and records, pouring through thousands of documents. It was "painful, deliberate, laborious" work.

"The day of Sherlock Holmes is over," Stern once explained. "You can't go out and solve the crimes of today with a magnifying glass."

But he learned one lesson Conan Doyle's detective would have appreciated: "You've got to look at the back of the check as well as the front—to determine if it was deposited or cashed.

"We developed a theory very early in this game. In the credit society that we are today, nobody just walks into a bank and takes out anything like four or five thousand dollars in cash—at least not for any legitimate purpose."

Stern got scant support from his potential witnesses. Supposedly reputable businessmen proved strangely reluctant to testify against the labor leader. They concealed facts, evaded answering as long as they could, often lied when they were forced to answer. A second grand jury had to be empaneled in Buffalo to investigate Joyce's attempts to obstruct the inquiry.

The investigation broke wide open in May when a Bechtel official came, under subpoena, from New York with some of the company's books and records. Leffler and Cosolo sifted through the documents. Leffler discovered a $20,000 check, made out by Bechtel's New York office, but billed against the New Jersey project for damage done during construction—and negotiated for cash! Stern issued subpoenas for every man whose name appeared on either the check or the voucher.

On May 31, Bechtel's brass showed up at Stern's office with their counsel—Paul Haerle of San Francisco and the local lawyer Haerle had retained, Frederick B. Lacey of Newark. Lacey said Bechtel would cooperate with the government.

"I sat with pencil poised, waiting for what was to come," Stern recalls. "I expected to hear about more payoffs to Weber."

Instead, "to my complete and utter amazement," Lacey proceeded to relate how Bechtel, at Colonial's request, had passed $20,000 in cash to the mayor and president of the city council of Woodbridge, New Jersey. "It was like looking for silver and finding gold."

So they set out to pan for gold. Stern called Henry Peterson, deputy chief of Organized Crime, and told him of the discovery. "He was delighted"—and gave the go-ahead to pursue it. Stern also apprised U.S. Attorney Satz. "Then we began to investigate."

The Bechtel payoff was only the tip of the iceberg. Colonial had asked Bechtel to pay out $60,000 in three installments. The first payment was made. Then Stephen Bechtel, Jr., president of the firm, got wind of the deal and refused to have any more to do with it. Colonial funneled the remaining $40,000 through a Bechtel subcontractor, Gates Construction Company.

"For the first time," Stern says, "we ran into something that was to repeat itself time and time again. The weakness in every one of these schemes is that, in the end, it must come out in cash. Find that cash coming out and you're halfway home.

"We also found something else that was to repeat itself. The price this cost society is much greater than the actual cost of the payoff itself. Forty thousand was needed to make the payoff. But Gates couldn't just send bills for forty thousand dollars to Bechtel, because they would have no offsetting expenses. They money would have to come out of profits, which are taxed at the corporate rate of fifty-two percent. So to make the forty-thousand-dollar payoff, they had to bill for eighty-four thousand. Roughly forty-four would go to federal and state taxes; the remaining forty to the corrupt public officials. For every dollar of graft that's paid, they have to build in costs of at least twice as much."

Stern issued a subpoena for all Colonial records "that reflect any payments, directly or indirectly, to the mayor or president of the city council of Woodbridge"—"We figured we'd let them do the work."

Colonial's top officials came to Newark with their attorney, David Wilentz. Wilentz was a former New Jersey attorney general, best known for his prosecution of Bruno Richard Hauptmann in the Lindbergh kidnap case. He was a power politically, the Middlesex County Democratic chairman and the state's Democratic national committeeman. His son, Warren, a partner in Wilentz's Perth Amboy law firm, was then running for the U.S. Senate against Clifford Case.

Colonial also decided to cooperate, claiming it had been the victim of a shakedown. Stern warned that they were coming in at their own risk, that if they weren't innocent, they'd be prosecuted. They took the chance and spelled out the details of the transaction: Not only had Colonial laid out $60,000 in bribes through Bechtel and Gates, it had previously paid $50,000 through another contractor, the Roland Tompkins Company.

"Once again, we almost fell off our chairs," Stern says.

The first $50,000 had been paid so Colonial could get permits to build a "tank farm" in Woodbridge without having to go through the formality of a public hearing at which local residents might vent their opposition. The second $60,000 had been paid to get easements to lay the line under a series of city-owned lots.

Stern decided that the corporations and their officers were not innocent victims, but culpable participants in a bribe plot. On February 23, 1967, the grand jury returned a nine-count indictment against four corporations—Colonial, Bechtel, Roland Tompkins and Gates—and five individuals: Colonial's top officers, chairman Ben D. Leuty, executive vice president Karl T. Feldman and vice president-operations Glenn H. Giles; as well as Woodbridge Mayor Walter Zirpolo and City Council President Robert Jacks.

The Colonial case pitted Stern against a formidable array of attorneys. Representing Mayor Zirpolo was Edward Bennett Williams of Washington, probably the nation's leading criminal lawyer. Leuty's lawyer was Simon H. Rifkind, a former federal judge and the driving force in the politically potent New York law firm whose partners included former Supreme Court Justice Arthur Goldberg. Other defense counsel included Adrian Foley, a former president of the New Jersey Bar Association, president of the state's Constitutional Convention and subsequently a law partner of Governor Richard Hughes; John Toolan, a former state senator and veteran trial attorney; Joseph Brill, one of New York's leading criminal lawyers; plus Wilentz and Lacey. Behind them were all the resources of their law firms—as many as 135 men in Rifkind's case. At times, as many as 19 attorneys clustered around the defense table.

By contrast, although he represented all the might of the United States government, Stern was virtually alone on the prosecution side. White had dropped out of the investigation with a back ailment, while Goldstein, who had filled in for him, was then with the U.S. Army in Thailand. For the 32-year-old Stern, it was only his third jury trial.

According to Stern, "Colonial came into the courtroom to overwhelm the United States government. I was determined not to let them get away with it. They had behind them virtually unlimited manpower, unlimited resources, unlimited money— a good percentage of the corporate wealth of this country."

He wasn't exaggerating. Colonial is a jointly owned venture of nine major oil companies—Cities Service, Continental, Gulf, Mobil, Phillips, Standard of Indiana, Sinclair, Texaco and Union—with assets in 1968 of more than $35 billion. Colonial's pipeline, which cost $390 million, was the largest privately financed construction project in history.

The defense attorneys filed 40 pretrial motions—enough to form a stack of legal papers nearly four feet high. The trial judge, a 73-year-old but still spry Eisenhower appointee with the Pullman-car name of Reynier J. Wortendyke, Jr., disposed of them all in a 30-page decision—all in favor of the government.

The trial opened on November 14, 1968. Stern started off with two advantages. First, Gates Construction pleaded guilty and its president, Robert Gates, agreed to testify for the prosecution. Second, the defense was split down the middle—Leuty, Feldman, Giles and the corporations claiming they were victims of a shakedown by Zirpolo and Jacks. In his opening address to the jury, Rifkind likened the government's case against Leuty to an attempt to prove that the sheep had attacked the dogs. Rifkind soon emerged as chief counsel for the "ovine" defendants, Williams for the "canine."

But Stern was also working under two serious handicaps. The first was dealt by the U.S. Supreme Court in the *Bruton* case. The judges ruled that in a multidefendant trial, statements made by one defendant could not be introduced if they incriminated another. This prevented Stern from reading into the record the grand-jury testimony of Leuty, Feldman and Giles, as he had planned. His only alternative was to sever Giles—the lowest-ranking of the Colonial officials—grant him immunity and use him as a witness against the others.

This pointed up the second problem. Many of his witnesses were officers of the defendant corporations and came into court represented by the defense attorneys. Although they admitted the facts, they put a different coloration on them—Colonial's contending that it was extortion, not a bribe; those of Bechtel and Roland Tompkins denying knowledge of the purpose of the payments.

For example, Giles, called as the government's first witness, testified on the stand that the payments were "a shakedown and not a bribe." Before the grand jury, he had said: "We were told that if we paid the money, they'd pass this thing over the residents' objections, jam it through."

William Fallow, business manager of Bechtel's pipeline division, testified that he had paid $20,000 in cash to Jacks, saw Jacks stuff the money in a desk drawer, had asked for and been denied a receipt—and still said he thought the money was going into the town treasury!

As a result, it was like pulling teeth for Stern to get a piece of proprosecution testimony into evidence from his own witnesses.

His star witness was Fred Stewart, rights-of-way manager for Mobil's pipeline division, who had been on loan to Colonial in 1963. He related how Colonial had decided to build its tank farm at Woodbridge—a 22-tank depot where the oil piped north from Houston could be stored until it was shipped out.

Woodbridge, which lay across the Arthur Kill from Staten Island, had a population of 78,846 and was the sixth-largest community in New Jersey. It had been cited by *Look* magazine as an all-American city. Its mayor, Walter Zirpolo, was a millionaire real-estate developer whose home had an indoor waterfall, a living-room swimming pool and a front lawn that fused into the fairways of an adjoining golf course. He was always nattily dressed and mustached.

Stewart told how he had gone to see Mayor Zirpolo in the summer of 1963 about getting permits to build the tank farm. Zirpolo told him: "I have promised the people that there will be no more tankage up there. This is an election year and we just can't entertain this thing until at least after the election."

Stewart returned to the mayor's office some time later. "Things haven't quieted down a bit," Zirpolo said. "I am still of the same opinion. Do not file any application yet."

"All right," Stewart replied, "but now this public hearing business. It seems to be our big obstacle."

"Yes, that is your big obstacle," Zirpolo said, ". . . and the people are going to fight you on this thing."

"Is there any way in the world to avoid a public hearing?" Stewart asked. "Is there another ordinance we could get under, just anything to avoid a public hearing? We need to do it."

"I'll tell you what," Zirpolo said. "I think it's time you ought to see Mr. Jacks. . . . I'd like for you to go up there today and see him because he is expecting you."

Jacks, a World War II marine hero, was president of the Woodbridge city council and a successful used-car dealer. He explained the situation to Stewart: "You have got to have friends on the council in order to get this thing put through. . . . You have got to have friends that will be able to pass this permit for you over the objections of the people. That's where you have got to get right."

"What do you mean by that?" Stewart asked.

"We've got to have campaign contributions," Jacks said.

"We don't make campaign contributions."

"You are going to have to in this instance if you [want to] get anywhere with your permit."

"We just can't do it," Stewart said. "It is unlawful. It is illegal. And we just don't and we just can't do it."

But after a pause, he asked: "By way of curiosity, just how much money are you talking about . . . ?"

"Fifty thousand dollars."

Colonial's top officials authorized the payoff—and two Roland Tompkins officers subsequently related how the money was raised and delivered.

The following year, Stewart continued, Colonial sought an easement to lay the pipeline under the city-owned lots. He again visited Zirpolo, this time in the mayor's private office in the Menlo Park shopping center. As he sat in the waiting room, Stewart could hear Zirpolo talking. But "when I walked in the office, the mayor wasn't there, but Mr. Jacks was sitting there behind a desk." Stewart explained the situation.

"This is all well and good," Jacks said. "We have got to have some money in this thing."

"What are you talking about?"

"I am talking about a hundred thousand dollars. That's what I'm talking about."

"We just got through paying you fifty thousand."

"Yes, but we have got to have more this time."

"That sounds like extortion to me."

"I don't care what you call it. We['ve] got to have it before you will ever get your permits."

Someone at Colonial—the government was never able to find out who—talked the price down to $60,000. Officials of Bechtel and Gates later testified about those payoffs to Jacks.

Another key witness for the prosecution was Harry J. Price (no relation to Harold Price of H.C. Price & Company). At the time of the trial, he was press secretary to Connecticut Congressman (now Senator) Lowell Weicker; in 1963, he had been a reporter on the Perth Amboy *Evening News* covering Woodbridge.

He testified that he had asked Mayor Zirpolo about rumors that a new tank farm was planned for the town. "That is the opposition, the Republican hogwash," the Democratic mayor replied. "There is no truth to that. They have no application of anything like that."

Price told how Zirpolo had given him a campaign flier headed, "Tanks? No Tanks!" in which Zirpolo pledged his opposition to any such installations. Stern introduced the leaflet in evidence—further support for his contention that the money was payment for services rendered.

For Stern, the trial was tedious and tortuous going, slowed by repeated defense objections and lengthy legal conferences at the sidebar or in chambers. It was a twofold strategy—first, to wear down the prosecutor; second, to fragment the evidence and make it difficult for the jury to see the total picture.

The proceeding was sidetracked so often by peripheral problems that Judge Wortendyke was finally prompted to remark: "*Infantry Drill Regulations,* edition of 1913, says something that I will never forget: Quibbling over the minutia of form is indicative of failure to grasp the substance."

The trial was also delayed by illness. Leuty was felled—and the trial proceeded several days without him. Judge Wortendyke caught cold and the trial was delayed for a week. Most significantly, Mayor Zirpolo suffered a heart attack and had to be severed from the case. The trial proceeded without him—and the eloquent objections of Edward Bennett Williams.

Stern rested on January 6, 1969. After a day spent hearing—and rejecting—defense motions for dismissal, Judge Wortendyke called upon the defense. Each defense attorney rose and rested.

Summations started on January 14. The lawyers for the "ovine" defendants tried to portray their clients as innocent victims. Warren Wilentz, who had taken over from his father, argued for Colonial "that it was a shakedown, that it was coercion, that it was duress and that these men . . . and this corporation had no intention to commit bribery."

Judge Rifkind was most flowery and eloquent in his description of Leuty as "a great, good and creative man . . . not a criminal, but the victim of the crime."

"The shadow of this accusation has darkened his life and the life of his family for over two years," he told the jury. "I submit to you in all sincerity it is time to lift this burden off his back, to let the sunshine of truth dispel the shadow of this unwarranted accusation. Yours is the power to do it and yours will be the glory when you wipe the tear off his lovely wife's cheek and restore them both to the rest they deserve after his prodigious labors and return him to the pride he should enjoy for his historic accomplishment."

Toolan, on behalf of Council President Jacks, made the most surprising summation of all. He made no attempt to deny that his client had received the money: "Elections in this country are run with cash. Every political party must have somebody in it who has the capacity to raise money. . . . Bob Jacks was that person in the Woodbridge political organization. . . . Now, this is an oil company coming through. He had to raise money either by going around and sandbagging local people, or you can get it on a one-shot deal with some big asset that is coming through, and you take advantage of it."

The final summation was Stern's. He reviewed the evidence unemotionally, reading large globs of the trial testimony to the jurors. He ridiculed the contention that the corporations and their officers were innocent victims: "They knew very well that what they were doing was illegal, and it was wrong, it was immoral.

"Ladies and gentlemen," he continued, "rarely if ever has the United States been able to pull back the curtain and to display before you or any jury the kind of naked corruption that we have displayed in this case, the intimate details of corrupt public officials met and joined, furthered and prompted by big businessmen who were equally corrupt for their own reasons. Ladies and gentlemen, I suggest to you that rarely if ever has the United States been able to prove such a deliberate, knowing, intentional and willful flouting of the law of the United States. . . .

"Ladies and gentlemen, these cases are rare indeed, and they are not easy to come by, and they do make history when they come. Let me suggest to you that the reason that they are rare and that the reason that they are not easy to come by and that the reason that they do make history . . . is because the men don't often get caught. . . . The reason they don't get caught is because generally they hide it too well, and if you doubt it, ladies and gentlemen, look how well it was hidden in this case."

The jury agreed. After three and a half days of deliberation, it found all defendants guilty. It was one of the few times in history that the government had successfully prosecuted *both* the givers and the takers in a bribe plot.

For Stern, the long ordeal was over. "I went through hell," he said afterward. "You don't know the pressures of these trials." After the Weber and Colonial investigations were settled in Newark, Stern gave up his flat on Capitol Hill and took an apartment on New York's Fifth Avenue, just off Washington Square. But during the trial, there was no time even for the half-hour commute via the Hudson Tubes. He moved into a hotel near the courthouse. For the three months of the trial, he put in nearly 18 hours a day. By trial's end, his weight had fallen to 145 pounds.

Sentencing did not come until six months later. Rifkind, who in his opening remarks said the defendants "proclaimed" their action, now admitted that Leuty had "committed a grave error when he failed to discern where the true path of his responsibility lay. . . .

"The story of his trial and tribulations and of his tragic conviction has been circulated the length and breadth of this land," he continued. "Its lesson has been studied . . . and learned in many executive suites, the cost in time, money and human spirit has been measured, and all the computers have been clacking out the answers in capital letters, and they said: Don't do as Ben Leuty did if ever you are confronted by the same dilemma."

Warren Wilentz argued that Colonial was "a rather young corporation . . . which I am afraid lost its way . . . somewhere around Woodbridge. . . ."

Judge Wortendyke was not impressed. He said the trial "was a liberal education to me of the amorality of business, politics and human relations in this democracy of ours.

"Apparently many such people seem to think that we must accept conduct such as the jury found in this case as part of our democratic way of life," he continued. "I may be a little old-fashioned and a bit narrow in my views, but I was astounded when I looked into the faces of the individual defendants and heard about the corporate defendants in this case. . . . [It] shakes my faith in business in this country."

When Jacks stood before him for sentencing, the judge said:

"I'll tell you this: If you had committed a crime of violence I would have given you the maximum period of imprisonment, because I have no patience with it."

What saved the defendants from prison was not the eloquence of their attorneys, but a hearing Judge Wortendyke had held the day before, taking testimony from "some of the most degraded occupants of Atlanta Penitentiary that I have ever run into." He hesitated at sending white-collar criminals into such an atmosphere. The individual defendants were given suspended sentences of one year and a day and placed on probation for five years.

But Judge Wortendyke imposed the maximum possible fines —$50,000 on Jacks and $20,000 each on Leuty and Feldman. The corporations were also fined the limit—Colonial, $90,000; Bechtel, $50,000; Roland Tompkins, $20,000. (Gates Construction and a sister company, Gates Equipment, which had also pleaded guilty, were fined $2500 each.)

The Colonial case had an ironic aftermath.

By the time Mayor Zirpolo recovered from his heart attack and was able to stand trial, Lacey was the U.S. attorney and Stern his first assistant. Stern wanted to try the case, but Lacey decided it might be a conflict of interest for his office to handle it. The prosecution was turned back to Washington. Justice Department attorney Frank Kiernan prosecuted the case before Judge Wortendyke, and Zirpolo was found guilty. But the judge ruled that Kiernan had committed an error in expressing his personal view of Zirpolo's guilt to the jury and declared a mistrial.

Meanwhile, the other defendants appealed their conviction to the third circuit court of appeals. Again, because Lacey had been associated with the defense, Washington handled the appeal.

In February, 1971, Stern was in Philadelphia arguing the

Addonizio appeal. He was leaving the courthouse when a clerk handed him a copy of the decision in *U.S.* v. *Zirpolo,* as the Colonial case was still titled, though the mayor himself was no longer a party to it.

Although the defendants cited many grounds for reversal, the court considered only one—discrimination against women in the selection of the grand jury. The facts were not in dispute: Federal grand juries in Newark were selected from a panel of 350 names, weighted in favor of men over women, 246 to 104; from this list, 100 names were picked at random and listed in sequence; the first 23 persons eligible and able to serve were empaneled for the grand jury. The panel that returned the Colonial indictment was composed of 18 men and 5 women.

No one knew when or why the practice originated. "Like Topsy, it just grew," the court noted. But it was "a patent violation of both the spirit and letter of federal statutory jury selection standards. . . . Any grand jury so selected has been improperly convened, and any indictment returned therefrom is void. Accordingly, any conviction based thereon shall not be permitted to stand."

The court did not apply the decision retroactively. Only those who had claimed such discrimination at the time of trial could claim it on appeal—and only the Colonial defendants had. It was thus a law affecting only the one case.*

"I was miserable," Stern recalls. "I felt badly that so much work had been put in for nothing. After all, this was the very thing that had brought me to New Jersey. I read the language that said we couldn't indict them again. I recalled a statute that said we could and decided it was probably a slip of the pen. I was determined that the next time I would not only try the case myself, but handle the appeal. I don't know if it would

---

* The Jury Selection Act of 1968 altered the method of picking grand juries, so subsequent defendants were not affected.

have gone any differently but if your own work is going to go bad, at least let it go bad under your own hands."

By this time, Lacey had been promoted to the federal bench and Stern was the U.S. attorney. He was no longer confronted with a conflict of interest in pursuing the case. He immediately empaneled a properly constituted grand jury and had the defendants reindicted. This time they had no fight left. The corporations pleaded guilty to one count, their officers *nolo contendere*. Fines of $10,000 were imposed on each.

The indictments against Mayor Zirpolo and Council President Jacks remained, but proceedings against them were deferred pending a state trial on identical charges. In the meantime, both men—long since resigned from office—were arrested for *passing* a $25,000 bribe to secure a zoning variance on a real-estate project in a neighboring community. They eventually pleaded guilty to both charges in the state court and were sentenced to two to six years in prison.

For Stern, the conclusion of the Colonial trial brought only a brief respite. He had to start preparing for the trial of Peter Weber, which opened on April 15, 1969, again before Judge Wortendyke.

The investigation into Weber's activities had been sidetracked by the Colonial case. But the grand jury eventually returned to it and returned two indictments (later consolidated) against the labor leader, charging him with conspiring to extort and violating the Taft-Hartley Act by taking payments from contractors.

Then the case was dealt a grievous blow—Roy Burgess died. According to Stern, "At that moment it looked as if the whole case was out the window." But he set out to prove the other eight counts—including the actual passage of the $14,000 from Price—through what was, in effect, the testimony of a dead man.

Throughout the trial, the courtroom was filled with the labor leader's supporters—"mugs, big strapping guys," as Stern described them. "When I walked down the aisle, they'd stand there and glower at me."

Some of them followed Stern and Goldstein—who had been discharged from the army in time to assist at the trial—after court recessed each day. "Weber used to tell me what I had done the night before," Stern says.

Unlike most defendants, Weber would josh with the man who was trying to put him behind bars. During one recess he told the prosecutor: "Hogan tried to get me, Bobby Kennedy tried to get me, they've all been trying to get me. They didn't do it—and you're not going to get me either."

Weber was represented by Joseph Hayden, a veteran of the Newark courtrooms. But after the first day of testimony, a new attorney showed up, Dino Bliablias, a peppery former prosecutor who had to be repeatedly admonished by Judge Wortendyke not to shout, gesticulate or badger witnesses.

Stern's first witness was Glenn Giles, the Colonial vice president, far more cooperative in the case against Weber than he had been at the trial of his colleagues and company. He said that Weber had called him at his Atlanta office and asked that the construction contract for the New Jersey leg of the line go to Price's firm. But the contract was awarded, under competitive bidding, to Bechtel.

In September, 1963, Weber's engineers walked off the job the first day Bechtel started work. Giles called Weber, who told the pipeline executive that there would have been no trouble if the contract had gone to Price. Giles then had State Senator Frank (Hap) Farley, the Republican boss of Atlantic City, set up a meeting with Weber. The union leader demanded the right to approve Colonial's contractors, and Giles gave in.

"I felt that if I did not adhere to this type of thing, we would continue to be harassed by strikes or slowdowns, work stoppages, featherbedding, whatever you might call it," he explained.

Giles was out of the office when another contract on the Jersey project was awarded to Osage, a company not on Weber's approved list. The union leader, learning of the award, told Giles: "Hell, yes, you are heading for trouble." Giles persuaded the company's management to drop Osage and award the contract to Napp-Grecco Company, even though its bid was $212,000 higher.

Stern's second witness was Harold C. Price, Jr., who told how his company had had trouble with Weber on previous New Jersey jobs. In 1963, he said, he sent Burgess to meet with Weber about the Colonial project. Burgess reported back that Weber wanted "tax-free cash." Price agreed to pay $10,000, a figure later upped to $14,000.

With the aid of Burgess's expense accounts—which he managed to introduce into evidence as company records—Stern led Price step-by-step through the details of each of the four $3500 payments. Price, of course, wasn't there when the money was passed, but he told how the cash was raised and given to Burgess, identified the records showing that Burgess had gone to New Jersey and told how Burgess reported back that he had delivered the money. His testimony was corroborated by another company official and by Burgess's secretary. Through them, a dead man told tales!

The next witnesses came from Bechtel. One testified that in 1961 Weber had asked the company for a $3500 "political contribution." Bechtel refused to pay—which apparently put it on Weber's blacklist. When Bechtel got the Colonial contract, it immediately encountered problems with Weber. Another official said that he met with Weber at Newark Airport to clear up the dispute and Weber suggested that if a river-crossing subcontract went to Joyce, the company wouldn't have labor problems.

That set the stage for the last phase of the government's case —Weber's relations with Joyce. Like most pipeline workers, James V. Joyce, president of the Western New York construction company, was big and muscular. But by the time of the trial, he was only a shell of a man. Broken by the prosecution, facing two indictments himself, apprehensive about future labor problems, throughout his first day on the stand he was nervous, mumbling and forgetful.

He testified that he'd agreed to pay Weber $30,000, about ten percent of the Bechtel subcontract. It was paid in installments, but he couldn't "remember the circumstances of every payment."

"If I paid somebody thirty thousand—or a thousand—I'd know it," Judge Wortendyke interjected.

That night, Stern and Goldstein ate at the Treat Restaurant (named for an early Newark settler, not the quality of its cuisine). Weber came over to their table.

"Hey, kid!" he said to Stern. "Watch out for that Joyce. That creep will be testifying against you next."

After dinner, the prosecutors returned to the office to review the next day's testimony with Joyce. Stern told him of Weber's remarks.

"Did he really say that?" Joyce asked.

Stern said he had.

"Let's get down to work."

The next day, Joyce was far more assured and precise, rattling off details of the payments—$2500 in Miami's Bal Harbor Hotel; $3000 at Newark Airport; another $3000 at Weber's home in Pompano Beach, Florida. Despite a vigorous cross-examination, the defense could not shake him.

Finally, Weber took the stand in his own defense. He was an impressive witness, booming out answers before counsel had time to object. Bliablias led him through his career in the labor movement, including work building the very courthouse where he was being tried.

He went on to testify that his relations with Price had always been bad—in part because the southern concern "didn't want blacks on the job." With several blacks on the jury, it was a blatant play for racial sympathy.

He said that Harold Price, Sr., since deceased, had offered him a $50,000 bribe ten years before, but he'd refused it.

"Did anybody take care of you in 1959 and 1960?" Bliablias asked.

"Yeah, my members."

"They paid your salary?"

"They did."

The colloquy opened a hole big enough for Stern to drive a bulldozer through on cross-examination.

Weber denied that Price, Jr., had offered him money. He suggested that if Price had passed cash to Burgess, Burgess had pocketed it for himself. He denied attempting to force Colonial to steer the contract to Price. He also denied attempting to influence Bechtel or taking kickbacks from Joyce. He admitted that Joyce's bagman, Thomas Stanton, had offered him money, but insisted that he had his aides throw the "garbage" out of the office.

Bliablias summed up: "Mr. Weber, you are acquainted with the contents of this indictment for which you are now under trial, are you not?"

"I am."

"Is any one word of it true?"

"It is all lies."

Then Stern took over for two days of cross-examination. First, he brought out that Weber's income—in 1959, 1960 and other years—wasn't wholly from his members, that Weber owned interests in a half-dozen companies, several of them contractors with Local 825 or companies that serviced the contractors.

When Weber tried to avoid direct admissions, Stern confronted him with contradictory testimony he'd given before the McClellan Committee. When Stern went on to question him about Florida hotel bills he'd charged to one of his companies, the labor leader's memory lapsed. He kept answering, "I don't remember."

The most telling part of the cross-examination came when Stern confronted Weber with minutes of union meetings that directly contradicted his testimony. Weber lamely tried to explain away the records as "typographical errors."

Finally, Stern questioned Weber about his "yacht"—Weber insisted it was only a "boat"—a 52-foot cruiser called the *Co-Pilot*, worth about $40,000. It sank in 1963—just before Weber allegedly made his demand on Burgess for "tax-free cash." The *Co-Pilot* was raised, but cost thousands to repair. Meanwhile, Weber had bought a 36-foot cruiser, *Co-Pilot II*, for $18,000. Payment was made with a cashier's check, presumably purchased with cash.

By the time Weber stepped off the stand, he was a broken man. The jurors did not dare to look him in the eyes.

The jury was out nearly two days. It came back at 2:20 on Saturday afternoon, June 7. The courtroom was jammed to standing room only with Weber's followers. There was a palpable tension in the air as they waited for the verdict. The key counts in the indictment were Numbers 5 and 6. Even if convicted and jailed on the other counts, Weber could remain in command of his local. But if he was convicted under them, he was through as a labor leader.

The clerk asked: "Do you find the defendant guilty or not guilty?"

The foreman replied: "On count one we find him guilty." It

was a Taft-Hartley violation involving a $3500 payment from Price.

"Count two?"—another Price payment.

"Guilty."

"Count three?"—the third Price payment.

"Guilty."

"Count four?"—the fourth.

"Not guilty."

"Count five?"—the Price extortion.

"Count five, not guilty."

There was an audible sigh of relief in the room.

"Count six?"—the Bechtel extortion.

"Count six, guilty."

There was a collective moan—and the jury's verdicts, finding Weber guilty on two or more counts of taking illegal payments from Joyce, were almost lost in the din.

On September 23, Judge Wortendyke sentenced him to ten years in prison and fined him $30,000. This time the verdict stood on appeal—and Weber went off to jail.

Stern had completed the Weber and Colonial cases, but as it turned out, he'd only just started his work at Justice . . . in Jersey.

4
A NEW TEAM TAKES OVER

Although it is called "The Garden State" and has long been famous for its truck farms, New Jersey is actually the most highly urbanized and most densely populated state in the Union. With a population of 7,168,164, it is the eighth largest.

It is also a "corridor state," devoid of personality and denied a community of interest, fragmented into hundreds of local governments, none large enough to impress its stamp upon the others. The largest city, Newark, has less than 17 percent of the state's population.

New York State focuses on New York City, Illinois on Chicago, Michigan on Detroit. New Jersey radiates outward. A majority of its residents live in New York or Philadelphia suburbs and exist in the metropolitan milieus. Many commute to work across state lines and feel closer kinship to New York or Pennsylvania than to New Jersey. The Garden State has no commercial television stations; its residents rely on broadcasts from New York or Philadelphia, which give short shrift to Jersey news. Similarily, no New Jersey newspaper echoes beyond its home base. The New York *Daily News* boasts the biggest circulation in the state.

The lack of common interest, the political fragmentation, the difficulty of mobilizing public opinion—all these made it easy for crime and corruption to flourish in New Jersey. When mayors, prosecutors and police chiefs in New York and Philadelphia pledged to "run the gangsters out of town," the refugees merely crossed the Hudson or Delaware rivers to New Jersey, ensconced themselves in hundred-thousand-dollar mansions and ran their illegal enterprises by remote control— while local officials hailed them as model citizens and good neighbors.

By the late 1960s, there were ominous rumblings about how deeply organized crime and official corruption were ingrained into the state's social and political fabric. Henry Ruth, a University of Pennsylvania law professor and a member of President Johnson's task force on crime, said that "official corruption in New Jersey is so bad that organized crime can get almost anything it desires." William Brennan III, the son of the Supreme Court justice, conducted an inquiry and concluded that "organized crime in New Jersey manages to work its way . . . into almost every segment of our society except the church." By the time of the Nixon Recession, the joke started going the rounds: "Business is so bad, the Mafia's laid off six judges in New Jersey."

The refinery odors of Carteret and the garbage dumps of Secaucus had long been familiar to travelers on the New Jersey Turnpike and Pennsylvania Railroad. So too was New Jersey's politics "a stench in the nostrils and an offense in the vision of the world," as the state's senior senator, Clifford Case, called it.

But nobody did anything about it—until Frederick B. Lacey was sworn in on September 2, 1969 as United States attorney for the district of New Jersey.

Although the signature on Lacey's certificate of office read "Richard Nixon," the presidential appointment was a legal fiction. In practice, U.S. attorneys are chosen by the local power in the president's party. Lacey was the choice of Senator Case, the only Republican to hold major office in New Jersey at the time.

Case is the epitome of an Eastern Establishment Republican, a GOP liberal who can draw Democratic votes. Then in his third term (he was reelected to a fourth in 1972), he was hardly close to the Nixon administration. He had supported Nelson Rockefeller for the presidential nomination in 1968 and in the few months since the inauguration had broken with the White House on such key issues as Vietnam, civil rights and the nomination of F. Clement Haynsworth to the Supreme Court. He had long felt that the administration of justice should be removed from the arena of partisan politics—a view far different from that of Nixon and Attorney General John Mitchell.

"I've been deeply concerned about corruption in government," the senator explains. "But until President Nixon's election, I didn't have any real voice in selecting either the judges or the United States attorney."

"Senatorial courtesy" mandated that no nominee in New Jersey could clear the Senate without Case's approval . . . and Case wanted Lacey.

Whether Lacey wanted the job was another matter.

Then 48, Lacey enjoyed the highest reputation in the New Jersey bar. He was a partner at Shanley & Fisher, one of Newark's largest and most prestigious law firms; its senior partner was Bernard Shanley, counsel to the president during the Eisenhower administration; its clients included some of the nation's biggest corporations.

Unlike most corporate lawyers, Lacey was a courtroom advocate, specializing in medical and airline-accident cases. Case, who had known Lacey for years, called him "one of the outstanding trial attorneys in the state—if not the country."

At six-foot-four, 225 pounds, Lacey had the rugged look of a retired football player, but he had the manner of a college don—a trifle pompous and pedantic. The son of a Newark police chief, he had been Phi Beta Kappa at Rutgers and editor of the *Law Review* at Cornell. He had served briefly as first assistant U.S. attorney during the 1950s. Though he wasn't active politically, his Republican credentials were impeccable.

Lacey had originally been suggested as a possible judicial nominee, but as they talked, Case came to consider him a better candidate for the prosecutor's post.

Lacey's chief reservation about taking it was financial. The job paid $29,000, only a fraction of what he made in private practice—and he had seven children, several at or approaching college age.

What changed his mind, he says, was a telephone call he received from William Sutherland, a 73-year-old Washington lawyer he'd known and respected. "When you're my age," Sutherland told him, "and you look back on your life, your pride will not be the size of the estate you are going to leave, but what you have accomplished. I know that you have an extremely lucrative law practice, but when you get to this point the money you didn't make won't seem to matter so much. What you might have accomplished in a few years as United States attorney could well be the one thing in your life you would be proud of."

Lacey agreed to serve—but he set several conditions. First, because of the financial squeeze, he couldn't give the four-year commitment the administration desired; he would serve only two, then return to private practice. The administration agreed.

Second, he'd made commitments to finish two cases—one, a personal-injury suit on behalf of two children injured in an explosion; the other, defending a claim against American Airlines from a 1965 crash near Cincinnati. He'd have to take leaves of absence to try them. In what Lacey terms "approval of the unprecedented," again the administration agreed.

His other conditions were harder to meet. Lacey wanted a free hand in picking his staff and he insisted that *he* call the shots for all federal law-enforcement activity in his jurisdiction. It was a freedom of action traditionally allowed only the U.S. attorney in the prestigious Southern District of New York.

"He's the man who put it all in motion," Lacey says of Senator Case. "Without his support we never could have done what we did. He told me I'd be completely free to pick my staff without regard to politics, solely on the basis of ability—and that no one would be permitted to interfere with anything that we elected to investigate and prosecute."

"The only thing I wanted," Case says, "was to get the best law shop in the country—which is what we got."

The Nixon administration, which had already made New Jersey a high-priority area for its investigations, with several units of the multiagency Organized Crime Strike Force already investigating mob activity in the state, accepted Lacey. "I didn't have any difficulty downtown with Fred," Case says. President Nixon submitted Lacey's name to the Senate, where it was approved without debate or opposition. "I don't think they know what they're letting themselves in for," said one of Lacey's law partners. "He's a dynamo."

While waiting for confirmation, the "dynamo" had already started spinning. His first action was to offer the job as his first assistant to the lawyer who'd licked him in the Colonial case—Herbert Stern.

"When I saw that kid in action, I knew he was one of the best and I wanted him on my side," Lacey said. "I recognized I was doing the unorthodox thing, but Senator Case thought it was an excellent idea."

Stern also hesitated about taking the new post. He and Jonathan Goldstein, his colleague at Organized Crime, planned to enter private practice and hang out a joint shingle in New York.

"I felt that my mission to New Jersey had been completed," Stern says. "We had a few shop steward cases left [from the Weber investigation], but all the significant aspects were over. Weber's power had been broken, the grip of the racketeers in that most important union had been snapped, the Colonial people had all been convicted. We'd done what we'd set out to do—and more. After seven and a half years as a public prosecutor, I felt it was time to do what I ultimately wanted to do, which was to go into private practice."

Unlike Lacey, finances were not a factor in Stern's reluctance. The $22,000 the first assistantship paid was a healthy jump above the $17,000 he'd risen to at Organized Crime, or what he could expect to earn during his first few years in private practice.

Lacey picked off Stern's reservations one by one. He'd made a commitment to Goldstein? Lacey solved that by offering Goldstein the post of chief of the office's criminal division.

He had no ties to New Jersey and no local "rabbi"? "I wasn't a regular anything," Stern says. "I wasn't a resident of New Jersey. I wasn't even admitted to practice in the state."

The jurisdictional difficulty was easily overcome: Membership in the state bar isn't necessary for practice in the federal courts; Stern could take the post, establish residency in New Jersey and take the state bar examination at his leisure— of which, he was to discover, he'd have precious little.

And on the political question, "Fred was adamant," Stern says. "He made it clear that he was not going to let any political considerations enter into the running of the United States attorney's office. And I must say that Senator Case was of the same persuasion."

So, on September 3, Stern was sworn in as Lacey's first assistant and Goldstein as chief of the criminal division.

The Organized Crime investigation had another pleasant consequence for the 32-year-old prosecutor. During the Weber trial, Stern met a former beauty queen from Bartlesville named Sandra Webster. He was quite taken with the Oklahoma girl and in the midst of a criminal case, romance blossomed. On August 20, 1970, Sandra Webster became Mrs. Herbert Stern. Three years later they became the parents of twin boys, Jason and Jordan.

"There are two ways to do this job," Stern says of the U.S. attorney's office. "You can sit here and wait for the agencies to refer cases to you, or you can go out and make them."

The first had been the way of Lacey's predecessor, David M. Satz, Jr. The second way was Lacey's . . . and Stern's.

"We decided we were going to run . . . and run—and keep on running," Stern continues. "We were going to be an active investigative office.

"We saw terrible things going on all around us, a perversion of our way of life and of the democratic processes of our society. We saw Newark strangled in the grip of unscrupulous public officials and of organized crime. Hudson County and Jersey City had been notorious for sixty years. Atlantic City cried out for action. And the state house—by reputation, they were running the state government the same way Addonizio was running Newark, and Kenny, Hudson County.

"Public officials sat like vultures ready to collect a tithe on every piece of public business. They had turned New Jersey into a—into a stink pot. It's hard to find the adjectives to describe it. The ordinary citizen who lived and worked here began to feel that there was no other way of life. Somebody had to do something about it."

At his swearing-in, Lacey declared that his first priority as U.S. attorney would be a war on organized crime and official corruption in New Jersey.

A war requires an army. Lacey found himself in command of a squad. The U.S. attorney's office was allotted 18 assistants—one fewer than when Lacey had served as first assistant 14 years before! Over the intervening period other prosecutors' offices in New Jersey had grown by as much as 300 percent.

The assistants were spread over three offices—two in Camden; two in Trenton; fourteen in the main office in Newark, a half-dozen in the civil division, the remainder in the criminal.*

The number was barely enough to handle the day-to-day caseload brought in by government agencies—the routine of bank robbers, auto thieves, tax evaders, dope peddlers, draft dodgers, mail frauds as well as land-condemnation cases and civil tax suits—much less investigate and prosecute organized crime and official corruption.

The chart illustrates the workload of the office for the fiscal year 1969–70:

	Criminal		Civil
	Cases	Defendants	
Pending—July 1, 1969	468	805	728
Filed	550	903	840
Terminated	372	516	728
Pending—June 30, 1970	646	1192	840

Of the criminal defendants disposed of, 4 were tried by a judge, 46 by a jury and 466 pleaded guilty.

Lacey immediately sought to augment the staff. It required an end run through the labyrinths of the federal bureaucracy. There is no budget for any U.S. attorney's office, only a master budget for all 94 U.S. attorneys' offices in the nation. Whatever New Jersey needed—from a Xerox copier down to an extra supply of carbon paper—required a requisition to Washington. If the item was as major as more men—even one assistant beyond the budget—it went first to Justice's Executive Office for U.S. Attorneys, where it was weighed against the manpower requests of the 93 other federal prosecutors; then to the deputy attorney general, where it was weighed

---

* In most districts, subsections are legal "divisions" with prescribed venue boundaries. In New Jersey, they are "vicinages," mere administrative conveniences; a case can be brought in or switched to any vicinage.

against the requests of the rest of the Justice Department; next to the Bureau of the Budget, where it was weighed against the requests of every other governmental department; and finally to Congress.

Though they've quarreled both publicly and privately with Mitchell and his successor, Richard Kleindienst, on other issues, neither Lacey nor Stern faults them on the question of staff. Justice cooperated on almost every request for more men. The number of assistants jumped from 18 when Lacey came in, to 40 when he left 17 months later, to 55 today, making New Jersey's the nation's fifth-largest U.S. attorney's office —after Washington, New York, Chicago and Los Angeles.

The present manpower allotment puts one or two men in Trenton, three to five in Camden, all handling both civil and criminal cases. The remainder are in Newark—three in the appeals division, four in the environmental, ten in civil; the rest, about thirty in all, are in the criminal division, though as many as a dozen at a time may be detached for duty in the special prosecutions section, which handles the major investigations.

Lacey recalls one telephone conversation when he reported a development on some case to Mitchell.

"Is there anything else?" the attorney general asked.

"We need more men," Lacey said.

At the next allocation, six of the eight new assistant U.S. attorney posts Congress had authorized for the entire country went to New Jersey.

The number of lay personnel increased correspondingly and Lacey acquired an administrative officer—Frank Costa, previously with the U.S. marshal's office in New York—to run the office's nonlegal side.

Also, after months of hammering away at Washington, the office finally got the seeds of its own investigative staff—two agents and an accountant.

No longer did the office have to rely solely on the FBI, IRS or other agencies to do its legwork. Only New York and Chicago were similarly blessed.

"I would like to increase it," Stern says of the investigative staff. "A modern prosecutor's office today needs investigators who can respond instantly to the prosecutor's authority, without any intermediate steps, people whose hours of work the prosecutor controls. I think it's essential."

All but a handful of Satz's assistants had left or submitted their resignations by the time Lacey took office. Normally, assistants are recruited through the political process. A good prosecutor will demand some degree of competence in those he hires, but party regularity is usually the first priority.

Lacey took a different course. He contacted the senior partners of New Jersey's major law firms and asked them to lend the office their brightest young associates for two or three years' public service—and some seasoning in the courtroom. He didn't require a reference from a political "rabbi"; he didn't even ask if they were Democrats or Republicans.

"It was a real shot in the arm," Stern says. "It brought in young, first-rate legal minds."

As the operation gained its own momentum, new assistants were recruited from law schools and the ranks of judicial clerks.

With the increase in personnel came a space squeeze. But the U.S. attorney's quarters on the fourth floor of the Newark courthouse—a vintage 1920s post office—were inadequate to start with.

"They were terrible offices, dark and dingy," Stern says. "The criminal assistants' offices were in a row and there were three doors in every one—one from the corridor and one to each adjoining office. On any given day, you could open all the doors and roll a bowling ball through every office.

"There was no security. There was no receptionist in the

passageway outside. Anyone could get off the elevator and walk into any office he wanted to. You could be sitting there preparing a witness on a sensitive organized-crime case and the lawyer representing the defendant might stick his head through the door and say, 'Howdy!'

"In the civil division, there was no ceiling. There were wires hanging and girders showing. It was a bloody awful mess."

Across the street, a new skyscraper federal building was rising, but the U.S. attorney's office had not been allotted space in it. It took a lot of bureaucratic string-pulling, but Lacey finally garnered the entire fifth floor for his expanding staff. In the spring of 1970, the U.S. attorney's office moved to its modern quarters.

In his first month after taking office, Lacey personally prosecuted a case, the only trial he was to handle from start to finish during his tenure. "Right at the outset, I thought I'd let them know I could try a case," he explains.

It was like Babe Ruth batting in the bush leagues. The defendant was Stanley J. Pollack, a Passaic County judge who had failed to file income-tax returns from 1962 through 1966. The charge was only a misdemeanor; Pollack had not evaded his taxes, since the money he owed had been withheld on his paycheck.

The trial lasted four days. Pollack, sobbing on the witness stand, said he'd been too busy to fill out the forms. He admitted that he'd been "lax and negligent," but denied any criminal intent. The jury needed only 90 minutes to return a guilty verdict. Pollack was later fined $10,000.

The prosecutor kept even busier after normal working hours. He went on a candidate's speaking schedule to enlist public support for his campaign against the underworld. In every speech the message was the same: "Organized crime is taking over the state of New Jersey."

"We went out and we spoke two or three nights a week," Stern says. "At lodges, Kiwanis clubs, Jewish temples, Methodist churches, Catholic churches, universities, law schools, bar associations, pounding home the message the length and breadth of this state, and occasionally out of state—trying to arouse the public, trying to persuade them that it didn't have to be the way it was, trying to convince businessmen that they didn't have to pay off, trying to bring the whole rotten system to a screeching halt."

A few samples from Lacey's speeches give the flavor:

> Unless you, as leaders, arouse an apathetic public to stem the tide of crime in this nation, our society as we know it is doomed. Organized crime is, in the vernacular, "taking us over." First, it corrupts law enforcement. Second, it corrupts unions and makes a mockery of the collective-bargaining process. Third, it corrupts the businessman.
>
> —November 29, 1969

> If the battle against organized crime is to be won, it is going to be won at the local, county and state levels. That is why your work will be so vital and so important. You can enlist public support. You can goad reluctant public officials who derive comfort from closing their eyes, stopping their ears and then declaiming, "We are tired of hearing that organized crime is taking over the state of New Jersey." . . .
>
> There must be a massive and swelling tide of public opinion to stop bribery and corruption. We must arouse the public—not lull them back to apathy. We have had enough of indifference, of indulgence and of law enforcement officers who do not know, or care to know the challenge which faces us. Businessmen and labor leaders must be quick to report violations of law. Above all, we

must sponsor candidates for public office who are men of impeccable reputation, of independence and courage.
—January 26, 1970

How powerful is organized crime? Can it run the cities, the counties, the states, the nation? The answer is, "Yes, in varying degrees." In some cities, its control is complete: it dictates who does business with the cities and on what terms. In other municipalities, it may only buy law enforcement protection. . . .

The late Senator Robert F. Kennedy called it the "enemy within," and attempted to alert the public as to the nature of this secret organization and the danger that it poses. . . .

It is . . . essential that the public be informed about it. It must come to understand that the existence of organized crime is not a myth, nor idle speculation; the public must come to the understanding that it does exist before it can take any action to protect itself against the threat which organized crime poses to our way of life.
—March 2, 1970

To many, Lacey sounded like the boy who cried "Wolf!" But he did more than merely *talk* about organized crime. He set out to clean up New Jersey. Within five months, his office rocked the state to its very foundations.

"The entire office went on the most fantastic schedule," Stern recalls. "You don't run these investigations without making massive commitments of manpower. There was nobody around to do the purely administrative work. Trying to get more men, interviewing the applicants when we got the authorization, trying to get the office moved, designing and laying out the new office and all the petty details—they were all done on the fly.

"Lacey and I were in the courtroom on DeCarlo. Lacey

and I were on the investigation of Addonizio. John Goldstein was running the entire office and conducting other investigations, including the investigation of Peter Moraites, the Speaker of the assembly, in a most sophisticated bank case.

"We were working at a fantastic, furious pace, just churning out work. It was probably the most hectic period in my life—and perhaps in the history of law enforcement in New Jersey."

5
A TALE OF TWO TAPES

The first step in the cleanup campaign was to clean up the calendar. Two of the major items on the agenda the new team of Lacey and Stern faced were carry-overs from David Satz's stewardship as U.S. attorney.* Both involved ranking Mafiosi.

Simone Rizzo DeCavalcante, dapper and swarthily handsome, was known in the newspapers as "Sam the Plumber," though he preferred the appellation "Princeton Sam." One nickname came from his legitimate front—a plumbing concern in Kenilworth, New Jersey; the other, from his residence in nearby Princeton township. He was the boss of a small Cosa Nostra family based in Southern New Jersey. According to the *New York Times*, he was "the smartest and smoothest and least vicious of the aging Mafia leaders in the East." Almost alone among them, he had never spent a night behind bars.

During the years that Stern was in New Jersey on the Weber and Colonial cases, another attorney from Organized Crime, Peter Richards, was building a case against the 59-year-old DeCavalcante. The indictment was filed in March, 1968.

As criminal actions go, it was hardly "a federal case." Two minor-league Mafiosi, Gaetano Vastola and Daniel Annunziata, had stuck up a crooked dice game in Trevose, Pennsylvania, near Philadelphia, and demanded a $20,000 payoff. The operators balked and sought DeCavalcante's help. Under DeCavalcante's mediation, the $20,000 demand was scaled down to $12,000. Sam the Plumber's "fee" was $3800. The government contended that the raid and sitdown had been engineered from the start by DeCavalcante. He was indicted—along with Vastola and Annunziata—for conspiracy to extort.

DeCavalcante's lawyer, a former assistant U.S. attorney named Sidney Franzblau, filed a number of pretrial motions.

---

* Satz stepped down in June, 1969. His first assistant, Donald Horowitz, served as acting U.S. attorney through the summer.

Among other things, he asked for the results of any electronic surveillance of his client. Under recent rulings of the U.S. Supreme Court, the prosecution was required to disclose this, and the government had dropped several major cases rather than reveal what it had overheard. But in this instance, the government complied. On June 10, 1969, Satz's office filed with the court clerk 12 volumes containing some 2000 pages of DeCavalcante's conversations.

Franzblau was astounded: "I've never heard of the government releasing such information before."

Most of the conversations had been overheard by the FBI's "criminal informant NK 2461-C*"—the bureau's code for a microphone planted in DeCavalcante's office between August 31, 1964, and July 12, 1965. It was one of 98 eavesdrops and wiretaps the FBI had placed in the homes and offices of Mafia members in that Valachi era. Their purpose was not to uncover evidence. The "bugs" were illegal and evidence obtained from them could not be introduced in court. They were planted as part of the government's intelligence effort— to pinpoint the members of the mob and determine their place in the underworld hierarchy.

The DeCavalcante tapes were a gold mine of information. Sam the Plumber had acted as mediator in the "Bananas War"—the Cosa Nostra "commission's" campaign to depose Joseph Bonnano, head of one of the five New York City "families." DeCavalcante's conversations gave the government not only a who's who of organized crime, but a blow-by-blow account of the underworld power struggle.

The tapes also supplied a few leads to the mob's link with New Jersey politicians. The name of Elizabeth's mayor, Thomas Dunn, repeatedly came up in the conversations, mostly when underworld underlings sought DeCavalcante's help in getting government jobs for friends and relatives.

Sometimes more important names were mentioned. On

December 30, 1964, DeCavalcante met with Joseph Zicarelli, better known as "Joe Bayonne," the mob boss of the Jersey waterfront. They discussed putting in "the fix" in a pending deportation proceeding against the father of one of DeCavalcante's *capos* (captains). Zicarelli noted that he'd once been friendly with Senator Harrison Williams, but after his arrest some six years before, Williams would have nothing to do with him. As a last resort, he continued, there were three or four federal judges, but the best bet would be to advise "Neal, the congressman"—Representative Cornelius Gallagher.

The DeCavalcante tapes also provided a rare look into the private life of a public enemy. There were discussions of legitimate business, domestic squabbles, arguments about the cost of weddings and charitable contributions, even whether to pay the boy five dollars for shoveling snow off the sidewalk (they didn't). But mostly, the talk was of crime. And most of it was penny-ante stuff—gambling, some shylocking, disposal of stolen goods.

One tape, though, disclosed more grisly matters. It came from a night of reminiscing by DeCavalcante, Angelo (Gyp) DeCarlo, called "Ray" by his friends, and Anthony (Tony Boy) Boiardo. DeCarlo and Tony Boy's father, Ruggiero (Richie the Boot) Boiardo, were old-time mobsters, powerful *capos* in the Vito Genovese family. Tony Boy had entered the family business.

"How about the time we hit the little Jew," Tony Boy recalled.

"As little as they are, they struggle," DeCarlo said.

"The Boot hit him with a hammer," Boiardo continued. "The guy goes down and he comes up. So I got a crowbar this big, Ray. Eight shots in the head. What do you think he finally did to me? He spit at me and said, 'You obscenity!' " [FBI's euphemism.]

"They're fighting for their life," DeCarlo observed.

That triggered DeCavalcante's memory: "Ray, you told me years ago about the guy where you said, 'Let me hit you clean.' "

"That's right," DeCarlo said. "So the guy went for it. There was me, Zip and Johnny Russell. So we took the guy out in the woods and I said, 'Now listen. . . . You gotta go. Why not let me hit you right in the heart and you won't feel a thing?' He said, 'I'm innocent, Ray, but if you've got to do it . . .' So I hit him in the heart and it went right through him."

The conversation had been overheard on a "bug" planted in "The Barn," DeCarlo's headquarters behind a restaurant near Mountainside, New Jersey. Although DeCavalcante outranked him on the mob's organization chart, DeCarlo had more clout in the underworld—just as the governor of Wyoming may outrank the mayor of Chicago in protocol, but not political power. At 67, pudgy and white-haired, DeCarlo ran much of the rackets in northern New Jersey. By the time the De-Cavalcante tapes were released, he too was inches away from indictment.

On November 26, 1968, the FBI in Newark received two handwritten letters from Louis B. Saperstein, a 63-year-old real-estate broker with a long history of shady financial dealings. The letters were dated November 21, but hadn't been mailed until the 25th.

One letter read:

> Federal Bureau of Investigation
> Newark, NJ
> Gentlemen:
>   I am writing you, maybe others can be helped by my plight. To-date, I am indebted to Ray (Gyp) DeCarlo, Joe Polverino (known as Joe the Italian) and Daniel

Cecere (known as Red Cecere), the total due these three is $115,000 on which I was charged and paid 1½ % interest per week, amounting to $1725 per week; the amount of $1725 was delivered weekly to Red Cecere at the Berkeley Bar. On September 13, 1968 I was severely beaten at a place in the rear of Weiland's Restaurant, Route 22, DeCarlo's headquarters. I was then told and given 3 months until December 13, 1968 to pay the entire accumulated amount of $115,000—the interest was then raised to $2000 per week which was delivered to Cecere every Thursday at the Berkeley Bar in Orange, NJ. This was delivered by Lenny Banks, my employee— on Nov. 14, 1968 I cashed 2 checks totaling $31,000 at Essex County State Bank and personally delivered to Cecere $30,000—under threat of death. Cecere, DeCarlo & Polverino, also stated many times my wife and son would be maimed or killed.

Please protect my family. I am sure they mean to carry out this threat.

Last night from my home I called DeCarlo at the Harbor Island Spa in Florida, and pleaded for time but to no avail, over the phone DeCarlo stated unless further monies was paid the threats would be carried out. Today, Lenny Banks delivered to Cecere $2000 at 11:30 am. Cecere called by phone while I was in Staten Island —& I had to send this money to-day.

Louis B. Saperstein

By the time the FBI looked into the case, Saperstein was dead. On the day he mailed the letters, he was rushed to the hospital with stomach pains and died the following day. The cause of death was listed as "cardiac shock induced by acute gastroenteritis."

On the basis of the letters, Satz obtained a court order to exhume Saperstein's body. The state medical examiner, Dr.

Edwin Albano, found it loaded with "enough arsenic to kill a mule."

But no one knew whether it was murder or suicide. The Essex County prosecutor, Joseph Lordi, haled all those mentioned in the letters before a grand jury, but the panel found "insufficient evidence" of homicide.

Then in March, 1969, a 32-year-old millionaire wheeler-dealer named Gerald Martin Zelmanowitz was arrested in Miami for interstate transportation of $250,000 in stolen securities. He was returned to New Jersey and hit with a similar charge involving a second $250,000 batch of stolen securities. Soon after that, Zelmanowitz told the FBI that he had information about the Saperstein case.

Since DeCarlo and his associates were known to be dangerous men, efforts had to be taken to protect Zelmanowitz and his family. "Most people are afraid to testify," Stern notes. "Ninety-nine percent of the time it's absurd that they should be afraid. But there is that one percent or less where a witness would really be in danger. And Zelmanowitz in the De-Carlo case was such a witness."

The Zelmanowitz family was kept hidden and was watched night and day by federal marshals. Even the fact that Zelmanowitz was cooperating with the authorities was kept secret as long as possible. He testified before the grand jury as "Mr. X" and his face was hidden from the panel by a screen.*

On August 28, 1969, five days before Lacey took office,

---

* Three years later, Zelmanowitz's "cover" was blown when officials of a San Francisco clothing company discovered that their ousted president was not the "military security" expert he'd claimed to be, but the confessed stock swindler who'd testified against Angelo DeCarlo. In a civil complaint, Zelmanowitz, who had been using the name Paul Maris, was accused of bilking the firm of at least $200,000. "My whole entire cover is being destroyed and torn apart," Zelmanowitz told a reporter. Two days later he disappeared . . . only to resurface a few weeks later as a witness before the Senate's Permanent Investigations Subcommittee.

extortion indictments were lodged against DeCarlo, Polverino, Cecere and another hood, Peter Landusco. They were charged under a section of the Truth-in-Lending Act.

Stern got the case. "I racked my brain for some way to get those letters into evidence," he recalls. "I knew that on their face they were hearsay. From the file I could see that Satz had toyed with the idea of a dying declaration, but it was impossible because you can only use that in a homicide case in the federal courts. Besides, it lacked the requirements of a dying declaration. I hit the books and came up with the theory that it could come in not for the truth of its contents, but for the state of mind of Saperstein. Since the indictment alleged extortion, one of the principal elements we had to prove was fear in the mind of the victim. There's a state-of-mind exception to the hearsay rule that lets in statements by a victim to a third party if they show he was in fear. Reasoning by analogy, I decided that if oral statements can come in, we could argue—perhaps successfully—that written declarations could come in as well."

The trial started on January 2, 1970. The courtroom was an armed camp, the doors guarded by federal marshals, all spectators screened by an electronic metal detector.

In the pattern they were to follow again in the Addonizio trial, Lacey and Stern divided the prosecution chores—Lacey delivering the opening and closing arguments to the jury, Stern presenting the evidence.

Unlike the Colonial case, the prosecution wasn't confronted with legal giants like Edward Bennett Williams or Simon Rifkind. DeCarlo and his associates were represented by men known around the courthouse as "mob lawyers"—lawyers Lacey once described as "men who turn up time and time again representing the same type of client." DeCarlo's counsel was Michael Direnzo, a New York lawyer whom, according to a cocounsel, DeCarlo had "known for a considerable portion of his adult life." Cecere's lawyer was Michael Querques, a veteran of the local courtrooms, who, it was learned in midtrial, had advised the defendants *during* the course of the alleged conspiracy; his counsel to a union of IRS employees had recently come under Lacey's fire. Polverino's counsel was Samuel Bozza, whose voice repeatedly appeared on what came to be called "the DeCarlo tapes."

From the DeCavalcante tapes, it was obvious that DeCarlo had also been "bugged." The defense asked for the transcripts, but it was careful not to repeat Franzblau's mistake. It asked that the disclosure be limited to the defense. Judge Robert Shaw, a no-nonsense Kennedy appointee who looked like Jack Dempsey in his heyday, ruled that *he* would read the transcripts and decide when and how they would be turned over.

After the jury of seven men and five women was empaneled, Judge Shaw ordered them sequestered for the remainder of the trial. The following day, over vehement defense objections, he filed the 1200-page transcript of the DeCarlo tapes with the court clerk, where it was in the public domain.

There was a mad scramble in the clerk's office as reporters climbed over tables, chairs and even each other to get a peek at the transcript. From first glance it was evident that the DeCarlo tapes were even more explosive than those of DeCavalcante. Page after page revealed the extent of DeCarlo's illegal empire and the political payoffs he made to keep it going.

Unlike many mobsters, DeCarlo made no pretense of putting up a legitimate "front." According to the tapes, he was once asked by Harold (Kayo) Konigsberg, a sadistic collector and enforcer for the mob: "Will you tell me why everybody loves you so?"

"I'm a hoodlum," DeCarlo replied. "I don't want to be a legitimate guy. All these other racket guys who get a few bucks want to become legitimate."

The heart of DeCarlo's underworld empire was gambling. "Craps is getting out of existence," he once told Konigsberg. "What's coming in?"

"Betting numbers, booking horses, sports. Sports is big, but so many crooked games. Basketball games are all crooked, and now and then you get a crooked football game. You get killed. You can't get anyone to take over a three-hundred-dollar bet on a fight except Demus."

DeCarlo's empire also encompassed shylocking—"strongest racket in the world," he said, "better than numbers or anything else and cleaner"—and the disposal of stolen goods, though he often got stuck with shoddy merchandise. Once, when DeCarlo was absent, another mobster said he'd "buy a barrel of sand on the Sahara Desert if the price is right."

But DeCarlo would have nothing to do with narcotics. He claimed that Vito Genovese was "framed" on the narcotics conviction that put him in Atlanta's federal prison—"Vito hated narcotics all his life"—and several times suggested stiffer penalties for dope pushers.

The mob's influence, as revealed by the tapes, extended deeply into legitimate enterprises. Gambling, where legal, was a favorite. All the top mobsters had "points" in the Las Vegas casinos and, under Batista, DeCarlo said, "the mob had a piece of every joint down there." Fidel Castro's seizure of power in Cuba forced the mobsters to seek new outlets in the Caribbean.

DeCarlo and Konigsberg once discussed the possible purchase of a hotel in Jamaica.

"I want you to sit down with these people," DeCarlo said. "One guy went to Europe who was here the other night. He said, 'Sure, if I thought there was any possibility of getting gambling, we would put the money up.'"

"You know who I'll get it from?" Kayo asked. "Frank Sinatra."

"I'm going down there next week," DeCarlo said. "I'll see Sinatra and have a talk with him."

A huge poster of Sinatra hung in The Barn and his name came up frequently in the conversations there. Once, DeCarlo related, "Tony Bennett came over to the Racquet Club [in Miami Beach] and says he's looking for this broad. I says, 'What do you want?'

"He says he wants this job [girl].

"I says, 'What are you talking about. Frank Sinatra sent a telegram wantin' this broad. She was a beautiful thing, a real job."

All the mobsters, it seemed, played "Godfather" to an Italian singer. During one conversation, Pete Fusco noted that he'd persuaded Joey Bishop to book a spot for his singer, Bobby Manaro, when Bishop substituted for Jack Paar on the *Tonight* show. DeCarlo doubted that Manaro could sing as well as his "kid"—Mickey Roselli—and to prove it played three of Roselli's records.

DeCarlo's illegal operations required protection—and he bought it, all over the state.

Policemen were frequent visitors to The Barn. One Hoboken detective was practically a regular.

"You guys gotta make a gambling squad in Hoboken," DeCarlo once told him. "The police commissioner and the chief get everybody together and tell them that there's nobody going to make any gambling raids except the gambling squad, and he tells the gambling squad before you make any raids you let me know. . . . Now, see, this way we're going to have everything our way. . . ."

"It will run perfect, if they don't let it run wild," the detective said. "You gotta have one decent game in the county."

"That's all, or you're going to have the federals in there."

One day in 1963, DeCarlo discussed the problem presented

by State Police Superintendent Dominick Capello: "Do you know how much Cappy wants?"

"No, how much?" said Louis (Lucky) Percello.

"He wants a thousand dollars for Long Branch and a thousand for Albany [Park]."

"For each town?" said William Rega.

"Yeah, each town," DeCarlo continued. "And for the whole county, he wants to make another price."

"Tell him——" Percello started.

DeCarlo interrupted him: "Do you want to hear the rest of the story? June, July, August and September, he wants double."

DeCarlo suggested a solution: "Here's what I figure: Let's move all the offices into Long Branch and we'll just pay him for Long Branch. . . ."

"If I had my way, I'd give him nothing . . ." Percello said.

"We used to pay him fifteen hundred for a crap game—fifteen hundred a month!" DeCarlo said.

"In Bayonne," Rega noted, "we paid him two thousand."

"He's no good," DeCarlo insisted. "He knows every racket guy in the state. We would have been better off with a dumb guy in there."

If the cops couldn't be bought, there were the prosecutors. Anthony (Little Pussy) Russo boasted that he'd bought off Monmouth County Prosecutor Vincent Keuper. And Tony Boy Boiardo said of Essex County Prosecutor Joseph Lordi: "Jerry Catena [Genovese's successor as head of the 'family'] is close to Lordi. They've gotten together several times."

But Lordi, it turned out, did the mob no favors. During one grand-jury investigation of the underworld, DeCarlo exploded: "I wish Lordi had called me. I'd [have] embarrassed him . . . by saying, 'I'm the one who okayed you for the job.' "

If the prosecutors couldn't be bought, there were the judges and the juries. When one small-time mobster was convicted,

DeCarlo inquired: "How come they didn't try to make [bribe] one?"

"Make who?"

"On the jury—one of the jurors."

"We had somebody."

". . . You should have had two or three," DeCarlo said. "Don't be cheap. Don't buy just one. Have them buy two or three. So it costs you twenty or thirty thousand."

DeCarlo explained his philosophy of an impartial judiciary to Anthony (Jack Panels) Santoli, whose brother-in-law sought appointment as a county judge:

"Sit down with the guy and tell him you want to do what's right. 'We don't want you to deal with eight million guys. You deal with one guy, he'll deal with you, that's all.' If Tony Boy gets a man in trouble, you want to do some business, pay him [to] straighten it out. Say, 'What the hell! We don't want to put a guy in there who won't take money. We don't want you to do it for nothing, we don't want no favors, we want to pay for whatever favors we get even if we get you the job. The jobs are made to make money with, not just to sit there. . . .' "

And if the judges and jurors couldn't be bought, there were the political bosses. DeCarlo told of going to see David Wilentz, the Democratic leader in Middlesex County:

"I went down myself. There's three guys—I don't know who they are or nothing. . . . They were breaking into cars at Howard Johnson's. You know, like you go in to eat, they break in your car and they'd steal stuff out of your car. They got caught on the job.

"I went down to Dave and told him that these guys want to give five Gs so they don't go to the can. . . .

"He said, 'Is this favor for you?'

"I said, 'No, it ain't no favor. They're gonna pay five thousand.'

"He said, 'But is it somebody you're interested in?'

"I said, 'No, I don't even know the guys. Why are you asking?'

"He said, 'If it was for you, it would be done for nothing. If it's for you, I'll go all the way. But if it ain't for you, I ain't gonna commit murder to do it.'

"I said, 'Well, they're willing to pay five Gs and I figured somebody could use it.'

"He said, 'The hell with the money. I owe you a big favor. I want to do something for you. I don't want money for it.' "

DeCarlo concluded: "I saved him from going to the can— nobody but me." It was not explained how.

The mob was bipartisan in its politics. It also had connections with Frank (Hap) Farley, the Republican boss of Atlantic City.

Frank Ruggieri told DeCarlo how he was brought into Farley's home by an Atlantic City police sergeant. As a convicted bookmaker, Ruggieri was barred from the local racetrack.

"Don't worry about it," Farley told him. "Tomorrow send your name with Joe. I'll call Ryder [the police commissioner] up myself. Don't worrry about it."

The next day the sergeant went to headquarters and left Ruggieri's name with the police commissioner. "Tell him to go to the track," the commissioner said.

Then there was the late Dennis Carey, the Democratic leader in Essex County—but relations with him weren't always the best.

"Carey double-crossed me," DeCarlo complained one day. "We gave him plenty of money and we didn't get one thing from him. A lot of it was Tony Boy's money. He never produced one thing he promised. The only favors we ever got were off Hughie and Rodino [the Newark-area congressman, Hugh

Addonizio and Peter Rodino]. Any favor we ever went to them for, we got it right away."

Of all the bosses, Hudson County's John J. Kenny was the most reliable for the mob. DeCarlo reported that Kenny gave them clearance to run gambling in Secaucus and when the game in Kearny was raided by a local cop, Kenny said, "I'll call the mayor"—and did.

In return, the mob did favors for Kenny. In 1962, Kenny phoned DeCarlo and asked him to contact Addonizio—by then mayor of Newark—and have him appoint one of Kenny's men administrator of Martland Medical Center.

DeCarlo agreed. "Well, what will I do with my man—make him call you or make him call Tom [Jersey City Mayor Thomas Gangemi]?"

Kenny's reply is not recorded, but DeCarlo continued: "I don't know if I can locate Hughie tonight, but if you see him down there, you tell him you was talking to me tonight and I go along with this a million percent. He knows I go along with anything you want. You talk to him the way you talk to me. . . . Okay, fine. . . . Okay, boy."

Of all the disclosures on the tapes—including DeCarlo's fantastic effort to infiltrate and take over the Masonic order—none was more sinister than the mob's role in electing Addonizio mayor of Newark in 1962.

A year before the election, Pete Landusco reported Addonizio's feelings about making the race: "And do you know what he said to me? . . . He said, 'I'm only [going to be] mayor for six years. I want to run for governor, that's my aim. . . . I'll be the first guinea governor the state ever had.' "

To become mayor, Addonizio had to defeat the incumbent, Leo Carlin. The trouble was, Michael Bontempo, president of the city council, also planned to enter the race.

"He's gonna . . . split the Italian vote," DeCarlo complained. "Carlin got him to do it."

So DeCarlo—and other members of the mob—sat down with Bontempo.

"Well, Mickey," DeCarlo said, "let's get down to business. What is it you want from Addonizio to work together? . . ."

"I've got to say this to you," Bontempo replied. "You say, 'We want to win.' Let me put it this way: Let the best man win. But here's the story and I say this to you, Ray, and I'm not pulling any punches. I think Mr. Addonizio made too damn many commitments with a lot of heels."

"Well, he must have made some commitments," DeCarlo said.

"Irving Berlin's [an Orange bookmaker] going to tell him what to do."

"Oh, no——"

". . . Don't say, 'no,' I'm telling you something. I'll bet you that Irving Berlin is closer to Hughie than you to Ray, Joe."

"Well, I won't deny it," said Joe DeBenedictis, the Democratic boss of Newark's North Ward.

"Irving's got him in the bag."

The conversation continued on this track for a while. Then DeBenedictis asked Bontempo what he wanted to get out of the race.

"I just told you—motor vehicle director."

The post, appointive by Governor Richard Hughes, was apparently beyond the mob's power to deliver.

"Now, look, you're in this business for the money, ain't you?" DeCarlo asked.

"At my age I am," Bontempo replied.

"You've got to be reasonable," DeBenedictis said. "We want to win. You've got to sit down with Hughie."

"I don't care if it's you or Hughie, as long as it's an Italian," DeCarlo interjected.

After Bontempo left The Barn, DeCarlo said, "We'll see if

we can raise ten thousand for him. We'll get all the bookmakers. The Boot will pay up five thousand."

A few days later, DeCarlo reported back on a meeting he had with Addonizio: "I told him, I said . . . Richie [Boiardo] and I were willing to give that lousy Mickey five Gs to get him out of the race. He said, 'Don't give him ten cents. . . .'

"I also told Hughie the other night also, I said, 'Hughie, you get elected, there's only gonna be one guy collect from all the bookmakers. If I hear that this guy pays you direct, this guy pays you direct and that guy—the hell with you! I'm walking. You can go and do business with everybody you want to and you're gonna wind up in the can sooner or later. . . .'"

They were prophetic words.

Apparently, Bontempo took the bait. DeBenedictis told DeCarlo a few days later: "We got rid of this jerk. I told you what I had to do with him. I had to give him five big ones."

Word of the payoff apparently reached another prospective mayoral candidate. On March 17, 1962, DeBenedictis reported to DeCarlo: "Nick Caputo's gonna file. . . . I heard about it, so I call him up yesterday. I said, 'Nick, is it true that you're gonna file?' I said, 'Why, you jerk, do you know what you're doing?'

"He said, 'Well, I can't win, but I can force a runoff. . . .'

"What he's asking for is out of this world. This is just between the four of us—he wants to be the administrator of Newark. . . .

"I had told Nick, 'You SOB . . . you're gonna pull this.'

"He said, 'Well, I'm only looking out for myself.'

"So I said, 'I'll tell you what I'm gonna do with you—I'm gonna break your two legs. Don't blame any racket men, don't blame any tough guys, I'm gonna break your legs for you if you file. I'm warning you now—I'll be the guy to break your legs.'"

"If he does," DeCarlo added, "we'll go and break his legs."

Caputo was dissuaded from entering the mayoral lists and Addonizio went on to defeat Carlin in the election. DeCarlo wanted one of his police proteges to become police director, but Tony Boy Boiardo vetoed him, and Irving Berlin's choice, Dominick Spina, got the job. After some of DeCarlo's "boys" beat up Berlin in The Barn, he no longer posed a threat to the mob's hegemony in Newark. And DeCarlo could boast: "Hughie helped us along. He gave us the city."

The startling thing was that the mobsters continued to plot so freely despite the strong suspicion that their every word was overheard. On one occasion, DeCarlo exclaimed: "I wonder if the FBI knows what we eat every night. They have a tap here or something. . . ."

Needless to say, publication of the tapes created a sensation. A few protested against release of the transcripts. Wilentz, denying that he'd ever met DeCarlo, called it "utterly outrageous that hearsay conversations between organized criminals . . . should be publicly released without the slightest regard, decency or fairness to those who are publicly smeared." Governor Hughes, with only a few weeks left in office, said: "There is a difference between rigid law enforcement and the dissemination of gossip and character assassination by braggarts and name-droppers." Prosecutor Keuper threatened to file suit for libel—against DeCarlo and Little Pussy Russo. The ACLU asked Lacey to indict the FBI for illegal eavesdropping.

The *New York Times* noted that "the activities and names of various people mentioned make interesting reading; but the method of disclosure scarcely makes for good law." The *Times*'s criticism irked Stern: "They printed more of the tapes than the local New Jersey newspapers. I find it perfectly absurd that a newspaper should condemn the release of material which it eagerly sought, rushed to be the first into print with and devote an excessive amount of space to. If they felt the material was improper and harmful, they were under no obligation to print it. When confronted with this, the newspapers say that the editorial department is different from the news department. That's like the government saying, 'Well, that's the left branch of government, not the right branch.' I just don't understand it."

One of the strangest criticisms came from the floor of Congress when Representative John Rarick, a white supremacist from Louisiana, denounced both Lacey and release of the tapes: "Many dedicated public servants, after decades of devoted service, were publicly smeared, for no apparent reason." But most of Rarick's attack dealt not with the question of crime in New Jersey, but with Lacey's son, who was working on a civil-rights project in Louisiana. Rarick introduced documents from Louisiana's Joint Legislative Committee on Un-American Activities calling Fred Lacey, Jr., a "Communist" and said the son's taint made it "impossible for Lacey to discharge his duties as United States attorney in a district where violence and subversion by the New Left are matters of record."

The charges against father and son were first aired by Frank Capell, editor of a right-wing "hate-sheet" called *Herald of Freedom*, published in Zarephath, New Jersey. He accused Lacey of "undermining public confidence in law enforcement officials and destroying the morale of police departments, thus giving aid and comfort to the Communists who are constantly trying to undermine the police."

Reprints of Rarick's statement and copies of *Herald of Freedom* were widely circulated in New Jersey by such organizations as Americans of Italian Descent. Rarick was invited to speak at an AID meeting in New Brunswick, where he called for Lacey's resignation and invited those who don't like things here to hop the first boat to Moscow—which was, as one observer noted, "a difficult navigational feat."

The prosecutor defended his son as "a boy, now twenty-five years old, whose ideals have led him to go to Louisiana, where . . . he lived with and helped educate young black children," while Senator Case denounced Lacey's attackers as men whose "Meanness of spirit . . . is exceeded only by their stupidity." The organized bar in New Jersey also sprang to Lacey's defense, and the furor soon died—but, while it lasted, it pointed up a curious alliance between the mob and the radical right.

While they may have harbored misgivings about how the data were obtained and made public, almost all who read the excerpts were shocked by their contents.

"I read them," Stern recalls. "I know Fred Lacey read them. It was shocking to read this material, to see how corrupt, rotten the city of Newark was; to see all this, to realize the background, the bribes, the hooks and lines, the reaching into various police and prosecutors' offices and into the court itself; and to see the absolute control of men like DeCarlo—murderers, extortionists, the vilest riffraff—had on the largest city of the most densely populated state in the nation. It was appalling."

Stern calls release of the tapes "the turning point" in the cleanup campaign: "It made the public realize just how rotten New Jersey was."

Meanwhile, back at the courthouse . . . Zelmanowitz outlined the extortion conspiracy. Among his various enterprises, he had engaged in arbitrage—the simultaneous buying and selling of stocks in U.S. and foreign markets, profiting on the fractional differences in price. The enterprise required vast capital. He persuaded Saperstein to put up $50,000.

When still more capital was needed, Saperstein took Zelmanowitz to The Barn to meet DeCarlo. Saperstein asked for $100,000. DeCarlo referred them to Cecere.

They met Cecere at the Berkeley Bar in Orange. Cecere agreed to put up the money on behalf of himself, DeCarlo and Polverino—not as a loan, but as a 50-percent investment.

It turned out that Saperstein owed them $50,000 already. Cecere wrote off that loan and increased the principal to $150,000—on which Saperstein had to pay one-and-a-half-percent "vigorish" (interest) a week. Thus, the mobsters were getting not only a 50-percent profit on their investment, but annual interest of 78 percent!

In 16 trading days, Zelmanowitz's arbitrage operation netted $85,000 profits. Then the IRS froze the account. While Zelmanowitz went to court to get the tax exemption that would enable him to resume trading, Saperstein was being pressed to pay the vigorish. He borrowed from Zelmanowitz and, with his consent, dipped into the principal to make his weekly payments to Cecere. When Zelmanowitz refused further credit, he disappeared.

He surfaced on September 13, 1968, at the New York Hilton, where he had registered under the name of "Stone."

"We just want to talk to you," Cecere told the broker. But Saperstein was not convinced. He threatened to jump out the window. He offered to make a $100,000 insurance policy payable to the mobsters and then kill himself, provided "you don't hurt my family."

Instead, Cecere and one of his thugs checked Saperstein out of the hotel and drove him to The Barn. Zelmanowitz followed in his own car.

· "When I got there," he testified, "Mr. Saperstein was laying on the floor. He was purple. He was bloody. His tongue was hanging out of his mouth. There was spit all over him. I thought he was dead."

"Was anybody doing anything to Mr. Saperstein?" Stern asked.

"Yes, he was being kicked and punched."

"By whom?"

"By Mr. Polverino and Mr. Cecere."

Zelmanowitz continued the narrative: "Mr. Saperstein seemed to come awake and he started to say things. He said, 'Stop hitting me.' He pleaded. He pointed to me and said, 'He is the cause of this. Hit him.' . . . He was lifted up off the floor and placed into a chair and in the chair he was hit again. . . . He was knocked off the chair . . . and picked up again and hit again."

At this point, DeCarlo entered the room. Saperstein pleaded with the mobster for mercy, saying he'd die if they hit him any more. Cecere and Polverino asked DeCarlo for permission to kill Saperstein. "This SOB stole our money," Cecere said. "I am going to kill him."

"You messed him up," DeCarlo said. "He is bloody. You will bring trouble to us here now. Why in the hell did you beat him up here? . . . Get outside. Take him outside. Maybe this place is even bugged."

DeCarlo's intuition was right, but the FBI's bug had been removed three years before.

The group gathered in a station wagon parked outside. De-Carlo laid down the new terms to Saperstein: "You will bring five thousand a week, every Thursday . . . and you will pay the entire sum, all the monies that are owed and due, by December twelfth or you [will] be dead."

Saperstein pleaded with DeCarlo to cut the vigorish to $3000.

"Forget about it," he replied. "Bring five or you're dead."

Only after the verdict was in did Stern disclose what was said next. After Saperstein left, Cecere said: "I hope he doesn't pay by [December 12]. I don't care about the money any more. I just want to take him down into my cellar for three or four days."

On both direct and cross-examination, Zelmanowitz admitted his numerous financial crimes. Under questioning by Querques, he confessed that he had engaged in "fraud," "deception," "dishonesty" and "chicanery." But the defense could not shake his eyewitness account of the threats and the beating; indeed, they did not even question him about it.

After Zelmanowitz, the trial slowed to a snail's pace. First, Landusco's attorney complained that release of the transcripts had caused his client "such anxiety and despair [that] I cannot effectively communicate with him. . . ." Next, Polverino wound up in the hospital with a kidney ailment.

"The strategy of the defense," Stern protested, "is to, by any means possible, delay and obstruct the orderly procedure of this trial." He accused them of trying "to provoke the court."

But Judge Shaw assured him: "I haven't been provoked up to this point and it isn't likely that anyone is going to provoke me."

Yet the trial was delayed for medical and psychiatric examinations of the two defendants, and another day was spent hearing the doctors' reports. Polverino was clearly too ill to continue. Judge Shaw also severed Landusco—not for psychiatric reasons, but because the examinations disclosed a diabetic condition that needed immediate treatment. The case continued against DeCarlo and Cecere.

The rest of the prosecution evidence was corroboration of Zelmanowitz. Hotel bills, airline tickets and telephone records were introduced in evidence. Saperstein's widow, Irene, testified that when her husband came home on September 13, "he looked a mess and his face was distorted. . . . It was swollen and very enlarged. His face was blown up and he was just a mess." In the weeks after that, she said, he was "very depressed and did very little talking, very little."

On cross-examination, the defense brought out that a few days before his death, Saperstein had wined and dined heavily and was too drunk to drive home—a hint that he might have died from overindulgence. To refute this, Stern summoned Dr. Albano to testify to the cause of death: "acute arsenic poisoning."

Saperstein's driver told of delivering the envelopes to Cecere at the Berkeley Bar. He also described Saperstein's condition after September 13: "His face was bruised. He had black-and-blue marks and he was wearing dark glasses."

Finally, Stern called the FBI mail clerk and presented Saperstein's last letters. This touched off two days of legal arguments. Judge Shaw finally ruled that the portions of the first letter that "reflect the state of mind" could be introduced, but not "the material as to the amount owed . . . and the interest charge." The excised letter was read to the jury. Once again a dead man told tales.

The defense dragged. The lawyers said their witnesses had disappeared, but it turned out that they hadn't made very strenuous efforts to seek out and subpoena them. When the witnesses were brought into court, it turned out that their testimony was irrelevant. But that took several days of hearing outside the presence of the jury.

Only two defense witnesses were heard by the jury—and their testimony lasted less than an hour. A lawyer whose office adjoined Saperstein's said that Saperstein was depressed because he feared he had cancer. He also said that Saperstein attributed his facial injuries to an auto accident.

The nurse at Saperstein's deathbed said that in his last conscious moments he said, "Somebody put some silvery stuff in my food."

"Is this a joke?" the doctor asked.

"I will tell you the whole story in a minute."

But he never did—and the nurse's testimony only added to the mystery of his death.

Summations started on January 27. Direnzo attacked Zelmanowitz's testimony, called him a "liar": "He takes an investor, he sells him a bill of goods. . . . That is his forte, that is his stock in trade, selling people a bill of goods—and he's got to sell it to you."

Querques made the astounding justification for Cecere's mauling Saperstein: "If Saperstein stole fifty-five thousand dollars from you and you found out about it . . . would you give him a punch? . . . Certainly you would. That's what the law excuses. The law calls that justifiable." Judge Shaw had to instruct the jurors to ignore Querque's weird reading of the law.

The following day, after Judge Shaw ordered each juror to sign a statement that he would consider the letter only for Saperstein's state of mind, the panel retired. They were back in less than four hours with guilty verdicts against both De-Carlo and Cecere.

Stern immediately moved to have them remanded to prison: "If the facts of this trial demonstrate anything, they have demonstrated that these defendants are brutal, sadistic men who can and will impose violence, have done so in the past and, I submit, pose a danger of imposing it now."

He quoted from the DeCarlo tapes and produced tax records to show that DeCarlo had no legitimate income. In 1964, he said, DeCarlo reported total earnings of $30,720, $24,740 of it from "miscellaneous." In 1960, when he owed $38,660 back taxes, he walked into the IRS office and paid cash.

Judge Shaw let the defendants remain free on bail until the March 4 sentencing. Then he threw the book at them.

"I think it is clear beyond cavil," he said, "that these defendants are indeed engaged in an organized criminal conspiracy. Whether you call it La Cosa Nostra, the Mafia or the Black Hand, it exists and these men are important members of it."

Both men were sentenced to 12 years in prison and fined $20,000 each. And both were remanded immediately.

"It was a frame-up from the beginning," DeCarlo told reporters as he was led off to jail. "You know it was and I know it was. It was a frame-up all the way."

The defense went all the way to the U.S. Supreme Court in a vain effort to get bail. Meanwhile, they appealed the conviction itself to the Third Circuit. The judges reversed the conviction—not, as Stern had feared, because Saperstein's letter had been read to the jury, but because Stern had introduced evidence that he'd died of arsenic poisoning.

"There was no evidence connecting [DeCarlo and Cecere] with Saperstein's death," the court said. "Thus it was not relevant to the charges. Even if it were remotely relevant, its use was so prejudicial as to render it inadmissible. The evidence was designed to divert the jury from its duty to decide the criminal charges before it. The extortion trial was converted into a murder trial."

But because of "overwhelming evidence of guilt," the court did not free DeCarlo and Cecere pending a new trial. They remained behind bars while Stern pondered his next move. Rather than prosecute the case again, he petitioned the Third Circuit to rehear the arguments *en banc,* before all nine judges. In a rare move, the court agreed; in an even rarer one, it reversed its ruling, Chief Judge Collins J. Seitz even reversing himself.

The court said that "the evidence of death by arsenic poisoning served a legitimate purpose—providing a link to determine Saperstein's state of mind."

The conviction stood. But one mystery remained: How did Saperstein die? That question probably never will be answered with certainty. "If I had to make a bet," says Stern, "I'd say it was suicide."

On January 2, 1970, the day the DeCarlo trial started, Sam the Plumber DeCavalcante was arraigned on a new indictment—on an interstate-gambling-conspiracy charge for allegedly masterminding a $20-million-a-year policy operation in Troy, New York.

Other than processing the papers, Lacey's office had nothing to do with the case. The investigation was launched by Washington and handled by the multiagency Strike Force. It was part of a nationwide sweep that netted 54 gambling figures, 17 of them in New Jersey.

Meanwhile, the office moved the extortion case to trial, but DeCavalcante succeeded in winning postponement after postponement while he switched lawyers. When the trial finally got under way on September 15, 1970. DeCavalcante and his cronies were represented by the trusty team of Bozza and Querques. The government's case, presented by Assistant U.S. Attorney George Koelzer, took six days; the defense offered no witnesses; the jury found all three guilty.

His cheek twitching nervously, Sam the Plumber stood before Judge Lawrence A. Whipple for sentencing on October 2. On each of the three counts in the indictment, the judge imposed a five-year prison term—to be served *consecutively*. Vastola got five years; Annunziata, three. All three were remanded immediately. Bozza and Querques appealed the conviction to the Third Circuit.

What happened next is in dispute. According to Stern, Raymond A. Brown, who represented DeCavalcante on the gambling case, approached the Strike Force with a deal: If the extortion conviction were affirmed, DeCavalcante would plead guilty to the gambling conspiracy. The proposal was referred to Stern, by then the acting U.S. attorney. "I disapproved it," he says. "I said, 'No, that favors the defendant. Let him either plead guilty right now or stand trial.' "

According to John Bartels, head of the Strike Force in New Jersey, "Stern had no role." Bartels said he threatened De-Cavalcante with treatment as a "special dangerous offender" if he stood trial—which could have meant a sentence of up to 25 years, to be served *after* he finished the 15 for extortion; whereas, "if he pleaded, he could only get five years and the chances were that it would be five concurrent."

Whatever the threat or inducement, on January 15, 1971, DeCavalcante pleaded guilty. The plea was taken in secret so it wouldn't prejudice the trial of his codefendants. Sentencing was set for March 15.

As it turned out, the gambling czar made a bad bet. On March 10, the Third Circuit reversed the extortion conviction. The court ruled that the government had not produced sufficient evidence of a conspiracy: "All the connecting links needed in the story to prove a conspiracy—that is, the existence of an agreement—are supplied only by the prosecution's argument." All that the government had proved, the court said, was a robbery by Vastola and Annunziata—not a federal crime—and that "DeCavalcante was merely a friendly arbitrator in a dispute between two groups of hoodlums—a role which, however unsavory, does not amount to a violation of [the statute]."

DeCavalcante was held in jail for five more days, then brought into court for the gambling sentence. He begged the court to let him withdraw the guilty plea, but Judge Leonard L. Garth refused and imposed the maximum penalty—five years in prison and a $10,000 fine.

Stern was not present for the hearing, but somehow he became the object of DeCavalcante's wrath. Later that year, Sam the Plumber was overheard talking about the prosecutor to a fellow inmate at the Atlanta penitentiary: "We missed him the last time, but we'll get him the next time." As a result, federal marshals mounted a round-the-clock guard on the prosecutor.

At the following holiday season, Stern received a card from DeCavalcante wishing him a happy Chanukah. On it the mobster penned a note with Mafia solicitousness: "Hope you and your family are in good health."

President Nixon also had a holiday gift for "Gyp" DeCarlo. On December 22, 1972, he commuted his sentence to time served—22 months. The stated reason was DeCarlo's health. "He's a very sick man," Direnzo explained. "He's got terminal cancer. He won't live long."

Significantly, Stern hadn't been consulted—or even informed. He learned of the president's action from newsmen at his office's Christmas party. "I was surprised to hear it," he said. "I was not aware that there was an application pending."

Some months later, in the backwash of Watergate, the FBI picked up a report that DeCarlo's release had been engineered by Frank Sinatra, once a camp follower of the Kennedys and Camelot who had since become a golfing buddy of Vice President Agnew and a spirited supporter of President Nixon. According to one account, Sinatra interceded with Agnew for the mobster's release; Agnew reportedly turned the matter over to an aide, who brought Sinatra to see White House counsel John Dean, who arranged the commutation—in exchange for $150,000 in campaign contributions. DeCarlo's release was among the matters being looked into by special Watergate prosecutor Archibald Cox, but by midsummer his investigators reportedly had "struck a dry hole."

6

THE UNMAKING OF MAYOR ADDONIZIO

On July 14, 1967, Newark erupted in racial rioting. In a decade of civil disorders, it was one of the worst. By the time an uneasy peace was restored four days later, 26 persons were dead, more than 1000 were injured and more than 1000 were under arrest. Much of New Jersey's largest city looked like An Loc after Tet. National Guard troops patrolled the streets in tanks. Block after block contained little but burnt-out buildings and looted stores. Property damage was estimated at more than $10 million.

Governor Richard Hughes reacted with what has become the characteristic ploy of public officials in time of crisis: He appointed a commission to investigate the causes of the riot and to make recommendations to prevent a recurrence. The "blue-ribbon" panel was headed by Robert D. Lilley, president of the New Jersey Telephone Company.

The Lilley Commission's report came out the following February. Among the causes it listed was "a pervasive feeling of corruption" in Newark. "There is a widespread belief that Newark's government is corrupt," the commission said. "A source close to Newark businessmen said he understood from them that 'everything at City Hall is for sale.' A former state official, a former city official and an incumbent city official all used the same phrase: 'There is a price on everything at City Hall.'" Among the commission's recommendations was that a special grand jury "investigate allegations of corruption in Newark."

It was a challenge no prosecutor could ignore. The grand jury was duly empaneled by Essex County Prosecutor Joseph Lordi. It quickly indicted Newark's police director, Dominick Spina, for failure to enforce the gambling laws, but he won a directed verdict of acquittal.

In time, the grand jury got around to Newark's mayor, Hugh J. Addonizio. Then 54, Addonizio was short, dumpy

and balding. A Newark native, the son of a clothing manufacturer, combat veteran of World War II, he had been
elected to Congress in the Truman upset of 1948 and reelected six times. He compiled a liberal, if undistinguished,
record in Washington before being elected mayor in 1962.
He was reelected in 1966, but even before the riots, the
Italian-Negro electoral coalition he had forged was falling
apart. The shocking revelations of the DeCarlo tapes were
a year away.

Addonizio appeared before the panel on May 7, 1969. He
invoked the Fifth Amendment and was brought into open
court. It turned out that the authorities were interested in
Addonizio's new summer home in New Shrewsbury, on the
Jersey Shore, and a $14,000 loan for it from Paul Rigo, an
engineer who had worked on many city projects. Addonizio
said he declined to answer because he felt he was the "target"
of the inquiry, but the judge directed him to return to the
secret session and answer the questions.

By the time Lacey and Stern came into office, the Essex
County grand jury had amassed more than 5000 pages of
testimony, but it had been frustrated in its attempt to pin
corruption charges on any city official. The new U.S. attorney
also started looking into Newark's civic cesspool, but at the
outset he was merely skimming the slimy surface.

Then the investigation broke wide open.

The county grand jury, probing the possibilities of bill-
padding on city construction projects, started checking Rigo's
records. What they didn't know was that Rigo was the key-
stone of Newark's substructure of corruption—the middleman
between the contractors, city officials and the mob.

When word of the grand jury's line of inquiry leaked out,
Tony Boy Boiardo's "bagman," Ralph Vicaro, warned Rigo:

"Keep your mouth shut and remember you have a pretty daughter in Suffern." After Rigo was subpoenaed to appear before the panel, he found a note in his car: "This could have been a bomb. Keep your mouth shut."

So Rigo lied to the grand jury. But the panel kept calling him back, each time inching closer to the truth—that he *was* padding his bills in an attempt to make up the ten percent he was kicking back. Meanwhile, IRS agents started poring over his books.

"I had . . . a three-way squeeze going," he explained later. "Boiardo's people on one hand. I had the Essex County grand jury on the other. And I had, now, the federal people in the act. I was getting desperate."

Rigo wilted under the "heat." He decided to cooperate with the federal authorities. Through an intermediary, an appointment with Lacey was set up, but two days later Rigo received an anonymous telephone call: "Keep the hell away from the federal building!"

Rigo fled south of the border—to Acapulco. Through Peter Flanigan, President Nixon's "Mr. Fixit" at the White House, an appointment was set up at Justice. Rigo flew to Washington and told his story to Will Wilson, then head of the Organized Crime section. Wilson summoned Lacey to the capital.

"Fred left on a Wednesday [December 3], carrying nothing, not even a spare shirt, and began to interview Rigo," Stern recalls. "On Thursday, he called me up and asked me to come down. I flew down there Friday morning."

With Stern went two of Lordi's assistants who had worked on the county grand-jury investigation, Donald Merkelbach and Michael Riccardelli.

The four prosecutors met with Rigo at the Justice Department. "He told his story," Stern continues, "these long involved payoffs over years, involving hundreds of thousands of dollars in cash systematically being paid over to public officials through organized-crime figures. He kept diaries that were coded in which he made notations of how much he was paying to whom. Agents of the Internal Revenue Service went and got them. It was basically the IRS that was supplying the manpower at this point.

"It became apparent to us that this was really hot. This was tremendous. Here was a man who had paid off a significant portion of the entire administration of the city of Newark—the incumbent mayor, members of the city council, the director of public works, the corporation counsel. We got corroboration for the first time that public officials were in league with organized crime. Before, there had been whispers, rumors, fictional accounts—but here it was."

Stern suggested that they immediately subpoena all those Rigo had named before a federal grand jury. Lacey agreed and telephoned instructions to Assistant U.S. Attorney John W. Bissell in Newark. Marshals fanned out all over northern New Jersey serving the subpoenas. Addonizio was hit at Newark Airport as he stepped off a plane returning him from a meeting of the U.S. Conference of Mayors.

Lacey wanted to go a step further. "You hear a wild story like this, you want to confirm it," he says. "I went down the list of those that Rigo had accused. I had known Gordon [Philip Gordon, Newark's corporation counsel] as a lawyer who bore a good reputation in the community and felt this was about the best litmus test I could apply to resolve whether Rigo was or was not telling the truth."

He telephoned Gordon and asked him to come to Washington immediately. Gordon flew down on the shuttle Friday night. Lacey and Stern met him at Washington National Airport and led him into the terminal's restaurant. At the table, Lacey gave Gordon a *Miranda* warning, then said:

"Phil, Paul Rigo has charged that illegal payments were made by him to the mayor and others, including you. What about it?"

Gordon proved to be the weak link in the conspiracy. With only a second's hesitation, he admitted that it was true.

"This, of course, was a most significant break in the case," Lacey continues. "It gave the stamp of truth to what I recognized would be difficult for many citizens to accept—that there had been a conspiracy between organized-crime figures and elected public officials in one of the nation's major cities."

On Saturday, Lacey and Stern returned to Newark. Over the weekend, Lacey conferred with Lordi, and the county prosecutor agreed to suspend his investigation and turn over all the grand-jury testimony he'd taken. He also agreed to lend the short-staffed U.S. attorney both Merkelbach and Riccardelli to serve as "special assistants" on the investigation.

The following week saw a parade of public officials into the grand-jury room. Gordon waived immunity and repeated under oath what he'd told Lacey in the airport restaurant—that on two occasions he'd received $2000 from Rigo. Both times, Rigo had delivered the money in two envelopes—$1000 for Gordon, another $1000 for Anthony Guiliano. At the time, both men were members of the city council; Guiliano later became a municipal court judge.

"It was wrong legally, morally and any way you want to put it," Gordon confessed. "It was wrong."

Addonizio was not so cooperative. He appeared on December 9 and invoked the Fifth Amendment. Lacey brought him downstairs before Judge Robert Shaw and asked that he be directed to answer. The questions were read aloud in open court:

"Do you know Ruggiero Boiardo?"

"Do you know Anthony Boiardo?"

"Do you know Paul Rigo?"

" . . . Did you receive any money from Paul Rigo or his associates?"

On the same day, before another federal grand jury, Newark's chief municipal court judge, James DelMauro, also invoked the Fifth Amendment when asked if he'd taken illegal fees for officiating at weddings. Thus Newark residents were treated to the simultaneous spectacle of seeing their city's chief executive officer and chief judicial officer both saying that honest answers would place them in criminal jeopardy. DelMauro escaped ouster proceedings by resigning from the bench. He was subsequently indicted for income-tax evasion.

The legal arguments on Addonizio's case continued into the following day. At one point, Addonizio interrupted his attorney, Bernard Hellring, and told Judge Shaw: "Your Honor, I'd like to take the stand."

The mayor was sworn in and the first question was put to him: "Do you know a man—personally—known as Anthony Boiardo, also as Tony Boy Boiardo?"

"I do know him—and my answer may tend to incriminate me."

"Well, I guess that disposes of that one," Judge Shaw quipped.

The judge reserved decision. A week later—December 17 —the parties filed back into the courtroom to hear his ruling. Judge Shaw started to comment on the case, but Stern interrupted him: "The grand jury having just indicted him—"

There was a mad scramble as reporters rushed to the telephones outside. When order was restored, Judge Shaw said: "In light of the fact that the grand jury has indicted Mayor Addonizio, a ruling on the question has become moot."

The action had been predicted—indeed hastened—by Attorney General Mitchell. On the day Addonizio took the stand in open court, Mitchell had addressed a bankers' convention in Boca Raton, Florida. He mentioned crime in New Jersey, then went on:

"In this state, within the next week or ten days, there is going to be a massive indictment of public officials on the local level; and also in this state, through the activities we have carried on, we're going to break up probably the largest gambling syndicate that's ever been broken up in this country." *

Though neither would say so publicly, both Lacey and Stern were plainly piqued by Mitchell's statement. Lacey got word of it at a press conference where he and Lordi were announcing the turnover of the county grand-jury records. All he would say about it was: "I don't comment on what Attorney General Mitchell says and I don't think he comments on what I say."

Again, though neither Lacey nor Stern will admit it, Mitchell's announcement forced the office to move faster than it had planned. It also presented a problem for Stern in drafting the indictment.

"I didn't have all the evidence at that time," he explains, "yet I was sure I would have it by the time of the trial. I had to devise an indictment to cover it."

The problem had been bubbling in his mind throughout the initial interview with Rigo and he had fallen asleep on it that Friday night in Washington. The next morning, while waiting with Lacey to catch the shuttle back to Newark, he suddenly burst out laughing.

"What are you laughing at?" Lacey asked.

"I just figured out how to draft the conspiracy count."

On the plane, he dashed off a rough version for Lacey,

* The second case Mitchell mentioned was the Strike Force's roundup of Sam the Plumber DeCavalcante and 54 others.

framing the first count as a catchall, charging a general conspiracy to extort money from contractors, engineers and suppliers. Under it, almost any evidence of corruption could be introduced in evidence. But "to treat it less broadly would have been unreal."

Given more time to mull over the problem, Stern might have spotted the hole the defense eventually did. In the Colonial case, the defense had argued—unsuccessfully—that it wasn't bribery, it was extortion. In the Addonizio case, the defense would argue that it wasn't extortion, it was bribery. In future cases, Stern was careful not to repeat the mistake: The indictments charged *both* bribery and extortion. A defendant trying to escape one crime by pleading another would be hoist by his own petard.

The indictment also alleged 65 specific acts of extortion, involving total payoffs of $253,000 from or through Rigo. Fifteen persons were named: Mayor Addonizio; Public Works Director Benjamin Khrush and his predecessor, Anthony LaMorte; Corporation Counsel Gordon and his predecessor, Norman Schiff; six current or past members of the city council—Frank Addonizio (a distant cousin of the mayor), Lee Bernstein, Calvin West, Irvine Turner, James Callahan and Judge Guiliano; Mario Gallo, a contractor; and three members of the mob—Tony Boy Boiardo, Joseph Biancone and Ralph Vicaro.

Several—including Addonizio—were also charged with income-tax evasion.

The Newark Chamber of Commerce immediately called for Addonizio's resignation, and state officials pondered the possibility of removing him. But Addonizio was determined to remain in office. That evening, free on a personal bond of $25,000, he showed up at City Hall for a council meeting.

"Will business go on as usual?" a reporter asked him.

"We will continue with an efficient and effective governing of Newark," the mayor replied.

Indeed, he was even planning to run for a third term the following spring. Not even the release of the DeCarlo tapes two weeks later daunted him.

After the New Year, while Lacey and Stern were tied up on the DeCarlo trial, Merkelbach and Riccardelli teamed with Bissell and assistants Garrett Brown and John Nulty to amass the volumes of evidence needed for the trial. As soon as the DeCarlo trial ended, they were rejoined by the office's two top men. "It was more than twenty percent of our effective force," Stern says.

Once again, the investigators got two major breaks.

First, they "broke" Irving Kantor. Kantor ran a family plumbing-supply business, but his role in the conspiracy came as head of a "dummy" concern, Kantor Supply Company. Kantor Supply supplied nothing—except cash. It was a check-cashing service, a "front" for converting the contractors' kick-backs into cash. Through this subterfuge more than $911,000 in cash was generated—in addition to the $253,000 listed by Rigo! Through Kantor's cooperation, another key element in the case was locked into place.

At the time, Kantor, aged 50, was dying of amythrophic lateral sclerosis, "Lou Gehrig's disease." "He was completely bedridden, paralyzed, unable to move a muscle," Stern says. "He could not even speak intelligibly.

"To say we 'broke' him is wrong. We couldn't threaten Irving Kantor. How can you threaten a man who is dying? We couldn't even try Irving Kantor. There were no threats or inducements. Irving Kantor simply decided he'd made a mistake and wanted to help his country. It was a most courageous decision."

Kantor's cooperation was one of the most closely kept secrets of the investigation, but federal marshals stood guard around the clock outside the helpless man's hospital room . . . just in case.

"Then," according to Stern, "we got what I thought was going to be one of the greatest breaks ever received by law enforcement in this part of the country."

Stern was getting ready to attend the swearing-in of a new federal judge when he received a call from Mario Gallo's lawyer, Dino Bliablias, asking if he could see the prosecutor as soon as possible. Stern "smelled what it was," so he skipped the ceremony.

Sure enough, Gallo was ready to cooperate. At age 44, Mario Gallo was one of the largest construction contractors in New Jersey and a major manufacturer of pipe and supplier of asphalt and gravel as well. "He had an empire," Stern says. His companies alone had funneled more than $576,000 through Kantor Supply.

Gallo was fearful of being seen with the authorities in New Jersey. Stern told Bliablias he'd be "happy to meet them any place they picked." A day or two later, the date was set— 7:30 P.M., February 9. But neither Lacey nor Stern was told where until a few hours before. The place was a suite booked under an alias at New York's Americana Hotel.

The whole scheme of secrecy was nearly blown when Lacey walked into the lobby and encountered the vice president of a company he'd once represented.

"I'm afraid he still will not understand my rebuff of his offer to join him for drinks and dinner," Lacey says. "And I'm afraid he's still miffed at my vague and ambiguous response to what I was doing there."

For three hours, Gallo sat with the federal prosecutors and outlined his information. According to Stern, "It looked as though we were not only going to solidify the Addonizio case, it had tremendous potential in terms of other cases."

At about 10:30, Gallo's lawyers asked to end the session because their client was exhausted. The meeting broke up with an agreement to meet again the next day, Bliablias to let the prosecutors know when and where.

The weather was so bad that Lacey stayed in New York overnight. The next morning he took a train back to New Jersey, picked up a copy of the *Newark Star-Ledger* at the Penn Station newsstand and glanced at the front page during the cab ride to his office. In the lower right-hand corner was a headline: "Contractor Killed in Crash."

At about the same time, Stern arrived at the office. His secretary, unaware of the previous night's development, looked up and said, "Did you hear? Mario Gallo's dead."

"I was just stunned," Stern says. Lacey calls it "the low point of our battle against organized crime and corruption."

"Had he lived," Stern says, "we might have been where we are today a year or a year and a half earlier—but we got there anyway."

After the session at the Americana, Gallo had headed home alone. It was early morning, the roads were streaked with sleet, and the driver was tired. His car skidded and crashed into a stanchion. He was dead by the time help arrived. His secret meeting with the authorities quickly leaked out and the newspaper accounts hinted of dirty doings. The FBI investigated the case thoroughly, but found no evidence that Gallo's death was anything but accidental.

The incident added a macabre touch to an already sensational case. Another followed on its heels. A few days later, Lacey and Stern were lunching near the courthouse when a man Lacey will identify only as "an organized-crime figure" approached their table and told Lacey that his life was in danger.

Death threats are something any prosecutor must learn to live with. Lacey had previously received anonymous letters and so many threatening phone calls that he'd had to get his home number changed to an unlisted one. An assistant in the office received an anonymous tip that Lacey's son would be beaten. The Newark home of Lacey's mother was burglarized—though this was more likely the act of a petty thief than a message from the mob.

But this warning could not be ignored. At John Mitchell's insistence, marshals moved into Lacey's home and for months he and his family lived under armed guard. Lacey saw it as a symbol of his success: "They have already learned that my office cannot be fixed. It cannot be influenced. And I tell them now: It cannot be intimidated."

Meanwhile, the Addonizio case was moving toward trial. The trial judge was George H. Barlow, a short, balding, mild-mannered jurist, newly promoted from the state courts to the federal bench. Among the matters he had to decide was when and where the trial would be held.

Though some defendants pressed for an early trial, Addonizio repeatedly moved for postponement—at least until after the mayoral runoff, June 16. In the election's first heat, Addonizio had trailed Kenneth Gibson, a black engineer, by nearly 20,000 votes. But Gibson's total fell short of a majority, and most supporters of the five eliminated candidates were expected to shift to Addonizio.

Surprisingly, the mayor—under indictment for extortion and depicted in the DeCarlo tapes as a pawn of organized crime—was running on a "law-and-order" platform, attacking "crime in the streets." As election day neared, the campaign focused increasingly on the racial issue and Newark's whites' fear of black violence. Although blacks and Spanish-speaking people comprised more than 60 percent of Newark's 381,930 population, whites remained a majority of the registered voters. Airing the evidence in court was bound to erode Addonizio's support among this white electoral majority.

Judge Barlow set June 2 as the trial date. Hellring objected vigorously on behalf of the mayor, pleading for a two-week delay. Stern opposed it. He said "the public had a right to know whether the charges were true or false before these men stood up for office." He had another reason, which he divulged to the judge only *in camera*: The government intended to call Irving Kantor as a witness; another two weeks and he might be dead or too far gone to testify. The date remained June 2.

Addonizio charged that the government was obstructing his reelection campaign in other ways. The terms of his bond forbade him to leave the state without the U.S. attorney's permission. Since Newark is covered by New York television stations, it meant that he could appear on live newscasts or taped interview shows only by Lacey's consent—and Lacey refused to give it unless Addonizio agreed not to discuss the pending case, a condition Addonizio understandably would not meet. Once the jury was chosen and sequestered, the restriction was lifted. Addonizio appeared on TV and promptly called the trial "a political prosecution."

The mayor wanted the trial held in his native Newark, but other defendants moved for a change of venue. Some of those standing for office even claimed they couldn't get a fair trial from the same citizens whose votes they sought. Boiardo's attorney, Thomas Wadden of Washington, a former partner of Edward Bennett Williams, urged that the trial be shifted out of New Jersey to some other district in the Third Circuit; he suggested the Virgin Islands.*

"You're talking to me as a golfer rather than as a judge," Judge Barlow quipped.

He ordered the trial held in Trenton, where jurors were less likely than those in Newark to be prejudiced by pretrial publicity.

So on Monday, June 1, a major portion of the U.S. attorney's office checked into Trenton's Holiday Inn for what turned out to be a two-month stay—Stern, Bissell, Brown and Merkelbach, plus a rotating retinue of secretaries, FBI agents and IRS accountants. Lacey commuted by car. As they had in the DeCarlo case, Lacey and Stern divided the prosecution chores—Lacey addressing the jury, Stern presenting the evidence. "Batman and Robin," one defense lawyer called them.

By trial time the defendants' ranks had been thinned. In addition to Gallo, Judge Guiliano had died since indictment— of natural causes at age 71. Turner, Schiff and Khrush were too ill to stand trial. Judge Barlow also severed West, Bernstein and Frank Addonizio because their lawyer, Raymond Brown, was tied up on a protracted trial in Jersey City.

The defense lawyers were a diverse crew. Addonizio's counsel, Bernard Hellring, was a roly-poly white-haired corporation lawyer. His strategy was to keep both himself and his client as far as possible from the other defendants and their lawyers—especially the mobsters. Addonizio himself commuted to court each morning in the mayoral limousine and hurried home each evening—until the election—to campaign.

Boiardo and his fellow mobsters were defended by three former colleagues of Edward Bennett Williams—Thomas

---

* The Third Circuit is composed of New Jersey, Pennsylvania, Delaware and the Virgin Islands.

Wadden, Thomas Dyson and Patrick Wall. They rented a house on the Jersey Shore and drove to Trenton each day with Gordon's lawyer, John Noonan, whose summer home was nearby. Noonan provided the trial's comic relief. "He never repeated a joke and he never stopped telling one," said a colleague. LaMorte was represented by Julius Feinberg, now a state judge, and Callahan by Stern's rival in the Weber case, Joseph Hayden.

It took three days to pick the jury. Then Lacey opened— astounding spectators with Addonizio's adage, "There's no money in being a congressman, but you can make a million bucks as mayor of Newark"; astounding the defense by announcing that the government's first witness would be Irving Kantor.

The next day, judge and jury, lawyers and defendants, plus the whole court entourage, trekked to East Orange for one of the strangest sessions in American judicial history. A makeshift courtroom had been set up in the auditorium of the Veterans Administration Hospital. The participants sat on folding chairs; the witness lay on a hospital bed, the tubes running out of him. Kantor was too weak to testify for more than ten or fifteen minutes at a stretch. The court attendant even had to lift his hand and place it on the Bible so he could take the oath.

Judge Barlow handled the initial examination outside the jury's presence, questioning Kantor, his wife and his doctor to determine his competence to testify and hers to act as "interpreter," since Kantor's grunts were unintelligible to anyone unaccustomed to them. Over defense objections, he ruled that Kantor "is in every respect competent and able to testify."

With Kantor's wife relaying his words to the jury, Kantor told how he had been introduced to Biancone in 1962. Biancone, an agent of Boiardo's, sought Kantor's help in converting kickbacks into cash. Kantor suggested that this be done through a dummy company and phony invoices for plumbing supplies to conceal the true nature of the transactions on the contractors' books. Biancone made a phone call to get approval.

" . . . He talked partly in Italian and partly in English," Kantor said.

"Could you understand the conversation?" Stern asked.

"The substance, yes."

"Just a second," Judge Barlow interrupted, summoning counsel to the makeshift bench. "Not unusual these days," he whispered, "we have a bomb threat."

Without telling the jury the reason why, the trial was recessed and the auditorium cleared. No bomb was found, but the incident heightened the drama of an already dramatic scene.

When the trial resumed, Kantor said that Biancone relayed the okay for the strategem. Kantor opened a bank account and ordered invoices—in the name of the nonexistent Kantor Supply Company, whose address was a vacant lot. When contractors' checks came in, Kantor would deposit them and mail out phony invoices to cover the amount. As soon as the checks cleared, he'd withdraw the cash, keeping five percent for himself, passing the rest to Biancone.

Stern calls it "a very difficult examination," but it was even tougher for the defense lawyers who had to cross-examine Kantor. Treading softly, lest they antagonize the jury, they went after him—but were unable to shake his story.

When the trial returned to Trenton, Stern called Joseph Patrick Foley, an engineer with Elson T. Killam Associates, which had bid on Newark's South Side Interceptor System. He related how he'd met LaMorte for lunch at Thomm's Restaurant on June 8, 1964. LaMorte introduced him to a "Mr. B," then discreetly left.

"He was a very soft-spoken gentleman," Foley said of

"Mr. B," "and he said that he is a businessman and I am a businessman. My business is engineering and his business is collecting moneys for—or political contributions, or what have you—for the city of Newark administration. He said his job was to keep the 'war chest' full. . . .

"I remember him saying to me—how could I . . . be so naive in this day and age in the engineering business not having to make kickbacks or shakedowns for work. I told him that it was not the practice of our firm to do anything of this nature and he just—he couldn't conceive that this was possible. He said that anybody that did work for the city of Newark had to give some percent of their fee for this."

But Foley, who had met "Mr. B" only once, could not identify any of the defendants as him.

Stern next called a bank official to the stand to identify some of the $911,000 in checks that had passed through Kantor Supply. He planned to have a second banker identify the remainder, but en route to Trenton, Paul Anderson, vice president of the First National Bank of New Jersey, was killed in an auto accident. Like Mario Gallo's fatal accident, it too was a one-car crash—ironically, only a few miles from the spot where the contractor had skidded to his death five months before. As in the Gallo case, the FBI investigated—again to find it only an accident. But newspapers had a field day with the story, further fueling the trial's "circus" atmosphere— "everything except sex," as Noonan put it.

Unlike the Gallo case, Anderson's death did not upset the prosecution's plans. "We got the word in the morning," Stern says. "I didn't tell the defense counsel that he was dead. I said, 'To save some time, let's just stipulate what's in these bank records.' They said, 'Okay.' If they hadn't, I would have just put another bank official on."

The stipulation left Stern without an available witness and the trial recessed early on Friday afternoon. Hellring sought to extend the recess into the following week so Addonizio could campaign on election eve and election day. Judge Barlow denied the request.

"May I ask for one day?" Hellring pleaded. "Just Monday."

"No day," the judge snapped back. "I am not conducting an election—I am conducting a trial."

Monday's witness was Peter Homack, president of Killam Associates, who picked up the thread of Foley's testimony. On July 14, 1964, he and the late Mr. Killam had gone to City Hall to discuss the South Side sewer project with La-Morte. They were intercepted by Biancone, who led them into the mayor's office, introduced them to Addonizio, then steered them back into the hall, where he made his pitch.

"Mr. Biancone indicated to us that a request was being made for five percent of our engineering fee to be paid in consideration of doing this work for the city of Newark," Homack said.

"Did he indicate why he wanted the money?" Stern asked.

"Yes, he indicated that he wanted the money for the political campaign—war chest . . ."

"Did either you or Mr. Killam make any reply to Mr. Biancone?"

"Mr. Killam shook his head. He indicated that we would not pay five percent."

"Was there further conversation?"

"Mr. Biancone said, 'How about four percent?' And we said, 'No.' Finally he said, 'Three percent?' and said to Mr. Killam, 'Won't you even make an offer? How much are you willing to pay?' Mr. Killam said, 'You do not understand. We will not pay anything.' "

Killam did not get the job. John Sepede became chief engineer on the project.

On Tuesday, June 16, Addonizio absented himself from the courtroom to vote. That night, he received the returns at his election-night headquarters—Thomm's Restaurant, where the mysterious "Mr. B" had made his pitch to Foley. Kenneth Gibson was elected, 55,097 votes to 43,048, to become the first black mayor in the Northeast. As the bad news came over the TV tube, Addonizio's followers shouted, "Kill the nigger! Kill the nigger!" No "niggers" were on hand, so they vented their wrath on newsmen, beating up an NBC camera crew and smashing its equipment.

Stern caught the results in his motel room, relieved that Addonizio lost, shocked that a man so steeped in corruption still received 45 percent of the votes. The prosecution had feared that if Addonizio were reelected, the courtroom would be thronged the next day with his cheering supporters. As it was, Wednesday was a day like any other in the trial. The jury was not informed of the results and Judge Barlow instructed counsel to continue referring to Addonizio as "mayor." But something intangible had changed. "It was like the steam just went out of him," one observer said of Addonizio after his defeat.

A string of contractors and suppliers took the stand in the week after the election to testify about kickbacks on the South Side sewer project.

Ralph Cestone of Verona Construction Company told how he had been approached by Sepede, who was putting together a package of contractors and suppliers willing to kick back $1 million. Cestone refused to go along—and the construction contract went to a joint venture headed by C. Salvatore and Sons.

Everyone on the project was kicking back ten percent—the engineers, contractors and suppliers. Then a hitch developed. The specifications called for pipe with rubber-and-steel joints, but the chief supplier, Mario Gallo, only made a pipe with inferior rubber-and-concrete joints.

The conspirators tried to enlist Interpace Corporation, a

major supplier of rubber-and-steel-joint pipe. Harry J. Gillespie, the firm's materials manager, told what happened:

Gillespie met LaMorte for lunch on October 22, 1964. "LaMorte told me the job was mine. I said, 'Thank you.' He said, 'We will require the usual.' I said, 'You mean ten?' And he said, 'Yes.' I said, 'I am in no position to commit. I will have to report back to my people. If they are interested, they will tell you.'"

As an afterthought, Gillespie asked who else knew that they were meeting.

"The man from Livingston," LaMorte replied—a reference to one of the Boiardos.

"I asked him, 'The father or the son?'"

"What did he reply?" Stern asked.

"The father."

LaMorte offered to drive Gillespie to meet Boiardo, but he declined. Interpace also declined to pay the kickbacks and the city fathers made plans to change the pipe specifications, so the contract could go to Gallo.

Gillespie tried to enlist some city council members in opposition, explaining that if concrete joints were used, ground drainage would seep into the sewer. The line was linked to a treatment plant of the Passaic Valley Sewerage Commission, the flow metered and Newark billed by volume. If concrete were used, the city would be paying to process rainwater!

Gillespie was not permitted to tell the jury what happened next. He received an anonymous telephone call: "Lay off the city of Newark or you'll get both legs broken or be floating down the river."

With Mayor Addonizio leading the way, the city council voted to change the specifications and Mario Gallo supplied the pipe.

Stern later introduced a chart illustrating the flow of money on the South Side project.

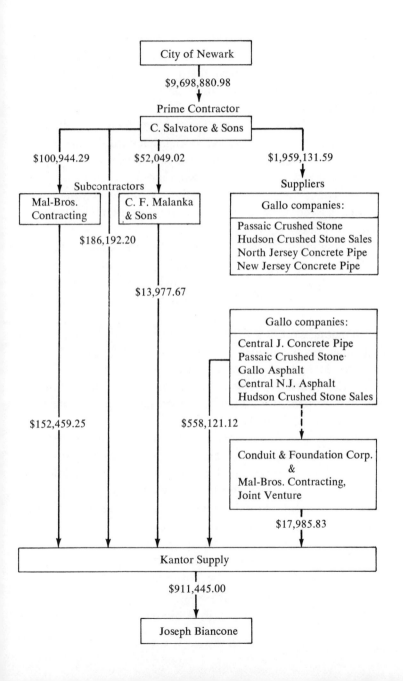

In 1965, the entire Northeast was parched by a severe water shortage. To tap an unused source of supply, Newark started a rush job on a new main, the Southerly Extension. Even in an emergency the mob and its municipal minions extracted their cut.

Cestone's Verona Construction was low bidder on the project. Since Cestone had refused to kick back on the South Side sewer, all bids were thrown out and new ones solicited. Again, Verona was low bidder and Newark's officials had no choice but to give it the contract. But they withheld payment until Cestone agreed to kick back. He capitulated and eventually paid $100,000.

The new main required high-pressure pipe, another product made by Interpace, but not by Gallo. So Biancone met with Gillespie again and asked how much Interpace would kick back on an order of 20,000 feet of pipe. Gillespie said a dollar a foot.

"Biancone said it was peanuts, wasn't worth talking about, that other people in Alabama were interested and we would have to do better," Gillespie said.

Charles Mack Albertson, former vice president of marketing for Interpace, told what happened next: He too was summoned to lunch with Biancone.

"He said that if we were interested in supplying pipe for the particular project that the only way we could participate is by paying a ten-percent kickback to him. . . . I told him the idea was ridiculous and that we would not participate."

But it was not too ridiculous to preclude another meeting with Biancone, this time over breakfast.

"I pointed out that . . . we obviously could not come up with the ten percent that he was asking for," Albertson said. "He seemed to recognize the position we were in and said, 'Well, could you pay five percent?' . . . I told him that I felt that we probably could pay a five-percent kickback. . . . He said, 'We will see that you get the contract for the pipe.' "

He said Interpace eventually paid $35,000 in kickbacks—first to Biancone, then to Paul Rigo.

That set the stage for the government's star witness. On the afternoon of June 20, Stern announced: "The government calls . . . Paul Rigo."

There was an electric shock in the air—and an electronic frisk at the door. Rigo's life had been threatened before and he had been under guard since December. All spectators who came into the courtroom were screened for weapons. The government even feared that snipers might try to pick off Rigo on the witness stand, so each day he testified, the blinds on the large window behind him were drawn, darkening an already dim courtroom.

The man who stepped to the stand was 45 years old, short, immaculately groomed and well dressed—"in showy good taste," as one observer said. Rigo liked to live well and enjoyed the use of a yacht and a helicopter that took off from a pad on his estate. His path to fortune had started only a few years before when he'd won $65,000 in the Irish Sweepstakes, quit his $12,000-a-year job and started his own engineering company, Constrad, Inc.

Although he'd never finished college, Rigo was an articulate witness. "That became very important to us," Stern says. "Although the public feeling about the case was that there was overwhelming evidence of guilt, virtually the only direct testimony to the guilt of Addonizio and the others was supplied by this one witness."

Rigo was given immunity and started his story. He was to remain on the witness stand for two weeks.

In 1964, after Sepede's death, Rigo became chief engineer on the South Side sewer project, in partnership with Sepede's partner, an elderly engineer named Charles Capen.

A few weeks later, LaMorte called him on a Sunday morn-

ing and asked him to come over right away. Rigo drove to
LaMorte's house. LaMorte met him outside, led him to his
own car and drove off.

"This is the most important meeting you will have in Newark," LaMorte told Rigo. "I am going to take you to the
man who really runs this town."

Rigo asked who.

"You will see," LaMorte said. "We are almost there."

LaMorte pulled up at the "dingy" office of Valentine Electric Company, led Rigo into the back room and introduced
him to a man named "Tony." Again, LaMorte discreetly left.

"Tony" told Rigo: "This job you have down there on the
South Side—that was set up by Johnny Sepede and me, and
Johnny Sepede and I had an understanding, and that understanding is that you pay ten percent of what you get on that
job."

"I can't pay you ten percent," Rigo replied.

"You will pay ten percent and you will pay it in cash."

"We can't pay you ten percent. What are we getting for
paying you ten percent?"

"There is a lot of mouths to feed in City Hall," "Tony"
said. "You pay me the ten percent. I take care of the mayor.
I take care of the council. I take care of anybody that has
to be taken care of down there."

At this point, Stern stopped the narrative and asked Rigo
to identify "Tony." Rigo pointed to Tony Boy Boiardo.

"I bargained, tried to get it down to five percent," Rigo
continued.

"No, it's going to be ten percent," Boiardo told him. "Everybody in Newark pays ten percent or they don't work in Newark
and they don't get paid in Newark. . . . Look what happened
to Killam. . . . He didn't pay. He is not in Newark and he is
going to sweat a long time before he gets what is owed to him."

There was the problem of how Rigo would raise the cash.

Boiardo suggested Kantor's operation, but that wouldn't work for Rigo, since engineers don't buy plumbing supplies. Rigo said he'd raise the cash his own way.

The conversation was cut short when Boiardo's wife called, summoning the mobster home for spaghetti dinner.

On the way back, Rigo asked LaMorte who "Tony" was.

"Don't you know?" said the incredulous LaMorte. "That's Tony Boy Boiardo. Don't you know Tony Boy Boiardo? Don't you know 'The Boot'?"

"I said, 'No. . . . Who are they?'

"He said, 'They are—' "

Stern interrupted: "Well, all right—"

And Judge Barlow interrupted him: "That's enough."

No mention of Boiardo's mob connections would be permitted in evidence.

Rigo kicked back—first to Gallo, then to Biancone.

During the water shortage, Rigo continued, he met with Mayor Addonizio, LaMorte and Schiff to discuss the Southerly Extension.

"Mr. LaMorte told the mayor that he had discussed the project with Mr. Boiardo and Mr. Boiardo approved of the project," Rigo said. "The mayor was quite upset and questioned me about why we had to use pipe other than Gallo's. The answer, of course, was that Gallo didn't make pressure pipe and we had to use Lock Joint [Interpace's old name] pipe.

"He said . . . 'If you have to use this Lock Joint pipe, Tony Boy better figure out a way to get something out of Lock Joint.' . . .

"Mr. Schiff made some kind of a remark to the effect, 'Will he get enough?'

"And the mayor said something to the effect, 'If he goes after it, he'll get enough.' "

Rigo started to work on the Southerly Extension, at first

without contract or pay. Since he was still kicking back on the South Side sewer project, he quickly felt the financial pinch. He took his problem to Addonizio, who told him that only Boiardo could settle the matter.

Rigo lingered in Addonizio's office and engaged the mayor in small talk.

"I don't know why in the world you ever left Washington and a nice job in Congress to come up here in this mess," he told the mayor.

"Simple," Addonizio answered. "There's no money in Washington, but you can make a million bucks as mayor of Newark."

Rigo took his problem to Boiardo, meeting the mobster at his home in Livingston.

"He was somewhat angry with me," Rigo said. "He said that we hadn't been making our payments, didn't know, couldn't understand why we were having money difficulties. . . . I explained to him . . . that if we didn't get a contract on that Southerly Extension job, I wasn't going to be able to pay ten percent, because we had more money eaten up in interest again and everything else, and we wouldn't have any money left.

"He told me, 'You pay your ten percent or I'll break both your legs.' "

Stern interrupted the narrative and asked Rigo to step off the stand and draw the floor plan of Boiardo's house.

"Here's a jury in Trenton listening to this thing," he explains, "a person like Boiardo saying the kinds of things he was saying. I was afraid it would be so shocking, so out of context with their particular world, they might not believe it. I had Rigo get off the stand and draw the interior of Boiardo's house. If the man had lied, it would be an easy matter to prove that that's not what the interior was."

The defense objected vigorously, fearing that Rigo would describe the statues "Richie the Boot" had erected of himself and his family out front and the ovens behind, where he supposedly disposed of mob victims' remains. But it turned out that Tony Boy lived in another town and Rigo had seen neither statues nor ovens.

Rigo eventually got the $300,000 engineering contract on the Southerly Extension and kicked back $30,000 to Boiardo's new bagman, Ralph Vicaro.

The mob soon found additional chores for him. Boiardo told Rigo that he'd have to collect the $100,000 from Cestone and later money from Interpace. When the Essex County grand jury started its inquiry, LaMorte summoned Rigo to City Hall and told him that because of the "sensitive situation," Boiardo could no longer personally pay off the city officials—Rigo would have to do it. The amounts were $10,-000 each to Mayor Addonizio and eight councilmen, $25,000 to LaMorte and, later, $10,000 to Corporation Counsel Schiff. The money would be paid in installments as the contractors received their checks from the city.

Rigo started keeping a diary to keep track of the payments. Each individual was identified with a code word or letter keyed to Boiardo's nickname for him. Addonizio was "the Pope"—because of his physical resemblance to Pope John XXIII; Cestone, "Chestnuts"; Schiff, "Swifty Morgan"; Bernstein and Frank Addonizio, "the Katzenjammer Kids."

Stern led Rigo item by item through the collections and payments. He calls it the "toughest" examination he's ever conducted.

"I had to change my game plan," he explains. "I had counted on introducing the diaries into evidence as business records and taking him through each payoff as reflected in the diaries. The defense prevented it. So I shifted my strategy."

Rather than use Rigo to confirm the diaries, he had to use the diaries to confirm Rigo. In addition, he led the witness through a long litany of personal outlays.

"I knew that they would try on cross-examination to say that he had generated that cash for himself," Stern continues. "I had to show that he had generated that cash to make the payoffs. I took him through every trip he ever made and proved that he paid for everything by check. When he needed cash, he wrote a check. This had the effect—at least it was my intention—of convincing the jury that whatever he was doing with that cash, he sure wasn't using it for himself.

"It was most difficult. I think through him I introduced a couple thousand exhibits. I had to show every one to counsel. I wound up running around the room one hundred, two hundred times a day. It was tough to keep it all straight. But it was vital."

On June 24, Lacey interrupted Stern's examination of Rigo to call for an *in camera* conference. Once closeted with the judge, the prosecutor relayed word of some events in Chester, New Jersey. Two toughs had visited the shop of Rigo's barber, Joseph Robert Stracco, and asked him when Rigo's next appointment was. It was an ominous question. Hitting a victim while he's sitting helpless in a barber's chair has long been a favorite method of mob executioners—*vide* Albert Anastasia's murder in the Park Sheraton barbershop.

Stracco refused to tell them. A few days later, his shop was burglarized and its fixtures destroyed. The men next approached Stracco in a bar and again asked him about Rigo's schedule. He still refused to tell them. A few days later, a car pulled alongside of Stracco's and someone fired a shot over the roof, narrowly missing a school bus unloading down the street. At Stracco's next encounter with the thugs, one told him, "Forget about it. It's all a mistake. When we win, you're invited to Tony Boy's party."

Although the events had occurred months before, Judge Barlow revoked Boiardo's $50,000 bail and remanded him for the remainder of the trial. He was influenced by other developments. The New York City police got word—whether by "tip" or "tap" has not been disclosed—that Stern's life was in danger, and the prosecutor was placed under 24-hour guard for the remainder of the trial.

Boiardo's stay in the Somerset County jail was brief. On July 6, the 56-year-old mobster suffered a massive coronary. From past experience, the prosecution had predicted that one of the defendants would have a "heart attack" before the trial ended. But this time the illness was not a case of jury jitters. Boiardo had to be hospitalized and was severed from the case.

A second defendant was also eliminated. To save time, the government had Xeroxed the thousands of documents it planned to introduce in evidence and distributed copies to defense counsel.

"They document you to death," one defense attorney complained. "They made it appear that we got everything and yet we got nothing. We had no idea of what half the documents were."

But the meaning of one was obvious. Government Exhibit Number 1 was a cashier's check for $1000 from Paul Rigo to Councilman Callahan.

Throughout the trial, Noonan kept needling Callahan's lawyer, Joseph Hayden: "What are you going to do when he puts Number One in evidence?"

Hayden would reply with something like: "I'll think of something."

He did. When the check was introduced and Rigo testified that Callahan couldn't wait for his regular cash payment and accepted a cashier's check instead, the councilman copped out. He pleaded guilty to the lesser charge of income-tax evasion and was severed from the extortion case.

Of the original 15 defendants, only five remained—Addonizio, LaMorte, Gordon, Biancone and Vicaro. According to Noonan, Gordon was offered the same deal as Callahan, but the government insisted that he remain in the case until his grand-jury testimony could be read into the record; it was the key corroboration of Rigo, but it could be introduced technically only against Gordon. Stern denies that such a "deal" was offered.

Rigo continued his account of the payoffs. By 1968, he said, he was feeling their pinch. He padded his bills to get back the ten percent, but "I never quite made it." He started looking for work in other states, but Boiardo "informed me that . . . regardless of where we obtained work, he would expect his percentage." When Rigo fled to Mexico, the payoffs stopped. As a result, Addonizio received only $4000 of his expected $10,000.

Rigo's direct testimony ended on June 29. Hellring had insisted on first crack at cross-examination, but he was out of town on a civil matter that day. To save time, Gordon's grand-jury testimony was read into the record out of turn—and Stern rested. According to Noonan, in an exchange that does not appear in the transcript, he sought to plead Gordon guilty to income-tax evasion. This time, Edwin Stern, a junior in Hellring's office and no relation to the prosecutor, objected—and Judge Barlow sustained it. Gordon remained a defendant, sitting silently throughout the trial, his head buried in his hands—as one news story described it, "three feet and 10,000 miles from Mayor Addonizio."

The defense hammered at Rigo for a week—without denting his story. Judge Barlow later described him as an "extraordinary witness": "I've never seen a witness in ten years on the bench who was more difficult for defense counsel to handle."

Back in Newark, on July 1, Kenneth Gibson was sworn in as mayor. Among his first official acts was firing Police Director Spina. Although his administration quickly raised the level of civic virtue, there was little Gibson could do to save the city's sagging fortunes. Newark was near bankruptcy and its property-tax rate was already at confiscatory levels. Worse, the population was polarized into black against white—a conflict symbolized in the persons of the white militant assemblyman, Anthony Imperiale, and the black-nationalist poet-playwright, LeRoi Jones, who had adopted the African name of Imamu Amiri Baraka. Between them, no compromise was possible nor cooperation permissible.

This too was Hugh Addonizio's legacy to his native Newark.

Ex-Mayor Addonizio was the first defense witness, the only one of the defendants to testify in his own behalf. Hellring quickly led him through his pedigree—up to his 1962 race for mayor. Addonizio said he'd made the race in order to be closer to his family and to be "helpful to my city that I felt was steadily going downhill." He also harbored "a secret ambition . . . to run for governor" and felt that the mayoralty would be a better springboard than Congress. And, he added, it paid more.

Hellring asked him about the "make-a-million-bucks-as-mayor" quote.

"That is absolutely false," Addonizio said. "I never made that statement to Rigo or anybody else."

He added that, if he'd wanted, he could have made a million in Washington.

Addonizio said his only business dealing with Rigo was the

$14,000 loan for his summer home, which he repaid. He called the rest of Rigo's testimony "absolutely false . . . a clear-cut lie." He denied receiving any money from Rigo. He even denied being at City Hall on the day one of the payments was supposedly passed. "If I was anywhere on a Saturday afternoon in June, I woud have to admit very frankly that I was at the racetrack. . . .Mr. Rigo never gave me five cents, not one red cent, not then or any other time."

He denied knowing Vicaro or Biancone, but admitted a 20-year acquaintance with Boiardo, ever since he'd been invited to Tony Boy's wedding in 1950.

"Since you first met Mr. Anthony Boiardo at his wedding, have you had any business transactions with him of any kind?" Hellring asked.

"No, sir. None whatever."

"Have you had any social or other occasions with Mr. Boiardo?"

"Yes, there have been a number of times . . ."

"Describe to the jury those social and other occasions. . . ."

"I met him at a dinner for Saint Anthony's Orphanage. . . . I also had occasion to meet him at the Pope Pius [XII] humanitarian award dinner. . . . I also met him once in New York. . . . I also had an occasion to bump into him once on an airplane. . . . I also had occasion to see him in Puerto Rico on several occasions."

A final question—Addonizio denied using the nickname "the Pope"—and Hellring was finished.

For the first time in the trial, Lacey took over the questioning, attacking Addonizio with such vigor that the ex-mayor repeatedly asked him not to shout—an admonishment echoed by Judge Barlow.

The first question was about Addonizio's gambling.

"I enjoy gambling," he replied. "I think it is very relaxing."

Had he reported his winnings on his tax returns?

"I assure you there were no gains. If there had been, they would have been reported in my income tax."

But he said he never lost more than he could afford.

Someone at the defense table started humming the folk song:

> *I'm a rambler, I'm a gambler,*
> *I'm a long way from home. . . .*

Lacey elicited the information that Addonizio had never picked up a hotel tab on his trips to Florida or the Caribbean. "I happen to have many, many good friends," the mayor explained.

Lacey turned to that Saturday in June when Addonizio was supposedly at the racetrack. Wasn't there a controversy about a police shooting that required his presence at City Hall that day? Addonizio couldn't recall.

But he admitted that the promissory notes for the $14,000 loan from Rigo had been backdated months after the transaction. And at the time he'd borrowed the money, he had $35,000 in the bank.

Lacey skipped to Boiardo's wedding: "Who invited you? His father, 'The Boot'?"

"Objection!" the defense screamed.

"I don't think that is necessary either, Mr. Lacey," the judge added.

Lacey brought out that Boiardo's best man had been Jerry Catena—not identified to the jury as Vito Genovese's successor as boss of a Mafia family. And Lacey was barred from asking further questions about the wedding guests, a veritable *anti*social register of New Jersey.

Addonizio denied knowing that Vicaro worked for a certain construction company. Didn't telephone records reflect calls to the company from Addonizio's home? "I have no idea."

A few more questions and Lacey was finished. Addonizio had been on the stand less than a day. The general feeling was that he'd been "destroyed."

Aside from Addonizio, the chief defense witness was Dr. Charles Capen, the partner first of Sepede, then of Rigo. He denied any knowledge of the payoffs, but said that Rigo "seemed very desperate for money." He also claimed that Rigo had cheated him of his share of the partnership's profits.

White-haired and distinguished-looking, Capen made an excellent impression on the jury. "It's hard for anyone reading the bare record to realize how devastating he was against us," Stern says. "Here's Rigo testifying about paying and paying, keeping a step ahead of the wolf, and here's the guy that brought him in, his partner, saying he knew nothing about it. He was a tough witness."

For three hours Stern questioned Capen, trying to poke holes in his story. He confronted the elderly engineer with a memo Rigo had sent him regarding developments on one city project: "This comes as the result of two regular meetings and many more of the kind you will imagine." Capen said he saw nothing wrong with that.

Stern sought to show that, rather than having been cheated by Rigo, Capen had profited from his association with him. His income jumped from less than $12,000 in 1961 to more than $81,000 after he'd teamed with Rigo.

The prosecutor finally elicited Capen's admission that Rigo could have been paying off without his knowledge. And then he cast a cloud on Capen's professed lack of knowledge by forcing him to admit that he'd cashed checks for Rigo.

As a final fillip, Stern showed that Capen's title of "doctor" was an honorary award for raising funds for the Newark College of Engineering.

The trial ground down to a close. Summations started on July 20. Hellring capsuled the case in a single sentence: "Will it be Rigo's word or the mayor's word?" He called Rigo "an impostor . . . a flimflam," whereas Addonizio—"He never flinched, he never hesitated, he never double-talked—he bared his life."

The other defense lawyers followed with denunciations of Rigo. Julius Feinberg for LaMorte: "I don't have to prove that Paul Rigo lied, that he cheated, that he was a thief—he has done all of this himself without any help from me." Patrick Wall for Vicaro: "[Rigo is] a witness on whose testimony no man should be convicted."

Noonan, whose client, Gordon, had admitted taking the money, had a tougher time. He argued that Gordon should be exempted from the extortion charge: "There's not one scintilla of evidence . . . that Mr. Gordon did anything other than accept money."

In reply, Lacey marshaled the evidence and argued that the prosecution had proved "cold-blooded, calculated, contemptuous corruption."

The jury retired at 4:55 P.M. on July 22. "Fred and I smelled that we had put in a powerful case and we were confident not only that we would get a guilty verdict, but that we would get an early one," Stern recalls.

At 9:40 P.M., Judge Barlow summoned the jury back and announced that he was discharging them for the night.

"Fred and I ran to the bench," Stern continues, "and started arguing, 'Why don't you ask them? Maybe they want to deliberate longer.' "

Judge Barlow asked them; they wanted to continue. The jury retired again.

At 10:08, they sent out a question: Could they make a recommendation for mercy?

"It was a doozie," Stern says. "We knew it was about Gordon."

It was also a most favorable portent for the prosecution.

Judge Barlow gave the only answer he could give—that the jury's concern was guilt or innocence, not possible punishment. Again, he started to discharge them for the night.

"Fred and I were gathering our papers,' Stern recalls, "when Fred said, 'What's going on?' I looked up and the marshal was bent over the clerk's desk. He was holding a manila envelope and he was asking for some Scotch Tape. Fred and I looked at each other and it struck us both at once—they must have a partial verdict. The only thing they have to seal is the verdict sheet. If it wasn't filled out partially, they wouldn't have to seal it. All they were doing was filling in the boxes. So we both leaped up to the front, asking the judge to inquire if they've got a partial verdict."

So the jury retired again. Lacey and Stern started for the corridor—Lacey for a stretch, Stern for a smoke. By the time they reached the courtroom door, the marshal waved them back to their seats.

The jury filed in and the foreman—Lyle G. Cook, a New Jersey Health Department employee—rose to read the verdict. "The jury finds the defendants, Hugh A-*don*-zi-o," he said, mispronouncing the mayor's name, "Anthony LaMorte, Joseph Biancone, Ralph Vicaro and Philip Gordon guilty of count one.

"The jury finds . . ."

And so on—64 times. (Two counts had been dismissed before the case went to the jury.) Judge Barlow finally took pity and told the foreman: "You may sit down if you wish, Mr. Guilty."

The Freudian slip summed up the evening: All five defendants were guilty on all 64 counts.

"It's like two hundred and two tons were lifted from my

shoulders," Stern said afterward. "In your mind is always the thought that one wrong word and you might have a mistrial— eight weeks out the window."

On September 22, 1970, ex-Mayor Addonizio stood before Judge Barlow for sentence.

"These were no ordinary criminal acts," the judge said. "These crimes were not the product of a moment of weakness, nor were they inspired by any of the defendants' desperate financial circumstances, nor were they the result of some emotional compulsion.

"These crimes . . . represent a pattern of continuous, highly organized, systematic criminal extortion over a period of many years, claiming many victims and touching many more lives. . . . The corruption . . . is compounded by the frightening alliance of criminal elements and public officials. . . .

"The criminal acts of these defendants were as calculated as they were brazen, as callous and contemptuous of the law as they were extensive. Nor can these defendants' criminal conduct be measured in dollars alone. It is impossible to estimate the[ir] impact upon . . . the decent citizens of Newark and indeed to the citizens of New Jersey in terms of their frustration, despair and disillusionment. . . .

"These very men . . . who as government officials inveighed against crime in the streets . . . pursued their own criminal activities in the corridors of City Hall. These crimes . . . tear at the very heart of our civilized form of government and of our society."

He sentenced Addonizio to ten years in prison and fined him $25,000. LaMorte got ten years and $10,000; Biancone, ten years and $25,000; Vicaro, twelve years and $10,000. (At subsequent sessions, Gordon was given three years; Callahan, one.)

The Third Circuit Court of Appeals upheld the verdict; the

Supreme Court denied *certiorari;* Addonizio and the others went off to prison.

Stern later consolidated the cases of the seven severed defendants and moved them to trial. But Boiardo, who had suffered a second heart attack, was still too ill to stand trial, and Stern didn't choose to conduct another lengthy trial against the lesser lights alone. The case, though, remains on the books and Stern says, "If we can ever get Boiardo back into court, we'll try it."

The Addonizio case may be incomplete, but to Stern the moral is clear: "You *can* fight City Hall."

7
MEMOIRS OF HUDSON COUNTY

After eliminating a corrupt regime in New Jersey's major metropolis, Lacey and Stern turned to the state's second city—Jersey City.

Frank Hague was elected mayor of Jersey City in 1917 and for more than 30 years, the city and surrounding Hudson County were his personal fiefdom. He built the Hudson County Democratic organization into a political powerhouse so strong not even Franklin D. Roosevelt dared challenge him.

"I am the law," Hague once proclaimed—and it was no idle boast. His tyranny was enforced by police nightsticks—and on occasion, Hague's own fists. Hague was something of a puritan. When he was at the table, no liquor could be served—which made political dinners a trifle tedious for many. He would not permit prostitution in Jersey City, and CIO organizers were run out of town. But gambling flourished, so much so that one downtown street was known as "Hague's Bourse."

Of course, the gamblers paid for protection, while public servants were assessed three percent of their salaries as "dues" to the organization and contractors had to kick back their tithe. Only a fraction of the money actually found its way to party coffers. Hague, whose salary never exceeded $7500 a year, was worth an estimated $8 million when he died in 1956. In that year, political scientist V.O. Key observed: "The plunder of Jersey City by the Hague machine . . . has made it the highest-taxed city in the United States."

Hague's downfall started in the spring of 1949 when one of his ward leaders, John V. Kenny, challenged his choice for the mayoralty. The two men were a study in contrasts: Hague—tall, gaunt, aloof; Kenny—a bantam of a man, gregarious, with an Irish twinkle in his eye. Although his ticket was called the "Freedom Party" and his chief issue was Hague's wealth and whip hand, Kenny was no reformer. He won his 22,000-vote margin by beating Hague at his own game. Where Hague paid $5 a vote, Kenny paid $15.

Although Kenny had ousted him from his power base,

Hague held on to the posts of Hudson County Democratic chairman and New Jersey's Democratic National committee-man. In the 1949 general election, he tried to install an under-ling as New Jersey's governor, but Kenny threw his votes to the GOP and Hague finally threw in the towel. He resigned his party positions and Kenny assumed full command in Hudson County.

The 25-year reign of "the Little Guy," as Kenny was called, was more benign than Hague's, but equally as venal. The rules of the game had not been changed; a new platoon merely took the field. Although Kenny soon left both his public and party posts, he remained the "boss," calling the signals in both the city and county, operating out of a penthouse suite in Pollak Hospital, where he had installed his son-in-law as admin-istrator.

"Everyone said that Jersey City and Hudson County were corrupt and had been for five decades," Stern says. "Every-body said that everybody who worked in Jersey City and Hud-son County had to pay off. So we decided to find out whether or not the charges were true."

The method Stern describes as "a pure imposition of scien-tific technique," developed and perfected in the Colonial, Weber and Addonizio cases.

"The first step was to find out from the businessmen whether they had to pay off. But we didn't know who the businessmen were. The first thing we did was subpoena all the records from the Jersey City Hall and the Hudson County Administration Building for public works for the past five years. From these records we determined who the successful bidders were and we subpoenaed all their records. Then we had teams of ac-countants and assistants analyzing their records, looking for that one critical thing—the cash coming out."

The first subpoenas were served on May 30, 1970, three

days before the Addonizio trial started. Before the case was concluded, the U.S. attorney's office had amassed more than 1,700,000 documents.

The investigators struck pay dirt quickly, getting several contractors to admit that they had kicked back. From them, a pattern of payoffs emerged—on city projects, through Bernard Murphy, Jersey City's purchasing agent; on county ones, through Frank Manning, the Hudson County engineer.

"The biggest break came when Frank Manning was broken," Stern continues. "Unless you're satisfied just getting the low-echelon guy, you have to go to the next level. And the only way you can do that is to persuade the bagman to break. We had a lot of money going in to Murphy, but he never would break."

Manning was the key to the case. A defense lawyer later called him "the most important single witness in the trial." Unlike most of those under investigation, Manning considered himself a professional, not a political appointee. He'd never relished his role as a bagman and had long sought a way out.

"It came to a sort of showdown in 1969," he said later. "It wasn't until then that I found myself determined to cast everything to the wind and get out if I had to, with or without pension, with or without any employment."

He got out, retiring at age 60 on a $12,000 pension. And he told all, meeting with the authorities at Lacey's summer cottage at Sea Girt, on the Jersey Shore. The fact that Manning was cooperating was kept secret—he even went before the grand jury as "Mr. X"—but Kenny suspected that he was the weak link in the chain.

A lot of legwork was required to discover where the money wound up. One lead came from an unrelated inquiry. Internal Revenue had been investigating Congressman Cornelius Gallagher, who had purchased more than $948,000 worth of municipal bonds—for cash!

"If you're going to charge a man with tax evasion," Stern says, "you have to prove that he's not just a conduit for funds, but that he's buying the bonds for himself. The only way you can do that is to find out who's clipping the coupons.

"When you have a bearer bond, it's not registered in anyone's name—that's what the phrase 'bearer bond' means. It's like money. Anyone can clip the coupons, walk into a bank, fill out a form and submit them for payment. And he can do it in any bank in the United States. Obviously, the IRS can't run to every bank in the country to find out who's cashing coupons.

"IRS did a fantastic job. They went back to the issuing municipalities to see where the coupons had come from, then checked back to determine who had cashed them. It turned out that something like four hundred thousand dollars of the bonds Gallagher had bought were in a Florida bank account and being clipped by the bank."

So the IRS agents checked at the First National Bank of Miami Beach and discovered that the bonds had been deposited—not by Gallagher, but by Jersey City's mayor, Thomas Whelan, and Council President Thomas Flaherty. The two Jersey City officials maintained joint numbered accounts which, at their peak, had deposits of $1,232,433.30—all in cash or in negotiable bonds purchased for cash.

A second cache of bonds was uncovered—and recovered—when IRS agents started checking the bank and brokerage records of William A. Sternkopf, Jr., the former Hudson County auditor who had gone on under Kenny's patronage to commissionerships first on the New Jersey Turnpike Authority, then on the bistate Port of New York Authority, which operates the metropolitan area's docks, bridges, tunnels and airports.

On one of Sternkopf's bond purchases, the records at Lehman Brothers, the giant Wall Street investment house, carried the notation that the bonds had been bought for John V.

Kenny. Tracing the trail of the transaction, the IRS agents discovered that Kenny had bought $700,000 in bonds through Sternkopf—all for cash, delivered to the bank by the Hudson County police chief, Fred J. Kropke.

Through a tip from a still-undisclosed informant, the U.S. attorney's office learned that $300,000 of the bonds were stashed in the suite of Pollak Hospital Administrator Paul Hanly, Kenny's son-in-law, and the remaining $400,000 at the Jersey Shore home of his granddaughter, Margo Hanly Hermann. Both were haled before the grand jury. Hanly took the Fifth Amendment, escaping ouster by resigning—only to have Kenny name his son, John, as his successor. Mrs. Hermann, after invoking the Fifth Amendment, was given immunity and she told where the bonds were. They were subpoenaed as evidence. Lacey said they represented "plunder unmatched by anything in my experience. You'd have to go back to the days of Boss Tweed."

As election day approached, it was clear that the net was closing on Kenny and his Hudson County cabal. But "the Little Guy" continued to spout defiance. "I wish that Stern was here," he said in early October, "so I could spit in his eye."

On October 29, Kenny threw a $100-a-plate dinner at the Jersey City Armory for Senator Harrison Williams, running for reelection against the Republican state chairman, Nelson Gross. Speaker after speaker laced into Lacey and the federal investigation. Congressman Gallagher called it "a Gestapo stalking through our county, an Anglicized version."

Among the Irish Catholic Democrats of Hudson County, anything *Anglican* is suspect.

Kenny also injected a racial motif into his remarks—of a different sort. He acknowledged buying the bonds: "I never knew that when you want to take care of daughter and children that it was an offense against the U.S. government. If that displeases Lacey or that great Jewish lawyer Stern, well, that's just too bad. I'm going to provide for the welfare of my children."

The *Newark News* said that Kenny had "reached depths of personal and religious vilification." Senator Williams had to issue a statement expressing his "deep regret" over Kenny's language, though he doubted that Kenny had intended an anti-Semitic slur. He hailed "the Little Guy" as "a great humanitarian."

Williams romped to an unexpectedly easy victory. Two days later, the "great humanitarian" John V. Kenny appeared, under subpoena, before the grand jury. He was accompanied by his attorney, the late Walter D. Van Riper, who had had firsthand experience of the Byzantine intrigues of Hudson County politics. As state attorney general during World War II, he had investigated gambling in Jersey City and had obtained several indictments. Whereupon the U.S. attorney's office, headed by a Hague hireling, indicted Van Riper—for allegedly selling black-market gasoline. Not surprisingly, both cases lapsed into limbo.

Kenny didn't spit in Stern's eye—he took the Fifth Amendment . . . or tried to. He refused to sign a waiver of immunity and asked permission to read a statement. He got it—but before he could get the words out of his mouth, Stern started firing a barrage of questions:

"Did you purchase those bonds?"

"Certainly I did."

"Did you purchase them for cash?"

"Yes."

"Through what means did you purchase them for cash?"

"What do you mean?"

"How did you buy them?"

"With cash—cash that I had saved for forty years."

"Who handled the transaction for you?"

"Well, I'm not supposed to answer any questions. . . ."

But he did—for eight more pages of transcript. Kenny insisted that the cash came from his private business concern, Terminal Industries, which cleaned cars on the Pennsylvania Railroad, and that his wife kept the money in a basement clothes-hamper.

Finally, Kenny managed to read the statement Van Riper had prepared: "Mr. District Attorney, members of the grand jury: I am advised by my legal counsel that in view of the fact that I am the target of this investigation and that an effort is being made to bring about my indictment, that if I were compelled to testify at this time it would amount to a violation of my constitutional rights. Therefore, acting on that advice, I most respectfully decline to answer the questions asked of me in this proceeding on the ground that to do so might incriminate me."

On November 16, a 34-count bribery-and-extortion indictment was lodged against Kenny and 11 others—Mayor Whelan; Council President Flaherty; Commissioner Sternkopf; Police Chief Kropke; Purchasing Agent Murphy; County Engineer Manning; plus John J. Kenny (no relation to John V.) and Walter Wolfe, both Hudson County freeholders (commissioners) and successively chairmen of the Hudson County Democratic organization; Philip Kunz, Jersey City's business administrator; Joseph P. Stapleton, treasurer of both Hudson County and the Hudson County Democratic organization; and James R. Corrado, secretary of Pollak Hospital.

The first two counts were catchalls, one alleging an overall conspiracy to bribe, the other to extort. The remaining 32 dealt with specific payments—$98,000 from Gerard Engineering; $68,282 from Warren George, Inc.; and $15,000 from Ashland Oil.

In addition, Kenny, Whelan, Flaherty and Murphy were charged with income-tax evasion.

As in the Addonizio case, the investigation continued long after the indictment, with the assistants compiling a veritable catalogue of contractors who had kicked back, or had been asked to.

Once again, they received a major break.

About six weeks before the trial was scheduled to start, John J. Kenny's attorneys approached Stern with an offer to cooperate. Secret sessions were set up at the Fifth Avenue Hotel in New York City. Like Mario Gallo, "Jack" Kenny, as he was called to distinguish him from John V., didn't want to be seen meeting with the authorities in New Jersey.

He had broken with John V. Kenny in 1969, when "the Little Guy" endorsed William Cahill, the GOP candidate for governor, while Jack Kenny stuck with the Democratic nominee, former governor Robert Meyner. Despite the political break, Jack Kenny maintained a personal loyalty to "the Little Guy." He was a gold mine of information, but, according to Stern, "one of the most difficult things we had to do was elicit his testimony about John V. Kenny."

He finally opened up and told Stern how he had approached "the Little Guy" at Newark Airport shortly after the indictment had been returned and asked him for $50,000 supposedly to "discredit" Manning. John V. Kenny made a phone call and the money was delivered that night. Jack Kenny kept the cash stashed in an ashcan in his basement.

"When I heard about that fifty thousand dollars," Stern says, "I realized that I had a tremendous piece of corroboration. It's difficult now, the case is over, there's been a conviction and everyone says, 'Of course, they're guilty.' But if you put yourself back then, you realize that the testimony of this man was incredible. While they may suspect things are wrong, our ordinary citizens have no conception of how massive, monumental, corruption was in Hudson County. Contractors were practically standing on line with envelopes in their hands. In retrospect, everybody agrees that's the way it was, but when you have to prove it in a court of law beyond a reasonable doubt, it sounds crazy. It *is* crazy, but it's true."

Stern persuaded Kenny to turn over the money. They met at the Gateway Motel in Newark. Kenny showed up with a shopping bag filled with cash. Stern had him sit on the bed and initial every bill so he could identify them in court. The bills ranged from five- to hundred-dollar bills. Some were worn tissue-paper thin and were so old that they bore the signature of Henry W. Morgenthau, the New Deal treasury secretary.

Securing John J. Kenny's cooperation required granting him immunity from prosecution. To Stern there was no doubt that this was the proper course: "It was clear to everybody that between prosecuting this one fellow and using him to rub out this whole miserable corrupt organization, there was just no choice."

But a problem arose because Jack Kenny was already under indictment by the state—for allegedly taking a $50,000 bribe to secure a zoning variance. Kenny was convinced that the indictment was revenge for his breaking with the organization. Given the Cahill administration's record of cooperation with the Hudson County Democratic machine—both before and after its disgrace—and its dogged determination to press the case, his belief seems justified.

Whatever the cause, granting federal immunity might preclude state prosecution. Stern decided to break the bad news as gently as possible. At the Legislative Correspondents Dinner at Newark's Robert Treat Hotel, he called aside New Jersey's attorney general, George F. Kugler, Jr., and told him of Kenny's cooperation and grant of immunity. At the time, Kugler seemed satisfied.

"Over the next couple of days," Stern says, "he was telephoning me furiously, telling me he didn't want to see him immunized as to their case. He specifically asked me not to question John J. Kenny about that transaction. I told him I wouldn't, but I also told him that I couldn't stop cross-examination; that he must realize that if they went into it on cross, he was going to get immunity. Apparently, he wasn't satisfied with the telephone conversation. So on the day the trial opened, he sent me a letter. I sent him a letter in reply."

The exchange did not end the imbroglio.

The trial opened on May 17, 1971. John V. Kenny, through his counsel, pleaded for postponement on grounds of ill health. At age 78, "the Little Guy" had just undergone a hernia operation. Judge Shaw denied the request, and Kenny came to court in a wheelchair accompanied by a nurse.

For Stern, the trial was the most grueling yet. Although frequent recesses had to be called so Kenny could rest, the court sessions often ran from 9:30 A.M. past 6:00 P.M., Monday through Saturday. And in the sticky spring weather, the courtroom air conditioners were inadequate to cool the crowds—mostly political hangers-on from neighboring Hudson County—who came to Newark each day. To save the two hours' commuting time each day, Stern checked into a motel near the courthouse. For him, the trial meant a series of 18-hour days.

"The role of a prosecutor in these cases is somewhat different from a defense attorney's," he explains. "A defense attorney just has to sit back and listen to the evidence. He's looking to poke a little hole somewhere and claim reasonable doubt. All the defense needs is a little crack in the door and you've had it.

"A prosecutor has to have his evidence completely prepared. Every *i* must be dotted and every *t* crossed. Otherwise, you're inviting a debacle. If your witnesses are not prepared, they'll fall apart on the stand.

"You're working against a presumption of innocence, proof

beyond a reasonable doubt, against men who are literally fighting for their lives, reputations, power. When you're dealing with an Addonizio or a Kenny, these kinds of cases are not equal contests. The mayor of Jersey City has the full resources of the Jersey City Police Department. He did not lack for investigative tools and devices. These were not people friendless and alone. These were rich, powerful, wealthy, influential men. We had to be perfect."

No prosecution is perfect. But Stern's seemed close to it. One of the defense attorneys compared him to the commander of the Third Army in World War II: Any general in command of such a well-trained, well-equipped force couldn't help but look good, and any prosecutor possessed of such evidence couldn't help but look good.

Stern disagrees. "The whole case was Manning," he says. "If Manning's testimony was believed, every single one of the defendants would be convicted—with the exception of Kunz, who was a very peripheral defendant. If he was believed, the whole rotten system was finished. If he was not believed, everybody walked out free and went back to business as usual. The whole case was put together with the idea of corroborating the testimony that Manning was going to give."

The corroboration was overwhelming. Stern boasts that the defense "didn't have one good day" throughout the seven weeks of trial.

Manning and John J. Kenny were severed from the trial at the outset. The first day's session was held in Trenton—to get a jury untainted by publicity. The panel was sequestered and the trial shifted back to Newark the next day where Stern opened, outlining each defendant's role in the conspiracy. Wolfe, Murphy, Manning and Flaherty he described as "bagmen"; Stapleton as the "bookkeeper"; Kropke, the "messenger"; Corrado, the "mail drop."

"And we will prove to you beyond a reasonable doubt that the leader . . . the mastermind of these conspiracies was the defendant John V. Kenny."

"These defendants," he continued, "knew that what they were doing was wrong, . . . they knew what they were doing was immoral and . . . they knew that what they were doing was criminal."

Most of the defense attorneys responded with the usual pieties about "presumption of innocence" and "reasonable doubt." But John Noonan argued that Walter Wolfe had a "diminished responsibility" because of injuries suffered as a marine on Saipan in World War II. He'd caught a shell fragment in his skull and was incapable, Noonan argued, of knowingly participating in the conspiracy.

"To Wally Wolfe," he said, "interstate commerce means taking the tubes over to New York to see a Knicks basketball game."

During the trial, Hudson County's Democrats reelected Wolfe as their chairman—a man supposedly unable to conform his conduct to the standards of society.

Corrado responded to Stern's opening by pleading guilty.

The first prosecution witnesses came from C.J. Langenfelder Sons, heavy-construction contractors in Baltimore which were interested in working on a $40-million reservoir project. The day before bids were to be submitted, Murphy called and asked to meet with a Langenfelder official. Project Manager James P. Crawford flew to Newark Airport in the company plane. Murphy climbed aboard and over cocktails made his pitch—seven percent to be kicked back in cash. On a $40-million contract, it meant some $2.8 million. Stern says it's the largest shakedown attempt he's ever heard of. Langenfelder decided not to bid on the project.

Hugh Platt, Jr., followed, telling how his company, Ray Palmer Associates, had modified some sewage-treatment equipment for Jersey City. When payment came due, Murphy called Platt and explained "that in case of this amount of money it is normal to take care of 'the boys downtown.' "

He asked for a ten-percent kickback and Platt agreed to pay. "I had little choice if we were going to get paid."

Ten percent came to exactly $2884.04.

"What did you do with the $2884.04?" Stern asked.

"I took it down to Mr. Murphy's office."

"All of it?"

"Took it all down."

"Including the four cents?"

"Took the four cents. He rejected it."

"He took the cash and gave you back the pennies, is that it?"

"Yes."

Herman Silverman, president of Sylvan Pools, told him his firm sold a dozen portable swimming pools to Jersey City's Department of Recreation to help defuse summer tensions in the ghettoes. On the bulk order, he gave the city a ten-percent discount.

On the way out of City Hall, Silverman was called by Murphy into the men's room. "We want that ten percent," he said. "We want it in cash."

Silverman agreed to pay. "I felt that [if] that was the price for doing business in Jersey City, we were going to go along with it," he explained.

To raise the $6000 kickback, Silverman simply billed Jersey City for a more expensive model than the pools he shipped. Frank LaRosa, Sylvan Pools' general manager, delivered the cash to Murphy in a parking lot.

Aaron Groveman of Ardsley Construction Company told how his firm had been interested in doing rehabilitation work on Jersey City's Roosevelt Stadium. But a company agent had been denied specifications for the project. Groveman called Murphy to find out why.

"He said, 'Jersey City is a political town and we have certain rules and regulations here, and since your company has never done any business with us before, I want to inform you as to what these rules and regulations are.'

"So I asked him to let me know what they were.

"He said, 'If you want to bid this job and you are the low bidder, you'll have to pay us ten thousand dollars.'

"I said, 'I see.'

"He said, 'Now that you know [what] the rules and regulations are, you can send over for the plans.' "

Ardsley got the award and Groveman went to Murphy's office to sign the contract.

"Mr. Murphy told me that he was the bagman and that I would pay him the ten thousand during the course of the job, and that I was to deal with him only and he was to deal with me only."

Groveman paid the $10,000 in four installments, the first in Murphy's office, the rest on street corners.

When Stern called John J. Kenny to the stand, Richard B. McGlynn, chief of the trial section of the state attorney general's office, interrupted the proceeding to announce that the state intended to proceed with its prosecution of the witness.

"If it can legally do so," Judge Shaw snapped.

His anger barely concealed, the judge told McGlynn: "I don't recognize that the state attorney general has any standing to challenge the action which I am taking . . . to immunize a witness who will testify in behalf of the government."

He warned McGlynn: "I will not permit any state official to interfere with the trial of this case in any manner whatsoever and anyone who thinks he can do it will be before me for appropriate proceedings. I can't make myself more clear, I don't think."

Kenny was given immunity. He was 51, a handsome man with a ruddy Irish face and dark hair tinged with gray at the temples. He spoke with the classic New Jersey accent— "I *coit*-nly did"—and his knowledge of Hudson County politics was encyclopedic. But he was not a good witness: His manner was feisty; his memory for detail was hazy; and he was not especially articulate—or politic. At one point, he likened himself to John F. Kennedy.

"I find the comparison odious," said defense lawyer Raymond Brown—and no doubt many on the jury did too.

Kenny told how he'd met John V. Kenny at his father's wake in 1944, allied himself with "the Little Guy" and rose through the patronage ranks until he became a freeholder in 1961 and county chairman in 1964. But they were figurehead posts. As he put it on cross-examination: "I was not able to do anything unless I had the approval of John V. Kenny."

He described how "the system" operated. He would hold checks due contractors on county projects until they kicked back, then he'd pass the payoffs to Stapleton. There were so many such payoffs that he could not remember all of them.

But he gave a few specifics. He told how Mayor Whelan had approached him at a political rally in 1964 and asked him to shake down a gambler named Lefty Marchitto—who had enjoyed Jack Kenny's "protection"—for a quarter-million dollars. Kenny went to the shoeshine parlor where Marchitto held court and relayed the mayor's message. "There was no reply but a laugh." But after some harassment by the authorities, Marchitto coughed up $15,000, which Kenny passed to Whelan.

Kenny went on to tell of shaking down the builder of a firehouse for $5000 and a sewerage construction firm for $50,000.

In 1965, he continued, Whelan thanked him for the money. "He said, 'We should get together and we'd do well and we ought to get John V. Kenny out of the picture.'

"I told him to go to hell."

Kenny continued his account, telling how he'd run into Dominick Galano of J. Rich Steers Construction at Pollak Hospital, which he described as "a sort of political headquarters." Galano, the son of a Hudson County freeholder, was interested in getting work on the New Jersey Turnpike.

"I asked Mr. Galano how large that contract would be," he said. "He told me in the neighborhood of ten million. . . . I asked Mr. Galano for a hundred thousand. He said, 'There is not a chance.' "

Kenny met later with Steers's President Gene Rau. "I asked him for seventy-five thousand and he said twenty-five thousand. . . . We agreed on fifty-thousand."

He said he passed half the money to Turnpike Commissioner Sternkopf, half to Stapleton.

Soon afterward, Sternkopf went from the Turnpike Authority to the Port Authority. Steers had a $4-million claim against the Port Authority for cost overruns on runway construction at LaGuardia Airport. With Kenny acting as middleman, Sternkopf agreed to expedite settlement in return for a $30,000 kickback. The payoff was divided between Kenny, Sternkopf and Kenny's brother-in-law, Edward Dooley, the Freeholders' clerk, who cashed Steers's check and paid the taxes on it.

Steers, Kenny said, also agreed to kick back $150,000 to get a contract for repair work on a Jersey City bridge, but by the time the payments came due, Kenny was out of politics and never collected.

He also told of receiving $225,000 in kickbacks from Sarubbi Construction, headed by Angelo Sarubbi, the mayor of nearby North Bergen, for work on Pollak and Mental Health hospitals. By the time the last installment of $35,000 was paid, Kenny had broken with the organization and he simply pocketed the money.

Kenny said he sought Sternkopf's advice on investing his ill-gotten gains. The commissioner suggested south Jersey real estate. The C.E.W. Corporation was set up, with brother-in-law Dooley serving as Kenny's "dummy," while Sternkopf handled Kenny's $81,000 investment.

Finally, Jack Kenny told of getting the $50,000 from John V. Kenny at Newark Airport. Stern opened a brown briefcase and spread the bills on the rail in front of the witness stand for Kenny to identify. Kenny did so and the prosecutor scooped up the cash in his arms, walked across the well of the court and dumped it on the defense table.

"Get that stuff away from me, whatever it is!" Van Riper shouted, while his colleagues jumped up screaming, "Objection!" and moving for a mistrial.

The defense attacked Jack Kenny with vigor, but he generally gave as good as he got. Stern's fear that he couldn't limit cross-examination proved justified. Van Riper's first question concerned the subject of the state indictment:

"Didn't you shake down the Reinauer Land Company for fifty thousand dollars?"

"I didn't—but Angelo Sarubbi did, and he brought me the money in a brown paper bag."

Judge Shaw later told Van Riper: "You definitely clinched the matter that he has immunity from state prosecution."

While Kenny was undergoing cross-examination, Stern received the first word of IRS's discovery of the Florida bank accounts. As the trial ground rules provided, Stern passed out copies of the bank records to opposing counsel. One could sense the complete collapse of Whelan's and Flaherty's defense.

After John J. Kenny left the stand, the trial reverted to a litany of kickbacks. Galano gave another account of the Steers payoffs, adding to Kenny's account of the abortive $150,000 kickback on the bridge-repair project: "I asked Mr. Dooley what the hell Jack Kenny wants a hundred and fifty thousand for, because as far as I was concerned he wasn't politically connected with John V. Kenny, and he had broken apart from the organization, and I just didn't understand why John V. Kenny would send Jack Kenny for a hundred and fifty thousand dollars. . . .

"He was quite frightened. He turned white and he said, 'Well, I hope he is not using me either, because my job at the county is at stake here.' "

Galano went to Wolfe, who had succeeded Jack Kenny as nominal chairman of the county organization. Wolfe said that Jack Kenny no longer spoke for John V. Kenny. Galano renegotiated the kickback with Wolfe—for $20,000. But there is no honor among bribers. He told his superiors at Steers that the price was $45,000 and pocketed $25,000 for himself.

Philip Schuster, from the Warren Brothers division of Ashland Oil, testified that a $400,000 claim against Hudson County for road materials was settled in January, 1970, for $208,000. A few days later, Manning asked Schuster to stop at his office. Schuster arrived and the county engineer led him into the hall.

"He told me he didn't like to talk in his office," Schuster said. "He was afraid that his office was bugged. . . . He then told me that I would have to come up with some money if I wanted to get this money from the claim. . . . He told me that he would need twenty-two thousand for the boss and two thousand for himself."

" . . . Did he identify to you who 'the boss' was?" Stern asked.

" . . . Yes, he did."

"Who did he identify his boss as?"

"He just called him 'the Little Guy.' "

"Did you know who in Hudson County was referred to as 'the Little Guy'?"

"Yes, sir."

" . . . Who is that?"

"Mr. Kenny."

"What is his full name?"

"John V. Kenny."

Schuster continued his narrative: "I told him it was impossible. We were a national company and we had no access to cash. . . . He said, well, maybe he could get the amount shifted down a little, but I would have to come up with something. . . . He told me this was Hudson County and this was the way things were done. . . . I said I didn't know how I could raise the money, but I couldn't raise that much. He said, 'I'll go back to the boss and see how little he will take and in the meantime you see how much you can raise.' "

The kickback was haggled down to $15,000—$13,000 for "The Little Guy," $2000 for Manning.

"Mr. Schuster," Stern asked, "did you want to pay fifteen thousand dollars in cash?"

"No, I did not."

"Did you want to pay anything?"

"No."

"Why did you agree to pay it?"

"Because I didn't think we could get our money any other way."

Schuster raised the cash through a subcontractor—paying out an extra $16,000 for the subcontractor's taxes—and went to Manning's office. "I tried to give Mr. Manning the money and he wouldn't accept it. He told me I had to give it to Mr. Wolfe." Schuster did so.

Soon afterward, the federal investigation started and the wheels of the conspiracy started to spin in reverse. In the grand-jury waiting room, Kropke tried to return the money to Schuster. The following day, he showed up at Schuster's office with an envelope that had to be delivered personally. But Schuster was out, so he left a note instead.

Throughout the trial, John V. Kenny had dozed off from time to time in his wheelchair and frequent recesses had to be called so he could rest. On June 7, the 78-year-old political boss was hospitalized with a distended bladder. The examination disclosed that he was suffering from a variety of ailments, including a prostate condition, heart disease and hardening of the arteries.

During the three-day recess to assess his condition, Stern had consulted electronics experts at Bell Laboratories and RCA. He suggested that the trial continue via closed-circuit television to Kenny's room in Pollak Hospital.

"While it may be novel," he told Judge Shaw, "I submit to Your Honor that it is an approach which does not derogate from Mr. Kenny's constitutional rights."

The judge ruled that the plan was "not workable": "I am not going to order the criminal trial of a man while he is lying in a hospital bed."

Despite Stern's disappointment at losing his star defendant, "the Little Guy" was severed from the case. The trial continued—more grueling than ever. With Kenny gone, the sessions ran longer and had fewer breaks.

The next witness was John Merrigan of Gerard Engineering, which had handled many projects in Jersey City and Hudson County—so many that Merrigan couldn't recall all the times he'd been forced to kick back.

Manning and Merrigan originally formed the concern—Gerard is Manning's middle name—to bid on a project in Bayonne. When that deal fell through, Manning pulled out of the firm. The original understanding was that Gerard would not be required to pay kickbacks. Then Manning brought word of the new terms: Gerard would have to kick back 20 percent on the first two projects, 10 percent thereafter.

Among the payments, Merrigan told of giving $20,000 in a

black bag to James Dolan, chief engineer in the Jersey City Department of Public Works, for delivery to Manning.

After the federal investigation started, Manning "asked me if I would take back part of the money which I had paid in kickbacks." Merrigan agreed. He met Wolfe for lunch at the King's Inn restaurant in New Brunswick. After the meal, Wolfe led him into the men's room and handed him an envelope.

"I was asked to give you this," he told Merrigan.

The envelope contained $18,000 in $100 bills. Merrigan put $17,000 in a safe-deposit box, which he later turned over to the U.S. attorney. Stern introduced it as evidence.

The session ran so late that the clerk's office had closed before the court recessed for the day. Stern agreed to take the $17,000—then in court custody—back to his office overnight for safekeeping. Noonan, ever playing the court jester, playfully plucked the envelope from Stern's pocket. Judge Shaw, who saw it from the bench, commented on the defense lawyer's "undisclosed talent." Noonan, of course, returned the money. "Otherwise," Stern says, "we would have had another case."

Merrigan's testimony was reinforced by that of Dolan and of David Muss, who had succeeded Merrigan as head of Gerard. Dolan told of collecting many payments and delivering the money to Manning—including the $20,000 in the black bag. He also related how he was called into Kunz's office after the federal investigation started. Kunz "asked me if I had heard the latest about Mario Gallo.

"I said to him, 'No, what is the latest about Mario Gallo?'

"He said, 'They found him with a rope around his neck. The same thing happens to you or anyone else who talks about what is going on in Jersey City.' "

It wasn't true. Kunz may have said it, but Mario Gallo had died in an auto crash.

The federal inquiry did not deter the cabal. Dolan related how he "asked Mr. Murphy if they were still following the same procedures, and he said, yes, he had received instructions from Mayor Whelan that the goodies had to keep rolling in."

Muss told of leaving $14,000 in payoff money in his room at Jersey City's Holiday Inn. When he returned to the motel, he found that someone in the cleanup crew had made off with the money. He had trouble raising so much cash again. "Flaherty came to me several times and emphasized that if we didn't . . . our bills wouldn't be paid."

Stern could have continued the litany of payoffs for weeks. "There was a vast amount of evidence that we never used," he explains. "When you have a John J. Kenny or a Frank Manning get up and say that thirty firms paid them off and list their names, we had spoken with all those firms, because what if they had come in and said, 'No, we didn't pay them'? But there's a judgment factor. When do you overprove a case? How many times do you slay the dragon? We had to call a halt somewhere. After all, we had a sequestered jury, locked up seven weeks, away from their homes, businesses and families." So he wrapped up his case with Frank Manning's testimony.

Manning was short, squat, his hair close-cropped. He told of being slowly sucked into the payoff conspiracy. He started out as Jersey City's chief engineer. He explained that as a professional employee, John V. Kenny exempted him from the usual three-percent salary kickback, but Judge Shaw barred any mention of salary assessments from being heard by the jury, since such kickbacks weren't interstate commerce and were thus outside the court's jurisdiction. Kenny also exempted him from kicking back on his private engineering projects.

But after Manning withdrew from Gerard Engineering, the agreement no longer applied to the firm. Not only was Gerard required to kick back, Manning was assigned the chore of collecting the payoffs.

Later, when Murphy and John V. Kenny had a brief falling-out, Kenny asked Manning to handle collections on other Jersey City kickbacks.

"Did you agree to do it?" Stern asked.

"Yes, sir, I did."

" . . . Did you understand that you were becoming a bag-man?"

" . . . Yes, I did."

Stern didn't ask why Manning had agreed. But the defense did on cross-examination. Manning attributed his acquiescence to "the Little Guy's" "Napoleonic influence."

Manning wound up collecting from "all the contractors in that year or so where I was still with the city of Jersey City."

In 1966, Manning became county engineer and his role as bagman on Jersey City projects was phased out. But he was quickly assigned to rake in the payoffs on county projects. When the money came in, he'd call John V. Kenny and inform "the Little Guy" that he had a "resolution" for him to look at —either a "city resolution" or a "county resolution." If it was "big money," it was a "lengthy resolution."

Manning told of delivering the first payoff to Kenny at his Terminal Industries office—$4800 in two envelopes. Kenny laid the envelopes on his desk and covered one with his hand. Then he called in Flaherty and handed him one envelope.

"This is your envelope from Gerard," he told the council president.

As soon as Flaherty left, Kenny called in Corrado and gave him the other envelope for delivery to Stapleton.

"Tell him it's from Gerard."

All the city payoffs were handled in this manner, Manning said, but Flaherty had nothing to do with kickbacks on county work.

Manning related how he'd received the $20,000 payoff from Merrigan through Dolan in four fat envelopes. Kenny wasn't in and Manning feared to leave so much money in his office overnight. He put the envelopes in his overcoat pocket. That night he had a dinner-and-theater date with his wife. When he checked his coat at Whyte's Restaurant in downtown Manhattan, he stuffed the money inside his shirt and kept it there while he ate dinner and sat through the show—"both very uncomfortably."

He corroborated earlier witnesses' testimony about specific payments and attempts to return money once the federal investigation started. He said he never kept any of the cash for himself, but was rewarded with three engineering contracts worth $80,000, two of them from Sternkopf. When Wolfe became county chairman, he took over the chores of collection and Manning finally got his wish—to get out of his role as bagman.

The engineer proved a tough nut for defense cross-examiners.

Murphy's lawyer, Robert Baime, asked him: "As of 1952, you became aware of kickbacks, is that so?"

"Yes, sir."

"So from 1952, was that the first awareness you had of kickbacks?"

"Yes, sir—other than salary kickbacks."

"Could I have that read back?" Stern asked. "I didn't hear it."

It's an old lawyer's trick. Stern heard the answer all right—he just wanted to make sure the jury did too.

"He heard it," Baime said.

"Read it back," the judge ordered.

The court stenographer read the answer.

"I ask that it be stricken," Brown said.

"I ask that it be stricken too, Your Honor," Baime echoed.

"Motion denied," Judge Shaw ruled. "If you want to frame your question so you describe a particular kind of kickback, that is one thing. But when you refer to kickbacks generally and the witness responded to that type of question, I will allow the answer to stand."

Thus, the forbidden subject finally came into evidence.

The prosecution came to a close as Stern presented bankers and brokers to testify about Whelan's and Flaherty's Florida bank accounts and Kenny's bond purchases. The government rested on June 22.

Wolfe led off for the defense. He was a big, muscular man who'd been an ironworker before entering politics. He gave the appearance of being an easygoing, likable clod. He answered counsel's questions with a breezy informality that kept the courtroom chuckling.

Here's how he described the Schuster payoff: Schuster came into his office with Manning and said, "Here, I want to make a contribution to the Democratic party."

"Are you sure this is all right for me to take, this thing?" Wolfe asked.

"Yes, it is. It is perfectly all right. I appreciate what you did for me."

Schuster gave him an envelope. "I didn't open it," Wolfe said.

Noonan suggested that Wolfe get off the stand, step to the easel and draw the layout of his office.

"I can't draw, Jack. Just let me explain. Okay?"

Wolfe said he took the envelope into Stapleton's office. "I said that Manning just brought some guy into the room and he handed me an envelope.

"He says, 'What is in it?'

"I said, 'I don't know.'

"I said, 'Manning went like that.' " Wolfe held up his hands with ten fingers extended. " 'I assume it's ten tickets [to the organization's annual $100-a-plate dinner].'

"So Joe said, 'You have a safe over there in that office?'

"I said, 'Yes, I do, but I don't know [how] to get in it. I'll find out.'

"So I went back and asked Marie [his secretary]. I said, 'Do you know how to open the safe?'

"She opened it. She knew the combination. . . . I took the envelope and I just threw it down with the Christmas decorations."

Months later, Wolfe continued, he opened the safe and found that the envelope contained $10,000.

"I brought it over to Mr. Stapleton and I said, 'Joe, there is something wrong. He went 'ten' "—Wolfe demonstrated again—" 'I assumed it was ten tickets.'

"I said, 'Let's send him ten tables to the dinner.'

"Joe said, 'No one ever took ten tables to the dinner. Besides, we couldn't give him ten if we wanted to.' Because he was making the chart up. . . . He said, 'Send him a table of tickets and send him the nine grand back,' which we attempted to do."

He said he asked Kropke to drive him to Schuster's office and when Schuster wasn't in, sent him a check by mail.

He similarly described Galano's $20,000 payoff as a "campaign contribution," and as for the men's-room transaction with Merrigan:

"Mr. Stapleton gave me an envelope outside the Freeholders' office. He said somebody handed it to him with a note on it—no, he asked me if I knew John Merrigan and I said, 'Yes.' He said somebody in the hallway gave him an envelope— 'Would you deliver it to him?' And I thought he said the Brunswick Inn, Jack, I swear I do."

". . . When you accepted moneys from Philip Schuster and

Dominick Galano, Mr. Wolfe, did you believe that you were committing a crime?" Noonan asked.

"No, I did not."

"Did you believe you were doing wrong?"

"No, I didn't believe I was doing wrong. I was trying to do a job for this dinner of ours. . . ."

Stern started cross-examination by asking Wolfe about his war wound.

"I'm not crazy," Wolfe shot back. "I'm not trying to say I am, pal. Remember it!"

Stern continued: "You know it's wrong for a public official to take money, don't you, Mr. Wolfe?"

"No, I don't, not where you are the county chairman."

"Do you know whether or not it is wrong to bring people into back rooms and give them envelopes with money in it?"

"I didn't know what was in the envelope."

Noonan also presented several psychiatrists and psychologists who testified to Wolfe's "diminished responsibility." During cross-examination of one doctor, who insisted that Wolfe suffered from "chronic brain syndrome," something Stern said touched a sensitive nerve. Wolfe suddenly jumped up and lunged for the prosecutor. He had to be restrained by counsel.

The next defendant to take the stand was Police Chief Kropke. A hard-jawed man with a bulbous red nose, his name naturally evoked parodies of *West Side Story*'s "Gee, Officer Krupke." The 60-year-old cop admitted making several deliveries as favors—of an attaché case filled with cash from John V. Kenny to his banker for a bond purchase; of the "dinner tickets" from Wolfe to Schuster. But he denied any evil intent. He finished his direct examination in tears, exclaiming, "I never took a dollar from anyone."

Then Stern took over for cross-examination. In 1967, when

Kropke reported income of $12,875, his wife bought a parcel of land for $13,000—cash; and $1137 in stocks—also for cash. Where had the cash come from?

From the household money, Kropke insisted.

Stern continued with the list of purchases—$400, $1168, $627, $461, $296, $6000, all for stocks, all in cash; $1500 for a new car; $13,000 on another land deal. He also showed that Krope's wife owned a $6800 diamond ring and a $4800 mink coat. She also bought $5000 worth of stock for cash.

Where had the money come from?

From a dresser drawer.

Even though he had three savings accounts and two checking accounts?

"Perhaps I am eccentric."

Where did the money come from?

"My wife saved it."

"Out of the household money?"

"Could be."

Few who heard him believed it "could be."

Kropke's testimony was interrupted for a character witness whose priority could not be denied—former governor Robert Meyner. He appeared on behalf of Sternkopf, whom he had named to the Turnpike Authority years before. He answered his direct examination with the usual platitudes of character witnesses.

Still, it was impressive. Meyner had been a figure of rare integrity in New Jersey politics—so much so that his comeback had been opposed by the Kenny machine two years before. He had a rugged, chiseled face and a Lincolnesque appearance; he was married to a distant cousin of Adlai Stevenson and had once been touted as a presidential possibility.

On cross-examination Stern elicited Meyner's admission that Sternkopf had been recommended by Kenny, but "when

I made any appointments, they were my appointments." Stern asked Meyner about the Larner Report, prepared by Judge Sidney Larner after a 1955 investigation of Hudson County, which found Sternkopf guilty of "dereliction of the performance of his duties" as county auditor, Had Meyner been aware of it when he appointed Sternkopf? The former governor said he was not familiar with the particular passages cited and that they had not affected his decision.

After Stern presented a rebuttal psychiatrist who said, "I found nothing at this time that made me feel that [Wolfe] should be considered anything except normal," Stapleton took the stand.

While the trial was in progress, the 75-year-old county treasurer had been hit with an 84-count state indictment, on charges of approving $392,000 in improper disability pensions for more than a hundred county employees.

Stapleton made a complete denial to almost all the charges.

"Did you ever receive money from any contractor that did business with the county of Hudson?"

"No, sir."

"Mr. Stapleton, did you ever conspire with anyone to violate any law?"

"No, sir."

"Did you ever receive any kickback money from anyone?"

"No, sir."

The only thing he admitted was passing the envelope containing the $18,000 rebate to Merrigan. He said he received it from an unknown man in the corridor of the county Administration Building and gave it to Wolfe.

A few more character witnesses took the stand—including Austin Tobin, executive director of the Port Authority, appearing for Sternkopf. Then Sternkopf himself was sworn. The 70-year-old commissioner admitted buying the bonds for John V. Kenny, but denied there was anything illicit or conspiratorial in the transactions. He denied receiving any kickbacks.

Stern was thwarted from asking his key questions on cross-examination. With the jury absent, he informed Judge Shaw of his proposed line of inquiry. Sternkopf and D. Louis Tonti, then executive director of the Garden State Parkway, Stern said, had reaped a $210,000 profit on a shady land deal. They had bought the land from ITT in 1964 for $90,000 and sold it to the parkway over the next four years for $300,000. Tonti's role in the transaction was hidden and his profits were secretly funneled to Italy for deposit in a Swiss bank account. It was a classic case of what George Washington Plunkett once defined as "honest graft"—not so honest under today's conflict-of-interest statutes. But Judge Shaw ruled that the transaction was outside the scope of the trial.

After a few more character and peripheral witnesses, the defense petered to a close on the last day of June.

Summations lasted three days, running into Saturday of the July 4th weekend. After the usual Sunday off, court resumed on the legal holiday, Monday, July 5, for Judge Shaw's charge. The jury retired at 1:40 P.M.

It was a scorching summer day—the temperature in the eighties, the air hot and sticky. The defendants, their lawyers, their followers—all but bookkeeper Stapleton—doffed their jackets and waited out the verdict in the deserted courthouse. Stern crossed the street to his fifth-floor office and had lunch at his desk, as usual. He was supremely confident.

"I had no doubt of what the verdict would be," he says. "I drew up a statement which I felt would summarize what the staff had accomplished. I didn't have long to draw it up. We were back across the street before I knew it."

Including a break for lunch, the jury needed only 3 hours and 35 minutes to digest and decide on seven weeks of testimony. It was barely enough time to fill in the 232 boxes on the verdict sheet—eight defendants, 29 counts (five counts were dismissed during the course of the trial).

Seven of the eight were found guilty on all counts. Only Kunz—against whom Stern admitted the evidence was weakest—escaped complete conviction; he was acquitted on 17 counts.

Sentencing came on August 10. Judge Shaw repeated the remarks Judge Barlow had made in sentencing Newark's Mayor Addonizio the year before. Then he went on:

"It really taxes the imagination to speculate on the amount of money involved in ten percent of all public contracts by Jersey City and Hudson County. . . . It seems indeed regrettable to the public that the cities become impoverished, unable to take care of their poor, unable to furnish the proper recreation for their people, unable to relieve some of the excessive burden of taxation, unable to do so because of a rotten system which is pouring money into the pockets of corrupt politicians."

"This is a vicious system," he said, "and the sentence should, among other things, serve the purpose as a deterrent. It should serve notice upon all politicians with like inclinations that when a crime is detected and there is a conviction, courts will not be inclined to deal lightly with it. . . . I find no ground for sympathy. . . . Sympathy or compassion should run in favor of the citizen who is the victim of this type of avaricious conduct."

The judge noted that he had received many letters asking for clemency, all with "the central theme [that] 'this was a way of life in Jersey City and Hudson County. . . .'

"I think the prevailing way of life should stop."

Judge Shaw's sentences were stern (no pun intended) for white-collar criminals. Mayor Whelan, Council President Flaherty and Purchasing Agent Murphy each got fifteen years; Sternkopf got ten years, plus a $20,000 fine; Kropke got five; Stapleton and Kunz each received six months, plus eighteen months' probation.

At separate hearings, Wolfe and Corrado each received five-year suspended sentences. Judge Shaw found Wolfe to be a man of "limited intelligence" who "just doesn't have sufficient judgment to avoid being misled by other stronger-minded individuals." Wolfe was freed with the stipulation that he not participate in politics or hold any office of public trust. Corrado was freed because he had cooperated with the authorities.

Stern said the case proved that "the forces of corruption and venality in the public service, no matter how powerful, can be overcome—that our system can be changed from within."

Changed it was. At the next elections—in November, 1971 —the Kenny machine did not even field a candidate for mayor of Jersey City. Dr. Paul Jordan, the 30-year-old director of a drug-treatment clinic, won on what was for Jersey City a real reform platform, promising to finish "the job started by . . . Stern."

Whelan and Flaherty decided to face the music. They pleaded guilty to income-tax evasion, received five-year concurrent sentences and $20,000 fines and went off to prison.

The five other defendants facing prison appealed. The Third Circuit Court of Appeals unanimously ruled against them: "The proof [of guilt] is overwhelming." The Supreme Court denied *certiorari*.

In the interim, Stapleton had gone on trial in the state court, was found guilty of squandering the county's pension funds and was given a one-year to 18-month sentence, *consecutive* to the federal term.

One matter remained—the future of John V. Kenny.

A month after the Hudson County verdict, "the Little Guy" was hit with a new indictment—for what Manning might have described as a "federal resolution." Kenny and three others were charged with extorting a $20-million subcontract on the $40-million automated post office in Kearny. The investigation was handled by a Washington Strike Force; other than processing the papers, Stern's office had nothing to do with it.

Putting the post office in the Jersey swamps had been President Kennedy's reward for Kenny's support in the 1960 election. But what "the Little Guy" had done with the reward had been the subject of federal scrutiny under three administrations. "They weren't satisfied with having gotten the world's biggest automated postal facility for Hudson County," said one Justice official, "they had to cannibalize it for 'the boys downtown.' "

The indictment charged that Kenny had conspired to force the $20-million contract for construction of the plant to Kearny Associates, a firm headed by North Bergen Mayor Angelo Sarubbi and John Luciani, and that "the boys downtown" had raked off $400,000 in cash from them. Kenny, Sarubbi, Luciani and a third contractor—Edward Hansen— were charged.

Meanwhile, Stern kept trying to get Kenny into court on the Hudson County case. For nine months, "the Little Guy" successfully pleaded ill health, never venturing from his suite in Pollak Hospital.

Although his machine had been destroyed and he had announced his "retirement" from politics, there were indications that Kenny continued to pull strings in New Jersey—especially through Governor Cahill, who still owed the Democratic ex-boss an electoral debt from 1969.

In April, 1972, Assemblyman David Friedland, a Democrat from Hudson County who claimed to be allied "privately" with Reform Mayor Jordan, complained to Stern about Kenny's "continued interference" in legislative matters. Friedland, a former Assembly minority leader, even suggested that the government tap a telephone in the State House to keep tabs on Kenny. Stern—who has not employed bugs in any corruption investigation—naturally declined.

Besides, the prosecutor was less interested in *what* Kenny was doing than in *that* he was doing it—that he was active politically and presumably fit to stand trial. From Friedland he obtained the names of three legislative colleagues who had also been in contact with Kenny. And from them he also secured affidavits as to Kenny's political activities. "The Little Guy" kept calling Trenton about congressional reapportionment, about the appointment of judges in Hudson County (whom Cahill duly named) and even about the choice of a Port Authority commissioner to replace the convicted Sternkopf.

Assemblyman Michael Esposito reported that Kenny had asked him: "Mike, how is everything in the legislature?"

"Quiet."

"Mike, keep it quiet."

But there was nothing to indicate that Kenny's activity was anything more than a political leader's normal concern for matters governmental.

"Did he ever ask you to do anything that was improper?" Kenny's counsel Van Riper asked Friedland at one court hearing.

"Not that I know of."

"Well, if it had been, you would have remembered that, wouldn't you, a moral man?"

"Mr. Van Riper, I don't know whether I am totally moral or not, or whether you are, or whether any man is."

"I'm not, I'll tell you that," Van Riper said.

"I try my best," Friedland replied.

Kenny came to court in a wheelchair on May 24 and escaped the ordeal of a trial by pleading guilty to six counts of income-tax evasion. Judge Shaw fined him $30,000 and sentenced him to 18 years in prison, pending a review. At Kenny's age, it amounted to a life sentence. But Judge Shaw indicated that he would reduce the sentence once he received the prisoner's medical reports. The ailing ex-boss was remanded immediately to the federal prison hospital in Springfield, Missouri.

The bribery and extortion charges remained open, but Stern said the case would never be tried. "If the court wants to, it can keep him in jail for the rest of his life," he explained. "There is simply no point in bringing further prosecutions against an eighty-year-old man."

All along, the problem of Kenny's failing health had plagued the prosecutor. "When we didn't prosecute him, they said we were too soft. When we did prosecute him, they said we were too harsh. The truth is, he should have been prosecuted twenty years ago."

Kenny's review of sentence came on November 27. By then, his physical condition had deteriorated sharply. In addition to his other ailments, he had undergone a prostatectomy, and to keep his failing heart going, a pacemaker had been implanted in his chest. He was too ill even to come to court to hear his fate decided.

Judge Clarkson Fisher—who replaced the late Judge Shaw on the case—said that Kenny's crimes "warrant most serious penalties. However . . . I just don't feel it in my heart and mind to inflict any further cruelty." He reduced Kenny's sentence to 18 months, with the prospect of parole as soon as his physical condition warranted. Kenny was released on March 1, 1973, after serving nine months behind bars.

"The Little Guy" was free—but "a way of life" had ended in Hudson County.

8
THE SENATOR ADVISES, THE PRESIDENT CONSENTS

Throughout the Hudson County investigation and trial, another drama was unfolding in Washington—one that would determine the future of the U.S. attorney's office in New Jersey.

Lacey had agreed to serve as U.S. attorney only through 1970, then return to private practice. Senator Case persuaded him to accept an appointment to the federal bench, instead. On October 7, 1970, President Nixon sent Lacey's name to the Senate. The action had been rumored for weeks and had provoked much speculation as to his successor.

Lacey left no doubt as to whom he wanted: "Should I leave the office at any time in the near future, I would hope that Chief Assistant Herbert J. Stern would succeed me."

"Batman and Robin" had proved an effective team, though their personalities and styles were markedly different. One lawyer likened them to Joe Louis and Rocky Graziano: "Fred's got class and style; Herb's a street fighter." But he said they pursued the same objective—"vigorous, nonpolitical prosecution of all wrongdoers."

Lacey is the first to admit that he couldn't have done the job alone. Stern had handled much of the detail work and had personally presented the evidence in the office's two major prosecutions—of DeCarlo and Addonizio. But Stern couldn't have done it on his own either. In the first place, he couldn't have gotten the nomination. Nor, as an outlander, could he have recruited the staff that Lacey did. He lacked Lacey's prestige, so vital in insuring the independence of the office and securing the support of the press and public. But Stern *was* in a position to carry on what Lacey had started. All he needed was the support of Senator Case.

Case, as it turned out, had never met Stern.

"He'd be happy to come down and meet you," Lacey told him by telephone.

"It isn't necessary," Case replied.

He'd read the reports of what the young prosecutor had done and he believed that Stern had "doubled the effectiveness of the office." On the basis of "his performance and Frederick Lacey's unqualified recommendation," Case submitted Stern's name to Justice.

"I had no difficulty making the strongest possible recommendation for Stern," he says. "I've never had any reason to regret it."

But somebody up there didn't like Stern. The administration did not second the nomination. The reasons were never made clear—either in public or private. "I don't think there was anything specific," Case says.

Observers were quick to point out some of the possibilities: Stern was too young; he was a "carpetbagger"; he lacked the proper political credentials—even that he was a Democrat. "I guess it's because I'm skinny," Stern quipped.

Actually, Stern considers himself a Republican of the Rockefeller "mainstream," but he hadn't registered as a member of either party in New Jersey. And "I've never been inside a clubhouse in my life."

There were rumors of personal objections: Stern's personality can be a bit testy at times. Supposedly, some of his old colleagues at Justice were jealous of the brash young man who'd moved so far so fast.

Even more ominous were the hints that both the federal and state administrations wanted someone more malleable in the post.

That the Nixon administration did not want independent agents in its prosecutors' offices was obvious. A similiar situation had arisen the year before, across the Hudson River in the Southern District of New York, seat of the most powerful and prestigious of all the U.S. attorney's offices, since Wall Street falls within its purview.

The Democratic incumbent, Robert M. Morgenthau, son of the New Deal treasury secretary, ran a patronage-free office that had aggressively attacked organized crime, political corruption and commercial chicanery. A House Republican task force on crime even urged that he be retained by the Nixon administration.

Actually, it had no choice. Unlike most U.S. attorneys' terms, Morgenthau's was not coterminous with that of the president. It ran to 1971. Morgenthau remained in office, explaining that he had a number of important matters to complete. Among them was the trial of former Tammany leader Carmine DeSapio and a tax-dodge investigation into the funnel.ng of funds from Wall Street to Swiss banks.

On December 17, 1969, Attorney General Mitchell demanded Morgenthau's resignation. At first, Morgenthau tried to fight. But without the support of Justice, which supplied his manpower and funds, he couldn't continue. He was replaced with Whitney North Seymour, Jr., an unsuccessful Republican congressional candidate and the son of a prominent Wall Street lawyer. The Swiss-bank investigation lapsed.

But Seymour, in time, was to show an independent streak. Among his last official acts was to obtain the indictment in the Vesco case—against his former boss, John Mitchell, and President Nixon's chief fund raiser, Maurice Stans.

In New Jersey, other political pots were boiling. When Lacey was nominated, Case had been the only Republican power in the state. Now there was a Republican governor, William Cahill, and a strong GOP state chairman, Nelson Gross, the party's candidate for the Senate. The White House clearly preferred dealing with this conservative combination than with the liberal Case.

The U.S. attorney's office had already crossed swords with this Washington-Trenton combination. In March, 1970, reports leaked out that Gross's "intercession" on behalf of officials of a Mafia-dominated Teamsters' Union local was under investigation. As the result of a Strike Force probe, three officers of the local had been indicted for embezzling union funds.

Gross labeled the report a "smear" by Lacey designed to deny him the GOP's senatorial nomination. He said that he'd merely inquired of Justice about the local before deciding whether to accept its manpower and financial support in Cahill's campaign for governor the year before.

Both Lacey and John Bartels, chief of the Strike Force unit in New Jersey, answered "no comment" to questions about the reports. But Richard Kleindienst, then deputy attorney general, said "to my knowledge" Gross had not interceded in the case and that he had "no personal knowledge" of any investigation of Gross.

"You'd think I'd be aware of it if one were going on," he added.

On April 1, Justice made it even stronger—curiously through an announcement by Governor Cahill at a State House press conference. He read a statement from Will Wilson, the assistant attorney general in charge of the criminal division:

> Having received newspaper accounts of an impending investigation of Nelson Gross because of his alleged association with labor unions or other matters, I reviewed the records of the attorney general's office and found there was no investigation under way or contemplated.
>
> Moreover, there is no evidence whatsoever to indicate that any actions of Mr. Gross have prompted any such investigation. Any statements and reports to the contrary are absolutely untrue.

Then he demanded that Lacey comment on the case.

The prosecutor replied that night in a statement which he personally telephoned to newspaper offices, from a pay phone

—to avoid taps, the newspapers hinted—because it was the only phone available, the prosecutor said:

> The policy of this office has invariably been to refuse to confirm or deny the existence of any criminal investigation. We, therefore, responded with a "no comment" when asked last week whether there was at that time an investigation under way concerning whether or not Mr. Gross had improperly interceded on behalf of Teamster Local 97 at a time when the Organized Crime and Racketeering Strike Force of the United States Department of Justice was probing that union.
>
> This policy is grounded upon obvious considerations, a departure from which is mandated only by extraordinary circumstances. Such circumstances are now presented by Governor Cahill's demands on this office for a statement. . . .
>
> I therefore state as follows: There is and has been an investigation in progress as recently as last week and it included the review of the books and records of Teamster Local 97 by an agent working under George Mack of the United States Department of Labor. The thrust of the investigation was whether, and to what extent, there was Teamster Local 97 political activity in last year's election.
>
> I have been informed that Governor Cahill released a statement purportedly coming from Assistant United States Attorney General Will R. Wilson indicating that Mr. Gross has never been the subject of an investigation by the United States. If Mr. Wilson has been accurately quoted, I must assume that the report of the foregoing labor investigation has not as yet reached Washington.

Two days later, the department backtracked. A Justice spokesman said there *had* been an investigation of Gross, that it had ended March 20—a week before the stories broke—and that Gross had been cleared.

Lacey labeled that statement "a falsehood." When asked if the investigation was still going on, he replied only that he had been ordered by the department not to discuss the case. In any event, no formal charges were ever leveled against Gross.

Obviously, neither Cahill nor Gross was enthusiastic for Lacey to be replaced by his chief assistant. Like Lacey, Stern was clearly his own man and not averse to rattling Republican skeletons, as well as Democratic.

Things did not bode well for his nomination.

Whatever the reasons, the administration sat on its hands. Justice did not even launch the background investigation that is the preliminary step in any nomination.

Within four days of submitting Stern's name, Case described the administration's reaction: "They just don't like him. I don't know why."

Two weeks later, he noted: "We haven't had such extraordinary ability in the administration of justice in New Jersey as we had under Frederick Lacey, and the operating job had been done in great measure by Stern." Still no word from the administration.

By the end of the month, Case felt compelled to issue a formal statement on the impasse:

> Over the past year the vigorous pursuit of organized crime and official corruption has brought new hope to the people of New Jersey. It is imperative that there be no slackening in the effort so successfully launched by U.S. Attorney Frederick B. Lacey and his assistants.
>
> For me personally it is gratifying to have had a part in bringing that effort about through my recommendation of Mr. Lacey for the U.S. attorney post and my support of his unfettered choice of his staff. Because I place such high importance on the continuation of this effort, sev-

eral months ago when the question of a successor to Mr. Lacey arose, I made it clear to the Department of Justice my sole concern was the selection of the best qualified man to replace him. And I asked for the Department's and Mr. Lacey's recommendations.

Mr. Lacey strongly recommended Mr. Herbert Stern, his first assistant, on the basis of Stern's exceptional professional qualifications and experience and most especially his part in the extraordinary accomplishments of the U.S. attorney's office in recent months.

Mr. Lacey's evaluation of Stern has been widely shared by the bar and bench, by the press and by the public. And I have repeatedly made known to the department my full support of Mr. Lacey's recommendation.

For reasons not known to me, the Department of Justice did not welcome the recommendation of Mr. Stern and has continued to block it.

Meanwhile, the highly merited appointment of Mr. Lacey to the U.S. District Court for New Jersey has stirred widespread concern that his departure may signal a loss of momentum in the fight against organized crime. Indeed there has been speculation in the press as well as in private that his elevation to the bench is a "kick upstairs" with the ugly connotation that there are people powerful enough to have a vigorous law enforcement officer removed by promotion from further pursuit of wrongdoers.

There is only one way to put an end to such speculation and, even more important, to ensure that the work of the U.S. attorney's office continues without interruption. That is the appointment of Herbert Stern as Mr. Lacey's successor.

I again urge the Department of Justice to support the nomination of Herbert Stern so that the work of the U.S. attorney's office will go forward with the same vigor and effectiveness that has marked it throughout Mr. Lacey's tenure.

In reply, a Justice Department "spokesman" said only that Stern was under "serious consideration" for the post.

Case decided that the only way to force the issue was to build a ground swell of public support for his choice. Throughout the ensuing weeks, the senator and his aides met with editorial writers throughout New Jersey—and in neighboring New York and Pennsylvania—urging them to devote their columns to the cause. Most fell into line.

For example, the *Newark News,* until its demise in 1972 New Jersey's largest paper, hammered home the point week after week:

> There are some, placing party affiliation foremost, who want Mr. Lacey's mantle passed on, above all, to a deserving Republican.
>
> We do not agree. Criminal infiltration of public office pays no heed to party lines. Neither should investigation and prosecution.
>
> Political dictation could be particularly harmful in this instance. . . .
>
> Politics aside, there is every reason to elevate [Stern] to the U.S. Attorneyship. . . . Any other priority would be a disservice to the office and to the people it is supposed to represent.
>
> —September 13, 1970

> [Stern] is a deserving successor who should not be denied appointment by petty political partisanship.
> —October 9, 1970

> The most that Herbert J. Stern has going for him as a possible successor to Frederick B. Lacey is outstanding competence.
> —October 26, 1970

> For reasons made anything but clear, the wheels are grinding grudgingly, if at all. It would be manifestly

more unforunate if party fealty and personal charm were given preference over proven ability. No one would love it more than the characters who were getting away with just about everything until the current team of federal prosecutors went to work.

—January 21, 1971

The Hudson County indictments added to the editorial barrage. The New York *Daily News,* one of the nation's most proadministration papers, noted:

We think highly of . . . H.J. Stern. So do a lot of New Jersey citizens. . . . The Stern record as a prosecutor is long and distinguished, although its owner is only 33.

With a background such as this, you'd expect Stern's nomination by the President and confirmation by the Senate to be a breeze; and we hope they may be—soon.

Every time such an editorial appeared, Case's office would Xerox a copy and fire it off to Justice. Meanwhile, the senator himself lost no opportunity to state his continued support.

On December 1, Lacey, already confirmed for the bench, entered the hospital for a gallbladder operation. For two months, Stern served as acting U.S. attorney. Case noted: "The announcement that Stern is acting U.S. attorney has assured me that there will be no letup in the effort to root out organized crime in New Jersey."

On December 6, Stern received a distinguished-service award from Justice for his work on the DeCarlo and Addonizio cases. It was his second such award; he'd received one two years before for successfully prosecuting the Colonial and Weber cases. Senator Case said the award "confirms my already deep conviction Stern has the qualifications to succeed as U.S. attorney for New Jersey."

Although editorial support was mounting, an electoral development clouded the picture. In the November election, Nelson Gross, running on a platform of 100-percent support for the Nixon administration, went down to defeat. Rumors quickly arose that he would be rewarded with the post of U.S. attorney.

Although Governor Cahill never suggested Gross—or anyone else—to Case, he made it clear that he didn't want Stern. He even asked Case if Stern was available "for some important job in state government"; reportedly, it was a post on the quasi-judicial New York–New Jersey Waterfront Commission.

"He's got an important job right now," Case told him.

The *Bergen Record,* the daily newspaper in Gross's home base in northern New Jersey's bedroom suburbs, reported that a $75,000 to $150,000 "slush fund" was being raised to deny Stern the nomination. "The bigwigs in organized crime would love to see him passed over," the paper editorialized. "They know what he can do."

The slush fund never materialized. Neither did Gross's nomination. "Nelson knew he wasn't going to get any appointment out of this office," said a Case aide. In fact, the Republican chairman and the Republican senator were barely on speaking terms. A month after the election, the Justice Department announced that "Gross is not under consideration" for the post. But no other nomination was forthcoming.

For Stern, the continued imbroglio meant treading delicately. "I was often asked about it," he says. "My answer was simple: I was gratified by the confidence and faith that Fred Lacey and Senator Clifford Case had shown in me, being so adamant that I should be the next U.S. attorney. I wanted very much to be the U.S. attorney. I felt it would be the culmination of my career as a prosecutor.

"But it was a matter entirely up to the president. I certainly wasn't about to say that he didn't have the right to appoint whoever he wanted. Of course, if somebody else were appointed, I would naturally go into private practice."

On February 1, 1971, Frederick B. Lacey was sworn in as a federal district judge. There was still no presidential appointment to fill the vacancy he had left as U.S. attorney. But there is a provision in the U.S. Code for such lapses. Just as a judge appoints an attorney to represent an indigent defendant, so the court—in the absence of a presidential nomination—names a lawyer to represent the U.S. government. The district court, with Lacey as its newest member, named Herbert J. Stern to be the U.S. attorney, pending a presidential nomination.

The swearing-in ceremonies were held in chambers, with Stern pledging to run the office "exactly the same way we've been going for the past seventeen months."

By contrast, Lacey's judicial swearing-in was formal and elaborate, held in the largest courtroom in Newark's courthouse, which was filled to capacity.

"I was asked to say a few words," Stern recalls. "I got up to speak and I instinctively looked over to the jury box. I saw Senator Case sitting there beside Senator Williams and Governor Cahill. I looked over at him and smiled, and he smiled at me. It was kind of funny, because we had never looked at each other's faces before."

In fact, Stern had seen the senator in the flesh only once before—when he was a spectator at Lacey's swearing-in as U.S. attorney. They would not meet formally until several months later, when Stern dropped in at Case's office during a visit to Washington.

Not quite three months past his 34th birthday, Stern was the youngest U.S. attorney in the nation—and the oldest attorney in the office. He had been a New Jersey resident for less than two years. He was not even admitted to practice in the state.

Ever since he'd been appointed as Lacey's chief assistant, Stern had planned to take the state bar examination. But court schedules didn't cooperate. The first time the exam was held —in February, 1970—he'd been too busy trying the DeCarlo case to cram for it. The second time—in July, 1970—he was on trial with Addonizio. The third time was two days after his appointment. Although he'd signed up—and paid—for the "cram course," he'd been too busy as acting U.S. attorney to take it.

It didn't affect his standing in the federal court, but it could create problems if he had to appear before a state bench—as the U.S. attorney must do from time to time.

Chief Justice Joseph Weintraub later explained that the New Jersey Supreme Court had three alternatives in the matter: First, it could require the U.S. government to engage a local lawyer every time it appeared in a state court. "That alternative quite obviously rejected itself." Second, it could admit Stern for his tenure as U.S. attorney. "We . . . had no such category of membership at the bar, and I felt it would demean the state to take so petty an approach to the United States of America." The third alternative "was the one we took, namely to admit him to the bar."

On February 3—two days after his appointment—the supreme court waived the bar examination and admitted Stern to practice in the state. He is the only man so admitted in New Jersey history.

Although he was officially *the* U.S. attorney, most newspapers continued to refer to him with the prefix "acting." Only in one respect was Stern denied the full prerogatives of the

U.S. attorney by presidential nomination. As the choice of the court, he was entitled to only 80 percent of the $36,000 salary for the post—$28,000. "But I had a hundred percent of the headaches," he says.

The question of the presidential nomination remained open.

Lacey was confident that it would go to Stern . . . eventually. "I never would have left the office," he says, "unless I had been given reasonable assurances that Herb Stern would be my successor. I stayed until after the Hudson County indictments and left only when it was clear that he would try the case. And the result justified my confidence. I was assured by Mitchell that after a few months of demonstrating that he could run the office as Number One man, they'd put in his name."

But some at Justice obviously had other ideas. "In May, the cherry blossoms come out, and who remembers winter?" one official said after Stern's appointment by the court. "In May, there might be another fellow who everybody thinks is right for the job."

Senator Case made it clear that no other name would be acceptable to him, and without his approval, no presidential nomination could clear the Senate. The result was a Mexican standoff—with the administration apparently unwilling to appoint Stern, but unable to get him out.

May and the cherry blossoms came and went—with still no word from Washington. In a rare political statement from the federal bench, Lacey again called for Stern's appointment: "On the record of the man, he is entitled to the job, and the people of New Jersey are entitled to him."

On July 5, the jury returned its guilty verdicts in the Hudson County case. Senator Case used the occasion to needle the administration again about Stern's appointment. He was echoed by newspapers throughout the state.

The Trenton *Evening Times:* "Mr. Mitchell and company have been roosting on the U.S. attorneyship for ten months now. . . . Mr. Stern has in that time more than proved his competence to hold it."

The Passaic *Herald-News:* "The case for Mr. Stern is simply that he has done a superlative job against men who were considered too powerful to touch until he came along. From the standpoint of practical politics, Mr. Stern has done such a good job that to replace him would be to invite the most unpleasant interpretations. The ordinary Jerseyman would probably conclude that Washington was not really interested in the drive against crooks in government and the mob. . . ."

Jerome Wilson, WCBS-TV's legislative correspondent, observed:

> If it were happening in New York instead of New Jersey—New York being the media capital of the world and New Jersey being some place between New York and Philadelphia—then they would probably be running Herbert Stern for governor by now.
>
> But Stern is the U.S. attorney for New Jersey, and while no one has really been watching, he has indicted, convicted and sent to jail a roster without parallel of Jersey political figures. . . .
>
> One of the ironies of the Stern career is that President Nixon has yet to officially name him to his job. Stern serves only under a temporary appointment by the district court. Not even a Jersey native, politically one supposes, Stern has little to recommend him.
>
> But for a national administration pledged to law and order, the limbo status of a man with this kind of record must pose something of an embarrassment.

Almost as if to flaunt his independence, Stern quickly launched the office's third "blockbuster" investigation into corruption in a Jersey community.

"The moment the Hudson County trial was over and we could catch our breaths," he says, "we moved against the Republican stronghold in Atlantic City and Atlantic County. We did the same thing there that we had done in Newark and Hudson—we started by subpoenaing all the records out of City Hall and the County Administration Building."

It was almost a direct slap at the administration. Atlantic City's "boss," state Senator Frank (Hap) Farley, had led New Jersey's pro-Nixon forces in 1968, splitting off half the state's delegation to the Miami Beach convention from favorite-son Clifford Case.

The office continued its activity on other fronts. On one day in August it returned bribery indictments against the Democratic state treasurer under Governor Hughes and a Republican state senator from Bergen County.

Some observers were incredulous. "Whoever heard of a Republican office-seeker invading Bergen to look for wrongdoing?" the *Hudson Dispatch* said. "And horror of horrors, even bearding the Republican untouchable, Senator 'Hap' Farley, in a probe of his Atlantic City activities."

Such activities put the administration in an increasingly awkward position. If it now attempted to appoint anyone but Stern, it would appear that it was trying to kill the investigation and hide its dirty linen.

The administration finally gave in. To this day, it's not known why it balked initially, why it resisted so long or why its resistance finally collapsed. Neither Justice nor the White House ever stated its reasons, and former Attorney General Mitchell, declined to discuss it.

Shortly after Labor Day, Mitchell called Stern and asked if he was still interested in the job. "He was laughing," Stern recalls.

Stern said, "Sure."

"Well, I just wanted to check with you before the president sends your name to the Senate."

On September 15, Stern was formally nominated. Senator Case issued a statement: "I am delighted that the president has accepted my recommendation. . . . The president's action strengthens not only Mr. Stern's hand as an individual but the whole effort to eradicate crime and corruption—an effort in which an extraordinary start has been made."

Stern said he was "honored by the action of the president for nominating me . . . and very grateful to the two men who recommended me—Senator Clifford P. Case and Frederick B. Lacey."

On November 8—Stern's 35th birthday—his nomination was confirmed by the Senate. He was sworn into office on December 4.

9
SONS OF
HUDSON
COUNTY

"Hudson County is the kernel from which all else grows," Herbert Stern says.

It's a slight exaggeration. But just as a hit movie spawns spin-offs and sequels, the Hudson County case led to a spate of other prosecutions for political corruption.

The first "Son of Hudson County" came indirectly through John J. Kenny. Through his cooperation, the U.S. attorney's office learned about the complicity of J. Rich Steers Construction. Not only had the company paid off in the Hudson County case, it had kicked back on other projects.

On August 12, 1971—barely a month after the Hudson County trial ended—the first indictments came down.

One accused Robert Burkhardt, a Democratic-party wheel horse who had served as assistant postmaster general under JFK. He had managed the gubernatorial campaigns of both Robert Meyner and Richard Hughes and went on to serve as the party's state chairman and as secretary of state for eight years under Hughes. President Johnson once considered him for the post of Democratic national chairman. He was accused of taking a $20,000 kickback for himself and extorting a $10,000 contribution for the party in return for getting Steers work on the Delaware Memorial Bridge.

The second indictment named Willard B. Knowlton, a Republican state senator from Bergen County and the former mayor of Tenafly. He was accused of taking a one-percent kickback for getting Steers a $10.6-million contract on the New Jersey Turnpike. Twenty-five thousand dollars was paid in cash, $81,000 by check for "fictitious legal services." In addition, Knowlton was charged with failing to file a 1968 income-tax return.

Burkhardt "categorically" denied the charge: "I have never taken a bribe in my life and I was never in any position to grant contracts on any construction job or in any other area of government in New Jersey."

Knowlton called a press conference and bitterly denounced

Stern and his staff: "If they're lawyers, I don't know where they got their training—they certainly don't know anything about any system of justice. . . . Man, if this is the United States of America, forget about it."

"I never took a crooked dollar in my life," Knowlton shouted. But he admitted getting the $81,000 in "legal fees," which even his fellow Republican, former Governor Alfred E. Driscoll, chairman of the Turnpike Authority, said "appears to be highly excessive."

Burkhardt subsequently went before the grand jury, where, among other things, Stern asked him about his income:

"Mr. Burkhardt, while you were secretary of state from 1961 through 1969, did you have any other business or occupation?"

"No, sir."

"I take it then that your total salary and earnings during those years was from your position as secretary of state. Is that correct, sir?"

"No, sir."

"Could you clarify the record for the grand jury, sir?"

"Yes, I supplemented my income in the stock market. I made—I can't recall exactly—but—"

"You may brag if you wish, sir," Stern said.

"Well, I was lucky in a couple of things, unlucky in others, but I did make some money in the stock market during that period."

"Did you have any other source of income during that period of time, sir?"

"Nothing substantial. There might have been a—nothing that I recall."

For those answers, Burkhardt was charged with perjury. The government contended that he'd received $123,950 in "public relations" fees from firms doing business with the state.

On May 12, 1972, Burkhardt, who once "categorically" denied the charges and later argued that he had "a right to lie," pleaded guilty to one count of conspiracy to bribe.

"Do you have anything to say in your behalf?" Judge John Kitchen asked him.

"No, sir, I don't."

But others did. Democratic Congressman Frank Thompson, Jr., wrote a letter urging clemency, and Judge Kitchen said he'd received similar letters from other prominent persons, whose names he did not reveal. He placed Burkhardt on probation for three years and fined him $5000. The *Newark News* called the sentence "a slap on the wrist."

Knowlton succeeded in severing the bribery and income-tax cases. He went on trial on the income-tax case in January, 1973. Assistant U.S. Attorney Milton Branch rolled out the evidence of the payoffs. Knowlton did not take the stand. But his attorney, George Koelzer, apparently persuaded the jury that Knowlton had, or might have, filed his 1968 return. He pointed out that his 1969 return included references to 1968 income.

"One hundred million tax returns are filed each year," Koelzer told the jury, "and do you believe that each one is in place?"

As if to prove his point, the IRS certificates that a "diligent search" revealed no trace of Knowlton's 1968 return disappeared from the court clerk's file in midtrial!

"It made the government look silly," Stern says.

Knowlton was acquitted. But, says Stern, "we still have the conspiracy-and-bribery case open and we're going to move it."

The next "Son of Hudson County" came from Stern's attempt to question Sternkopf about his land dealings with D. Louis Tonti, the former executive director of the Garden State Parkway. Reporters immediately sought out Tonti, then head of a construction company in Woodbridge, who called the accusation "hogwash."

In effect, he was daring the prosecutor to act. "The die was cast," Stern says.

On July 7, two days after the Hudson County trial ended, Tonti was subpoenaed before a federal grand jury where he invoked the Fifth Amendment.

According to Stern, the evidence against Tonti was cold, but no federal statute was broken. The conflict of interest was punishable only under state law.

"I referred it to the state," Stern says. "They never proceeded on it."

"However, I realized that if the man was doing a deal like this, he had to be selling a lot more than that in public office. We had heard reports about his activities. So we began to investigate him. We used the same techniques that we had used in Newark and Hudson County. And we came up with several firms that had paid him off, some by using the same technique he'd used in the land deal—checks made payable to Giovanni Paolini [Tonti's contact in Rome] and deposited in Tonti's Swiss bank account."

On April 19, 1972, Tonti, Paolini and Philip May, chief engineer on the parkway, were indicted for extorting more than $200,000—$144,000 from Frederick Harris, a New York engineering firm; $46,000 from Automatic Toll Systems and $10,000 from Seacoast Builders.

Tonti pleaded guilty to conspiracy to bribe. He stood before Judge George H. Barlow for sentencing on March 13, 1973. The judge asked if he had anything to say.

"Just that I'm sorry, Your Honor."

It was a sad end to the career of a man who had earned an international reputation in highway engineering—he had served as a consultant on Italy's Rome-to-Milan expressway.

But Judge Barlow said he was "no different than any common thief." He sentenced Tonti to three years in prison and fined him $10,000.

Stern prepared to move the case against May for trial, while Paolini remained in Rome, a fugitive from American justice.

"By this time," Stern says, "we had unraveled that great ball of string that had been strangling the state for so many years. As soon as one strand began to fall, we'd pull out another and another."

In January, 1973, a week before Tonti pleaded guilty, what might be termed a "Grandson of Hudson County" was born. Just as Steers's cooperation in the Hudson County case had led to the indictment of Burkhardt, so Harris's cooperation in the Tonti case led to the indictment of John A. Kervick, state treasurer in both the Meyner and Hughes administrations.

Kervick was charged with extorting six-percent kickbacks on Harris's contracts with the Garden State Parkway, New Jersey Turnpike and Delaware River Port Authority—three percent for himself, three percent for unnamed "political organizations." According to the indictment, he received $113,200. Kervick, too, pleaded guilty.

The Kervick indictment loosed a spate of rumors that Stern was going after other targets in the Hughes administration, possibly even Hughes himself. One report even hit the airwaves that Hughes had come within one vote of a grand-jury indictment.

Stern labeled it "an unmitigated falsehood." "I will proceed against anybody," he said, "regardless of position, power or influence, if he's violated the law of the United States. But I'm not going to sit by and let anybody, through whispers, gossip or innuendo, try and destroy another man's reputation."

Meanwhile, in the state courts there was the "Stepson of Hudson County." Actually, it involved the son-in-law and grandson of John V. Kenny—Paul and John Hanly, successively administrators of Pollak Hospital.

The case came from the cooperation of James Corrado, who had pleaded guilty at the outset of the Hudson County trial. Since his evidence involved only state crimes, Stern turned it over to the Hudson County prosecutor, Geoffrey Gaulkin. Long a loyal servant of the Kenny machine, Gaulkin had once denounced the federal investigation as "McCarthyism," but he followed through on the evidence Stern gave him.

The indictment was handed up on December 23, 1971, six hours after the Hudson County freeholders reappointed John Hanly hospital administrator. Father and son were charged with using hospital employees as domestic servants in their Florida winter home.

They went on trial the following May, but the jury deadlocked. They were retried in the fall, and this time the jury returned guilty verdicts. On December 8, Superior Court Judge Samuel Larner sentenced both father and son to two to three years in prison.

John Hanly went on trial again the following month—on charges of padding the hospital payroll with two "no-show" employees, one the wife of a Hudson County freeholder. He was found guilty and Judge Larner imposed another two-to-three-year sentence, consecutive to the first.

Three generations of Kenny kin were behind bars.

There was the "adopted son" of the Hudson County case—the investigation of Congressman Cornelius Gallagher, whose bond purchases had led to the discovery of the Whelan-Flaherty bank accounts.

In 1968, *Life* magazine, armed with some secret FBI files, made a series of startling disclosures about Gallagher's underworld connections—including the bizarre story of how a loan shark named Barney O'Brien had dropped dead (of natural causes) at Gallagher's home and how Gallagher, fearing to be linked publicly with the dead gangster, summoned Kayo Konigsberg and had him secretly dispose of the body. *Life*'s revelations had little effect on the Hudson County voters; Gallagher was reelected easily in 1968 and 1970.

But the net was closing in on him. A team of IRS agents headed by Marvin Sontag and James Killeen started investigating Gallagher's dealings with Joseph (Joe Bayonne) Zicarelli as disclosed in the *Life* articles. As a result, Zicarelli was charged with evading taxes on nearly $916,000 in illegal income.

Almost by accident, the agents stumbled on the fact that Gallagher had been purchasing huge amounts of municipal bonds—all for cash. Pinning down the exact amounts required months of work. Stern called it "a monumental job—the most backbreaking kind of chores."

The agents discovered that Gallagher had purchased $942,000 in municipal bonds between 1961 and 1968, all but the earliest under phony names—"George E. Connors" or the initials "G.E.C.," the reverse of his own, or "Rickey," his wife's nickname, from her maiden name of Richter, or the initials "R.I.K." Gallagher had paid taxes on none of this money.

To seal off possible defenses to a charge of income-tax evasion, the agents had to prove that Gallagher was not acting as the agent for others, but that he was using the money for himself. They were able to show that he had cashed some of the bonds, used others as collateral for loans and clipped the coupons on still others.

By 1972, Gallagher had cashed $201,000 of the bonds. Another $408,000 had been traced to the Whelan-Flaherty account in Florida. That left $333,000 still unaccounted for.

On March 27, 1972, Gallagher went before the grand jury clutching a suitcase filled with $333,000 in municipal bonds.

He claimed that they belonged to the Hudson County Democratic organization.

"I was in a position of a trustee holding bonds for the Democratic party," he explained. "My sole contact in the Democratic party passed on, died, though he was alive when this investigation began and anybody had access to him, and that was Mr. Ben Schlossberg. I have never in any way been involved in any extortion or crooked plot or kickback or graft or anything else. I happen to consider myself an honest person. I have worked pretty damned hard all of my life and I still do, but I did not want to bring the wrath of the party down on me because I need their goodwill in order to survive politically. . . .

"Now I just want to say this, Mr. Stern: I am a trustee of those bonds and I would like to say right now, I don't know what to do with the bonds because Mr. Schlossberg is dead and I don't know who to contact and I don't know whether a party still exists. It seems to me that the Democratic party has been totally devastated in the state of New Jersey. I don't know who speaks for the party, who is the party, whether it can survive.

"I have a problem. I would like to pass that problem on, Mr. Stern, because right here are the contents of my trust, right there, and I give them to you, to the grand jury, to the court or anybody. [The bonds] have been a problem to me. . . . I didn't know whether I am to protect my trust or whether or not I am supposed to go on and try to hedge on this whole business. I don't want to hedge. I have a problem and I want to answer every question truthfully. . . ."

"Suppose you start letting me ask you some questions," Stern said.

"Yes, sir."

"Fine. Now Mr. Schlossberg died in 1968. That is a fact, isn't it?"

"That is a fact."

"He died in November of 1968. That is a fact, isn't it?"

"That is a fact." . . .

"Now all of this time you say you were the trustee of these bonds, is that right?"

"Yes, sir."

"Now in 1968, when Mr. Schlossberg died, in November of 1968, did you know who the head of the Democratic party of Hudson County was?"

"All I know——"

"Answer the question!" Stern snapped.

"Yes, I did."

"Who was that man?"

"Mr. Kenny."

"In 1969, as you maintained those bonds with the problem you say you had about who to turn them over to, did you know who the head of the Democratic party was in Hudson County in 1969?"

"Yes, sir."

"Who was that man?"

"Mr. Kenny."

"In 1970, all the time that you had those bonds that you have now in your suitcase as a matter of trust from Mr. Schlossberg, as you were looking around for anybody to give them to, did the Democratic party have a head in Hudson County?"

"Yes."

"Who was that man?"

"Mr. Kenny."

"Now, in addition to Mr. Kenny, is there not a state chairman of the Democratic party?"

"The state chairman of the Democratic party had very little to do with the Democratic party in Hudson County."

"Congressman, is there a state chairman?" Stern snapped.

"Yes, there is."

"Is there one by law? Is he elected by the county committeemen?"

"Yes, he is."

"Is there also a chairman of the Democratic party of Hudson County?"

"Yes, there is."

"And he is by law, is he not, Congressman, the head of the Democratic party of Hudson County?"

"Yes, he is."

"Now is it your testimony, Congressman, that since the death of Mr. Schlossberg in 1967 [sic] you have had a problem and that problem has been that as trustee of these bonds which you say are the bonds of the Democratic party of Hudson County, you did not know who to give them to, who to bring them to, and so today, in a grand-jury investigation as to your tax liability, you are bringing them here now to turn them over to the grand jury?"

"Yes, sir." . . .

"As trustee of these funds, is there any document or record on file anywhere in the Democratic party reflecting that these assets of the Democratic party are in your hands?"

"I don't know."

"Did you ever sign a receipt when you got them from Mr. Schlossberg?"

"No, I did not."

"So if I understand you correctly, you are walking around with that suitcase right now containing bearer municipal bonds which you say are the property of the Democratic party and that there is no document located anywhere in the Democratic party to show—"

"Now I don't know whether there is, Mr. Stern," Gallagher interrupted.

"—or any receipt signed by you to show that you are in

control over a substantial amount of assets of the Democratic party?"

"I don't know whether there is. I just know I have never signed a receipt. I am not sure what is floating around or what instructions Mr. Schlossberg left with anybody. All I know is I have been waiting for somebody—"

"To come to you?" Stern suggested.

"Yes."

"And no one has?"

"No one has."

"Not in five years?"

"That's right. . . ."

"What is the face value of the bonds that you have in that suitcase?"

"I haven't counted them. I think it is about three hundred and fifty thousand dollars or three hundred and seventy."

"That is like money, isn't it, Mr. Congressman?"

"Mr. Stern, you know it is like money." . . .

"Those bonds you've got there, you are the trustee of them? They are not your bonds?"

"They are not my bonds."

"Fine."

"I might be indicted for stupidity or insanity, Mr. Stern, because you know that if I did not consider this mine, I am under no obligation to bring these things in here today. But I don't know what to do and I want to answer your questions truthfully, Mr. Stern."

"You got the bonds in 1967 from Schlossberg?"

"Yes."

"You are the trustee?"

"Yes."

"Could you tell us why he made you the physical trustee of them?"

"He trusted me." . . .

"Congressman, all the time that you had these three hundred and seventy thousand dollars' worth of bonds after Schlossberg died, you were troubled by the fact that, as you have told us, you didn't know who to give them to?"

"That's exactly right, Mr. Stern. I am still troubled. I don't know whether I am doing the right thing or not in regards to my trust."

"Who did you make contact with in the Democratic party in order to find out about that?"

"Nobody."

"So troubled though . . . you told nobody in the Democratic party?"

"I don't know who the Democratic party is anymore."

It sounded like a comedy skit—so much so that a few weeks later the New Jersey Legislative Correspondents set the patter to music at their annual dinner. The names of the protagonists —Gallagher and Stern—made the song selection simple:

"Oh, Mr. Gallagher. Oh, Mr. Gallagher.
There's a briefcase full of bonds you must explain.
   Tell us who you have to thank
   At that Hudson County bank
Where you tried to hide behind a phony name."

"Oh, Mr. Stern. Oh, Mr. Stern.
Those securities are none of my concern.
   I just held them for a guy
   Who was kind enough to die."
"Why, that's bullshit, Mr. Gallagher."
"Try to prove it, Mr. Stern."

Stern set out to prove it. On April 11, Gallagher was indicted on four counts of perjury—for claiming that the $534,-000 worth of bonds he'd purchased between 1960 and 1967 were party property—two counts of income-tax evasion and one count of conspiring with Mayor Whelan and Council President Flaherty to help them evade their income taxes.

The following day, Gallagher called a press conference at his Washington office to denounce the charges:

> This is a political indictment aimed specifically at discrediting me at a time congressional redistricting is the major issue in New Jersey. It is also directly related to the terrible smears published in *Life* magazine, which have been totally disproved. I have retained Edward Bennett Williams as my counsel, and I believe I will be vindicated. . . .
>
> What makes this case different is that this is a political matter. . . .
>
> I intend to speak out on the floor of the House in the very near future and disclose the operations of a monolith which operates totally free of any constitutional or congressional restraint. What was done to me was done by the total corruption at the highest levels of the American secret police. I was selected as a "target" because I opposed those illegal and corrupt methods. A target is a man who opposes unrestricted power, and the monolith then sets out to invent a crime to smear the target and to punish him for his opposition.
>
> I am informed that over $11 million in taxpayer dollars have been spent to destroy me. I have undergone the most relentless investigation in modern political history for nearly four years, ever since leaked federal raw investigative files were handed to *Life*. Any citizen—officeholder, local policeman, anyone—who disagrees with our new caesars will be the victim of this terrible repression. I have spoken out against it for nine years and for four years my family and friends have been subjected to a terror equal only to the oppression in Nazi Germany. In the days to come, I shall speak out on this —I will name names.

I expect to be reelected, but perhaps more important, I will lay out for the first time on the public record the full story of the new surveillance subculture and those who would pervert democracy in the lust for uncontrolled power.

On April 19, Gallagher took the floor of the House on a "point of personal privilege" and for an hour rambled on, attacking *Life* and the FBI, especially J. Edgar Hoover ("an American Beria") and the bureau's PR man, Cartha (Deke) DeLoach, who he said were trying to "blackmail" him out of Congress. But he said nothing about the charges in the indictment.

Gallagher's district disappeared in the congressional redistricting and he lost the Democratic primary to his Jersey City colleague, Dominick Daniels. On December 21, with only ten days left in his congressional career, he walked into Trenton's federal courthouse and pleaded guilty to evading $74,000 in 1966 income taxes.

The other counts were not dropped, though Stern indicated they would be at the time of sentence.

"Furthermore," Stern told Judge Barlow, "the defendant Gallagher through his attorney has asked, and we have acceded to his request, that he be given a period of approximately five months between now and the time of sentencing to come into the offices of the United States attorney and make known such information as he has which can be of assistance to the agents of law enforcement. We have represented to him that if he does that, we will make known to the sentencing court whatever help he is to the United States, if during that period he chooses to be. . . ."

"Is that so, Mr. McNelis?" Judge Barlow asked Gallagher's attorney.

"That is so, Your Honor," Charles McNelis replied. "I would

adopt the statements made by Mr. Stern. They are precisely the arrangements we have discussed. They are my understanding."

"Is that so, Mr. Gallagher?"

"Yes, sir," the congressman said.

But back in Washington the next day, Gallagher had a different tale to tell. He issued a statement:

> Contrary to the latest public relations releases out of Newark, I have made no arrangement whatsoever to give Mr. Stern or the FBI or any other group or agency any information, real or fictional, on any person at any time or in any place.
>
> I have checked with my attorneys and they have advised me they have made no such arrangements.
>
> Mr. Stern advises them he would be interested if I wished to cooperate and assist them in the quest for information and that he would make such cooperation known at the time of sentencing.
>
> I neither agreed to this nor have I discussed it with my attorneys. To say anything else is a lie. To portray me as a cringing animal about to bargain my future at someone else's expense or happiness is a lie. To insinuate that I will add to the growth of a secret police is a lie. To give the idea that I shall participate in spreading the reign of terror or investigative insanity and inflicting it on innocent people or anyone else is a lie.
>
> The indictments timed prior to the redistricting decision, which wiped out my district, ruined me politically. The various harassments, investigations and intimidations with the late and unlamented J. Edgar Hoover and *Life* magazine over the years have ruined me financially.
>
> I do not, however, feel that "big brother" and the public relations apparatus in Newark should be entitled to my soul. My whole life has been lived as a man in war and peace and I will continue to live in that manner for the rest of my life.

I am neither a Judas nor an informer, nor shall I become one to save my own skin at someone else's expense. . . .

True to his vow, Gallagher never showed up to provide any evidence against others.

Indeed, the ex-congressman managed only to dig a deeper hole for himself.

There had been an *in camera* hearing in the case in September, an outgrowth of Gallagher's motion for disclosure of any eavesdrop evidence against him. In the hearing, Gallagher—who had been privy to such information as chairman of the House Foreign Affairs Subcommittee on Asian-Pacific affairs—disclosed details of National Security Administration "bugging" of foreign embassies in Washington. In the interest of "national security," Judge Garth ordered all parties to the case not to discuss the matter again, and then impounded not only the transcript, but his order.

On March 22, 1973, Gallagher sent a rambling, 13-page letter—which he apparently typed himself, on two different typewriters, XXXing out the "law office" on his legal letterhead—to Chief Judge James A. Coolahan, asking that Judge Garth be removed from the case.

"The personal prejudice of Judge Garth combined with his close working relationship with Mr. Stern is making a mockery out of Justice," he wrote.

He claimed that Stern and the judge had combined to prevent his taking a trip to the Far East "at the request of the Congress of the United States."

"I have always understood it to be a cardinal rule of the Judicial System that a defendant cannot engage in 'Judge shopping,' " he continued. "I believe that Justice equally demands that Mr. Stern not engage in Judge shopping or that Judge Garth not engage in defendant shopping. The boldness in this latest action on their part is appalling and totally violates the integrity of the Court."

He quoted an unnamed congressman as calling Judge Garth "the house prostitute of the U.S. attorney in Newark." He said he'd pleaded guilty only because "that would be the only way to terminate Judge Garth's lock on my life."

He concluded:

> I am stripped of my career, I am disbarred, I am financially ruined, my home of 27 years involved in a foreclosure proceeding, part of a shakedown by the two Government witnesses—I have pleaded guilty to income-tax evasion and I must accept what is my due.
>
> Why then is it so important to the point of unbelievability that Judge Garth must retain permanent possession of my fate. Why is it necessary that Mr. Stern have a stacked court. [punctuation sic]

In between, Gallagher made a series of specific charges— that Judge Garth had shown prejudice against him in a land-condemnation case; that Stern and Judge Garth had colluded to gerrymander him out of his district. And finally he raised the "bugging" issue again—in what form cannot be determined, since those two pages of the letter were impounded.

Gallagher's attorney, Charles McNelis, later incorporated the letter in a motion for reassignment of the case to another judge. Judge Coolahan referred the matter to Judge Garth, who remained in charge of the case.

The judge summoned both Gallagher and McNelis into court on April 9, denied the motion for reassignment, then directed both attorney and client to show cause why they should not be cited for contempt of court for violating his order not to discuss the September hearing.

Gallagher kept asking to be heard, but Judge Garth refused, instructing him to speak through counsel. For his part Stern said: "I'm sick and tired of listening to charges which are as vile and as vicious as they come from a man who is equally venal. . . . I have never, in all my years of practice, seen anything as contemptuous of a court, of a process of law, where judges are branded liars and allusions are made which not only, as Your Honor said, are unsubstantiated, but unsubstantiable."

Strangely, after he was carted off to prison, Gallagher made another U-turn and *claimed* the $333,000 worth of bonds. The government was more than willing to turn over the money to him—after extracting $199,000 in income taxes and $10,500 for his fine. Presumably, Gallagher's lawyers got much of what was left.

Where had the money come from? Since Gallagher refused to cooperate, that question will never be answered fully. But Stern says, "If we had gone to trial, we would have been prepared to prove some transactions." What they were he won't say.

Finally, there was the "bastard son" of Hudson County— New Jersey's bribery prosecution of John J. Kenny.

After the Hudson County trial, when it became apparent that the state intended to proceed with its prosecution, Kenny's attorney, Donald Robinson, sought an injunction from Judge Shaw preventing it. Stern submitted a brief that the federal grant of immunity barred state action. Judge Shaw agreed and issued the injunction.

Eighteen months of litigation followed—without a ruling on the basic legal issue.

New Jersey's attorney general, George F. Kugler, Jr., appealed Judge Shaw's ruling to the Third Circuit, which reversed him—neither on the law nor on the facts, but on his timing. The court held that no order should be issued until *after* the state had placed Kenny in jeopardy . . . if then.

So *New Jersey* v. *Kenny* shifted back to the state arena. Since the charge had been brought by the state—not a county prosecutor—the trial was held in Trenton. Mercer County Court Judge George Y. Schoch ruled that the federal immunity did not apply, since Kenny had "volunteered" his testimony about the zoning-variance bribe.

Robinson attempted to appeal the pretrial ruling first to the Appellate Division, then to the state Supreme Court, but both benches declined to hear it. Another round of appeals in the federal courts was equally fruitless.

So in February, 1973, Jack Kenny went to trial. The chief witness against him was Angelo Sarubbi, the former mayor of North Bergen, himself under indictment for extortion in the Kearny post-office case. He testified that he had paid Kenny $50,000 to get the Hudson County freeholders to grant a zoning variance for two builders. The jury needed only six hours to find Kenny guilty, and Judge Schoch imposed the maximum sentence—six years.

But another round of appeals started—and the ultimate decision on Kenny's freedom remained open.

With so many "sons" around, there was bound to be a dispute about the inheritance—the hundreds of thousands of dollars in cash and bonds that the government had seized from Hudson County's corrupt officials.

As in any probate, the first claimant was Uncle Sam. The IRS filed a tax lien against the $700,000 worth of John V. Kenny's municipal bonds. Another lien was lodged against the $1.2 million that had been in the Whelan-Flaherty accounts—though the money was never found. A third lien was filed against Congressman Gallagher's hoard of bonds.

That still left a considerable pile of cold cash. On November 2, 1972, Stern turned over to Hudson County $9000—money found in Police Chief Kropke's office, but never introduced in evidence at the trial. "It's particularly appropriate that this money goes to the people of Hudson County, who were the real victims of corruption there," Stern said. Another $10,595 —seized from Stapleton's office and, again, not introduced in evidence—was turned over to the Hudson County Democratic organization (under new management), which used it to defray its expenses in the presidential election.

That still left $90,590, the bulk of it the $50,000 John V. Kenny had passed to John J. Kenny. Stern filed an interpleader asking the court to rule on who should get the money. The final decision is pending.

10
STRANDED
IN THE
SLUDGE

One day in October, 1971, shortly after his formal nomination by President Nixon, U.S. Attorney Herbert Stern was leafing through the morning's *Newark Star-Ledger*. His eye lit on an account of how 19 communities along the Jersey Shore saved their sewage sludge from the summer months and piped it into the Atlantic Ocean during the winter.

The sludge was the solid effluent left after the towns' primary sewage treatment—straining and filtering. This mass of metal particles and human feces was then mixed with water and forced through pipes ending less than 1000 feet from shore. The liquid effluent, chlorinated and diluted, was emptied into the ocean daily—and presumably rendered harmless by the dissolved oxygen in the seawater.

"I became incensed about it," Stern says. "It was barbaric. It smacked of something out of the dark ages. It's not the way a progressive society should be eliminating its wastes.

"The New Jersey Shore is the greatest natural asset the state has—not just for its scenic beauty, not just for recreation, but for the fact that it is the main tourist attraction in New Jersey. Hundreds of thousands of people come to New Jersey each year just to bathe on the shore."

Although the office had brought a few such cases previously, the newspaper account spurred Stern on an aborted career as an antipollution crusader. At the outset, the campaign offered vistas as wide as the fight for law and order. Just as crime and corruption fouled New Jersey's political climate, industrial wastes and human sewage polluted its waterways. The Passaic and Hackensack Rivers were practically open sewers. The Raritan, honored in song by generations of Rutgers University students, enjoyed the unenviable reputation of being the nation's most polluted stream. New Jersey's border rivers—the Hudson on the east and the Delaware on the west —were no better.

"There was only one statute that gave us any jurisdiction—

the Refuse Act of 1899," Stern says. "The problem was that we were dealing with municipalities and we were dealing with sewage. The Refuse Act of 1899 makes it illegal to discharge anything into a navigable body of water. But there is an exception—and that exception is for municipalities for sewage going through municipal sewer systems.

"So the first problem we had was, was this sewage or wasn't it? There was nothing we could do about the liquid that was flowing straight through after it got this wonderful primary treatment. That was clearly liquid sewage exempted from the statute. Much as we deplored the continuation of that, there was nothing we could do about it. But we believed that the sludge was solid, and we could argue that this did not fall within the exemption. So we could move against it.

"But we didn't go directly to court, because that—in our view—would not have been responsible. We did some preliminary surveys. We ascertained that there was a viable alternative—at least a short-run alternative—which would have been to barge the sludge twelve miles out to sea, where it would not wash back onto shore. The total cost to all nineteen communities would have been something in the neighborhood of three hundred to four hundred thousand, which isn't very much for the alleviation of a condition like that."

Stern sent a letter to the mayors of the 19 communities —Allenhurst, Asbury Park, Avon-by-the-Sea, Bay Head, Belmar, Bradley Beach, Deal, Lavallette, Long Beach, Manasquan, Neptune City, Neptune Township, Point Pleasant Beach, Sea Bright, Sea Girt, Seaside Heights, South Belmar, Spring Lake and Spring Lake Heights:

Dear Mayor ————:

The Department of the Army has by letter, a copy of which is enclosed, officially apprised me that your community follows the practice of discharging untreated or poorly treated solid human wastes (sludge) into the Atlantic Ocean approximately 1,000 feet from the beaches where many bathers swim during the summer months. These discharges occur between December 15 and March 15 of each year and have been continuing for many years. The Army Corps of Engineers has also advised me that it has not issued any permit to your community for this discharge.

I am writing to you with respect to this matter because of the potential hazard to the health and welfare of the people using New Jersey beaches and the deleterious effect on the environment of such discharges. This is not a purely local matter. The beaches in your community and the beaches along the entire New Jersey coast annually attract summer visitors from many other communities within this State, and from other states as well. I, and I am sure, you, wish to assure that all persons enjoying your beaches may use them safely, and without danger to their health or the health of their families.

I realize that your community, other communities and the State of New Jersey have been working on the creation of regional sewage authorities to remedy the existing situation. While this remedy may be the permanent solution to the problem, it is apparent that necessary sewage treatment plants will not be operational in the near future.

Because of the nature of the discharge, there is the possibility that the annual discharge by your community violates Section 13 of the Refuse Act of 1899, 33 U.S.C. Section 407. As you know, it is my obligation as United States Attorney for the District of New Jersey to enforce this Act, and to that end, to conduct whatever investigations are necessary and to institute whatever measures are warranted. It seems to me, however, that whether there has been a violation or not, the direct discharge of vast quantities of fecal matter so close to our coastlines is an intolerable practice. At this time I am asking your community to voluntarily refrain from discharging this sludge and to secure other acceptable alternatives for its disposal.

The Corps of Engineers has issued and is currently issuing permits for the barging and dumping of sludge, such as the sludge your municipality accumulates, approximately 12 miles out into the Atlantic Ocean. The Corps, as the enclosed letter notes, will give every consideration to a request by your municipality for authorization to barge and dump your sludge at approved locations in the Atlantic.

I am not an advocate of ocean dumping. I am also aware that New Jersey may require that any ocean dumping be considerably farther out to sea than 12 miles. For an interim period, however, it is certainly more desirable to discharge sludge 12 miles out at sea rather than 1,000 feet from beaches which are used by so many people.

Before making a final decision as to the applicability of 33 U.S.C. Section 407, I am soliciting you, and the chief executives of other communities similarly situated, either to take immediate steps to find interim alternative means of disposing of the sludge that is stored during the summer months, or to apprise me of any reason which makes it impossible for you to do so.

I would ask that you provide me with a prompt response to this letter so that we will be able to resolve this matter before December 15, 1971.

If you have any questions please contact Assistant United States Attorney Richard W. Hill, telephone (201) 645-3158.

Very truly yours,

s/Herbert J. Stern
Herbert J. Stern
United States Attorney

Enclosure

"The results were rather disappointing," Stern says.

Of the 19 communities, only four indicated a willingness to stop dumping sludge. The others refused.

"There was a lot of publicity about it," the prosecutor continues, "mostly emanating from down there. They objected to it. They screamed about it. We would get arguments, 'Well, this has been going on for fifty years.' It was the same kind of argument we got when we went into Jersey City—as though a bad practice is justified by its longevity. We were equally adamant that we were going to do something if they didn't."

The "something" meant going to court. "We had a choice," Stern says. "We could proceed against them criminally or civilly. We determined that it would not avail us very much to proceed against them criminally. First of all, it would take quite a while to fix the criminal responsibility on any given person. Second, to proceed criminally would not have ended the condition. We decided that the strongest possible remedy we could employ was an injunction—enjoin them, bar them from dumping, actually stop them cold."

The suit was filed January 14, 1972. Judge George H. Barlow issued a series of temporary injunctions delaying dumping and started hearings on whether or not to make the order permanent.

"We faced two problems," Stern says. "We had to prove that the material was solid, not liquid. And we had to prove not just a violation of the statute—we had to prove irreparable harm."

The Environmental Protection Administration served as the office's investigative arm in the case.

"They did a magnificent job," Stern says. "They overflew the area in helicopters and took videotapes of the material being pumped out of the pipes. We gave permission for one community to pump out for the purpose of experimentation. We forced yellow dye through the pipe. By observing what happened to the dye after it left the pipe, we were able to ascertain that any material pumped out from those pipes, within the relatively short time of about twenty minutes, was right up to the beach.

"One community was permitted to flush out its tanks as it normally would have done. We got videotapes of that which show clusters of birds alighting on the water and feeding off the fecal and other material as it flowed onto the beach. It was really frightening.

"Then the EPA and private chemists that we engaged did scientific analyses of the water—of the toxic levels of the water after the tanks had been flushed from this one community. There were polio viruses, meningitis, hepatitis."

On February 17, Judge Barlow issued an opinion that "the discharge of sludge into the Atlantic Ocean . . . constitutes immediate and irreparable harm and produces a destructive impact upon marine life and upon the environment generally [and] presents a dangerous health hazard." He "permanently enjoined [the defendants] from all future deposits or discharges of sludge into the waters of the Atlantic Ocean."

Says Stern: "I believe it was the first time anywhere that the United States government enjoined a municipality—totally enjoined them—from discharging."

Stern, who was in Philadelphia arguing an appeal in another case at the time, hailed the ruling "for bringing an end to a practice which is universally recognized as being unclean, unsanitary, unhealthy and intolerable."

And the prosecutor received rare kudos from Ralph Nader for his handling of the case. But the consumer crusader coupled his praise with a plea for stronger legislation in the field:

"The U.S. Attorney should be given more autonomy and a skilled staff of technical experts who know how to find remedies to such problems. With better laws on the books, Mr. Stern could do a much better job."

On the following Memorial Day weekend, Stern was sitting at his lakeside home near Bloomingdale, New Jersey. Again, he was reading the morning's *Star-Ledger*—this time, an account of how a barge loaded with more than one million tons of raw sewage was being towed north from Virginia to be dumped off the Jersey Shore.

"I read this and I was infuriated by it," Stern says. "Here we had just gone through a lawsuit to stop New Jersey from polluting New Jersey's beaches and Virginia is going to pollute our beaches."

When Stern went to work Monday morning, he alerted Z. Lance Samay, chief of the office's new environmental-protection unit. Samay contacted the U.S. Army Corps of Engineers and found there was no permit to dump the sludge. The Hampton Roads sewage plant in Newport News reported that it was planning to dump the sludge off the Jersey Shore "because that's where everything's dumped."

Through the coast guard, Stern drafted an ultimatum to the tugboat *Mary Ann*—either turn back or be slapped with a federal injunction. Samay quickly drafted the injunction and a coast-guard helicopter stood ready at Newark airport to speed the 27-year-old "pollution prosecutor" first to Trenton to get it signed by Judge Barlow, then to serve it—if necessary—by dropping it from the air onto the vessel.

But at 12:30 P.M., the coast-guard station at Cape May, New Jersey, made contact with the *Mary Ann* off Chincoteague Inlet, Delaware, about 60 miles from its proposed dumping area, and the captain agreed to turn around.

Once again, the Jersey Shore was saved.

Soon Stern started shooting at bigger game.

"You've only to look at the Hudson River," he says, "to recognize it is one of the foulest waterways in the United States. If I remember the statistics correctly, there are three hundred and fifty million gallons of raw, totally raw, untreated sewage poured into the river every day from New York City and another six hundred million gallons of poorly treated sewage from New Jersey. They built the World Trade Center [the Port Authority's twin-tower complex in downtown Manhattan]. Over nine thousand bathrooms in that place flush directly into the Hudson. I think Attila the Hun could have devised a better way to get rid of the garbage."

The campaign to clean up the Hudson was a joint effort with Whitney North Seymour, Jr., the U.S. attorney for the Southern District of New York, Robert Morse, U.S. attorney for the Eastern District (Brooklyn, Queens and Long Island), and the Environmental Protection Administration.

"I must give Mike Seymour credit for it," Stern says. "It was really his conception.'"

On July 18, the three prosecutors announced that they had filed identical suits in all three districts against a total of 35 governmental, individual and corporate defendants—including New York City and its mayor, John V. Lindsay; the state of New Jersey; the Passaic Valley and Jersey City sewage-treatment commissions and their members; the mayors and municipalities of Bayonne, Edgewater, Hoboken, North Bergen and West New York, New Jersey.

The civil action sought an injunction against the dumping of metal or chemical wastes and raw or undertreated sewage into New York Harbor or its tributary streams.

"I do not think that this lawsuit will, in and of itself, bring an end to all of the pollution in New York Harbor and its adjacent waters," Stern said, "but I do believe that this is the proper place to at least begin.

"In this suit, for the first time, all of those responsible for controlling the pollution of this major body of water will be drawn together in one courtroom where, under the supervision of the federal judiciary, it is my hope that effective measures will be implemented."

Jerome Kretchmer, then New York City's environmental-protection administrator, best known for his unsuccessful campaign against dog litter—and a defendant in the case—called the lawsuit "absurd, frivolous and political." But Samay, who had done most of the "scout" work on the case, termed it "perhaps the largest, if not the most significant, environmental lawsuit in history."

The cases against the New York defendants were consolidated in Brooklyn, those against New Jersey's in Newark. Final decisions are pending.

Meanwhile, Stern, on his own, started hitting corporate polluters in New Jersey with criminal actions. It was dangerous ground. The year before, Seymour's executive assistant, John M. Burns III, had filed criminal charges against corporate polluters in New York and was preparing a similar case against General Motors, for polluting the Hudson from its Chevrolet plant in Tarrytown. GM's attorney, Lawrence E. Walsh, took his case directly to the Justice Department. The administration owed Walsh a few favors since Walsh, as chairman of the American Bar Association's committee on the federal judiciary, had given his stamp of approval to President Nixon's nominations of F. Clement Haynesworth and G. Harrold Carswell to the Supreme Court. Justice ordered that the criminal complaint be dropped, and as soon as the civil case was settled, Burns was fired.

But Stern reported that he had "no problems with Justice—I never had any problems with Justice."

In the largest environmental criminal action, Toms River

Chemical Corporation was hit with a 206-count information *
for dumping its wastes into the Atlantic Ocean. If found guilty,
it could be fined $515,000.

Other criminal informations were filed against Continental
Oil ($2000 fine); Rollins Terminals ($4000 fine); Iron-Oxide
Corp. ($900 fine).

Even Humble Oil (now Exxon), which had assisted the U.S.
attorney's office in the shore sludge case, was hit. "They came
forward and offered to give gratis to the shore communities,
two tanker-trucks to help them cart away their sewage sludge,"
Stern says. "Unfortunately for them, they violated the statute
later on—undoubtedly inadvertently; it was an oil spill. So,
while we appreciated their help and commended them publicly, they violated the statute and we handed down an information against them."

The antipollution campaign came to an abrupt end. In October, 1972, Congress—with only 11 dissenting votes in
the House—approved the Federal Water Pollution Control
Act Amendments, a $24.6-billion program to clean up com-
pletely the nation's waters by 1985. But somewhere along
the line, a "sleeper" clause was slipped in suspending enforcement of the 1899 Refuse Act for two years. As long as a
company filed for a permit with the Army Engineers, it could
continue to pollute.

"That effectively took us out of the ball game," Stern says.
"A lot of big industries rushed in, filed for a permit—and
they're off the hook as far as this office is concerned.

"That act was the whole basis of our jurisdiction. We had
so many plans under way that were completely shut off by the
Congress. We were planning actual campaigns to take particu-

* Unlike most criminal cases, a grand jury does not have to' vote an indictment in the environmental cases; the U.S. attorney merely files an "information" in court.

lar waterways in this state and within a reasonable period of time totally clean them up."

The aborted campaign would have been too much for the facilities of the U.S. attorney's office and the Environmental Protection Administration. Stern had started to line up student volunteers at New Jersey colleges and universities to do the legwork and use the schools' laboratories for the chemical analyses.

The campaign had to be cut back to a handful of students from Seton Hall Law School who are surveying which polluting industries have not filed for permits. Stern planned to institute charges against them.

"We will use that act to the maximum of the jurisdiction left to us," he says. But basically the campaign was stranded in the sludge.

11
STERN'S "FRENCH CONNECTION"

Investigations of political corruption and campaigns against pollution rate the headlines, burn up the manhours and ultimately prove the most satisfying part of the prosecutor's job. But they're only a small percentage of the caseload handled by Stern's office.

As in any U.S. attorney's office, most of the prosecutions are of common crimes like mail fraud and auto theft, tax evasion and narcotics. In addition, there are civil actions with titles like *U.S.* v. *10.66 acres of land*—land condemnations, mortgage foreclosures or defending the government against the claims of those whose cars collide with mail trucks. In recent years, a large percentage of these "routine" cases involve Selective Service violations.*

The office has to be selective about which cases it will prosecute. "We are not set up to handle volume," Stern ex-

---

* The office's most sensational—and bizarre—draft case was that of the so-called Camden 28. The case, investigated by the FBI and the Justice Department's Internal Security Division, was turned over to Stern's office for prosecution—a thankless task, as it turned out. The "Camden 28" were members of Catholic Resistance, an antiwar group, who had broken into Camden's Federal Building in 1971 and destroyed draft records. Seventeen of them went on trial before Judge Clarkson Fisher in February, 1973, two floors below the office they had raided. Judge Fisher permitted an extremely informal, even unjudicial, atmosphere, with defendants singing on the witness stand and jurors posing questions. Stern, fearful of "another Chicago," did not press for proper decorum. The defendants did not deny the charges, but claimed they'd been "entrapped" by the FBI's informant, who had supplied the leadership, expertise and even the tools for the raid. In a strange turnabout, the informant, Robert Hardy, testified for the *defense,* calling the defendants "the finest group of Christian people I have ever been associated with." After a trial that lasted more than three months, Judge Fisher charged the jury that if they felt that the government had gone to lengths "offensive to the basic standards of decency and shocking to the universal sense of justice," they could acquit. Although the defendants admitted their act and although it had been witnessed by some 60 FBI agents, after three days of deliberation the jury found all 17 not guilty. One member of the panel explained afterward: "There was a strong feeling among the jurors that they wanted to join the defendants in taking a stand against the war." Stern's office then dropped the charges against the remaining 11 defendants.

plains. "If we took everything that the agencies brought to us and did not defer it to the state, we would be out of business very quickly. There are only nine federal judges in the whole state for eight million people, and they hear not just criminal cases, but all the civil suits involving the government and civil suits between private parties. In Essex County alone there are seventeen judges who hear nothing but criminal matters. So we defer many cases to the state. With a few exceptions like income tax or Selective Service, any federal crime is also a state crime."

Even if federal agents effect the arrest, many prosecutions will be handled by local authorities. The U.S. attorney will not prosecute stolen-car cases unless more than one auto is involved. Similarly, most narcotics violations are turned over to the state courts.

The office has set up a screening system to process the cases brought by federal agencies. Each week one assistant—with another serving as "back-up" man—pulls "duty." He's available to federal agents around the clock, and during office hours receives citizens' complaints. The agents—from the FBI, IRS, Secret Service, post office and other agencies—present their evidence for review. The "duty" assistant can authorize an arrest or send the case back for further investigation, or he can direct that it be turned over to local authorities.

Occasionally, though, a federal agent must act in a pinch, making an on-the-spot arrest without taking time for a legal review. One such case led Stern into an international imbroglio—his "French connection."

On April 5, 1971, a dapper Frenchman named Roger Xavier Leon DeLouette—described by one observer as "a poor man's Cary Grant"—arrived at dockside at Port Elizabeth, New Jersey, to pick up a Volkswagen camper he'd shipped across the Atlantic. Lynn Pelletier, a 22-year-old Customs inspector on the job only a few months, gave the car a cursory once-over. Her eye was attracted by a loose screw on one of the floorboards. She lifted the panel—and discovered packages containing 44 kilos of raw heroin. The narcotics had a street value of $12 million—one of the largest caches ever seized by the government.

Often, when the papers print news of smuggled goods being discovered in a routine search, it's a "cover" story; Customs had been tipped off exactly where to look. But in this instance, Stern swears the discovery *was* accidental.

DeLouette was arrested on the spot. Since he was a French national, under a recently concluded international agreement, he was taken to the French consulate in New York City and questioned by both French and American narcotics agents. He quickly "came clean."

The prisoner said he was 47 years old. He had a wife from whom he was separated and six children. He also had a 22-year-old mistress, Marie-Jose Robert, who was pregnant by him. He was an agent of the Service de Documentation Extérieure et de Contre-Espionage—the SDECE (Foreign Intelligence and Counterespionage Service), the French equivalent of the CIA.

DeLouette had been an intelligence agent since 1946, having served in Greece, Algeria, Cuba and the Ivory Coast. By 1970, he was back in Paris—and in desperate financial straits. On his foreign assignments he had received a 3500-franc-a-month salary (about $636), plus a cost-of-living allowance. In France there was no cost-of-living allowance and 3000 of his 3500-franc salary went for the support of his wife and children. That left only about $90 a month for himself.

As he explained later—in a not always felicitous translation:

"During the month of June of 1970, I telephoned at the office of the Invalides and spoke to M. Fournier [Col. Paul Fournier, the mysterious head of the SDECE], but he was not there. I left a message in the name of Delmas, which is my code name, asking him to return my call, which he did. . . . I explained to him my problems and he told me he would see what he could do. . . .

"A few days later he telephoned me again and asked me if I would be willing to make a short trip towards the Italian border for a small special matter. I agreed and he made an appointment with me in the café which is located at the corner of the Rue de Grenella and Boulevard de la Tour Marbourg, by telling me that I would meet there a man whom I had already met from the service. I went to this appointment and I did in fact meet a man whom I did not know well, but whom I had occasion to see, who worked in the accounting section. . . . He asked me to go to Modane, to cross the Italian border and on the other side to turn over an envelope which he gave to me in which there were 17,000 and some odd [American] dollars. He told me right away that these dollars were counterfeit."

As instructed, DeLouette went to Modane, met an intermediary named Marcel and waited for his contact.

"At approximately 9:30 [A.M.]," DeLouette continued, "he [Marcel] stated that the meeting had been canceled and that he had been told to instruct me to return to Paris. I rested there during the morning in the hotel and after lunch I returned to Paris. I received a telephone call from Fournier the next day . . . who told me that the meeting had been canceled, but since I was going to Algeria from time to time I could transport this money directly to Algeria. . . .

"Having learned the severe police action against counterfeiting in Algeria [the death penalty, DeLouette said at one point], I did not accept to transport this money to Algeria. He asked me to keep them [the counterfeit bills] for the time being. . . . I left the money in my bureau drawer. . . .

"During the month of August 1970 I had no contact with Fournier. During the month of September I called him back. . . . I telephoned him at the Invalides. When I spoke to him, I explained to him my situation which was worsening. . . . He told me that it was rather difficult now in view of the situation at the time and especially the situation with SDECE at the time [the French government was going through the shake-ups of its post-Gaullist Thermidor] to solve my problem. But he promised me that he would not forget me, that he would try to get me out of it.

"Around the 15th of December—maybe before then—he telephoned me to ask me if I would accept an assignment, a very special assignment which included certain risks. This was a time when my personal situation was at its worst and when I would have accepted everything.

"On my agreement, he set up a meeting at the Café le Paris at the Champs Elysées with a man of whom he gave me a vague description, but he told me this man would be alone at a table and that he would have a *Paris Match* magazine with a pair of gloves placed on top of the magazine. The meeting was set up for me two days after the telephone call.

"I went to the meeting . . . and, as agreed, at a table inside the café there was a man, approximately thirty years old, a little smaller than I am . . . dark-complected, distinguished-looking and dressed in a very elegant manner and a very conservative manner. . . .

"This man told me—first, I understood that he also belonged to the service. That is to say, when he referred to the service, he said 'we' and 'us.' He told me that for special matters they needed to smuggle drugs to the United States. He told me that Fournier had told him I could be trusted, that should I refuse I would not speak of this matter.

"He outlined the basic principle without placing any conditions and it was after my agreement that at that time he explained the details. He told me then that there were fifty kilos of heroin that had to be smuggled to the United States by car. . . ."

There was some discussion about which make of car to use. It was finally decided that a Volkswagen camper or minibus was best.

"The main thing," DeLouette continued, "was the sum which I was to receive for this operation. . . . We agreed on a figure of 300,000 francs [about $54,340]. This person then told me to organize all the details of the trip and that we would see each other at the beginning of January. . . ."

DeLouette obtained his visa, arranged to purchase the camper—in Switzerland, to escape French excise taxes—and have it shipped to the United States.

On February 15, he continued, "I received a telephone call from Fournier, who asked me if everything was in agreement. When I answered in the affirmative, he gave me another meeting date with the same individual I had met the first time.

"This meeting was to take place at the Café le [Roi] on Rue François, Premier. . . . I went to the meeting. I gave the dates at which I would receive delivery of the automobile and along with this date, the possible date at which the auto would be shipped, the possible date of the delivery of the automobile in the United States and the date of my departure and of my arrival.

"I stated that since the automobile would arrive on a Saturday, I would not be able to take it out of Customs before Monday morning and therefore I would not be able to deliver the 'merchandise' before Monday.

"He told me . . . at that time a person who would not be him, who would be someone else, and that he could not tell me who it would be at that particular time, would contact me at the hotel where I would be staying. . . .

"He also told me not to worry, that if the person was not present at Monday's meeting, that I should wait for him on the next day. I remember in fact telling him, 'I hope this won't happen because I don't want to be in possession for too long a period of time of the merchandise.' "

The man gave DeLouette approximately $5500 for the purchase of the camper and he picked it up on March 1.

On March 15, Fournier again called DeLouette and directed him to drive to Pontchartrain, a town about 25 miles from Paris, the following day.

"I would be met," DeLouette continued, "by a man with a new green Simca Chrysler, driving it or sitting at the wheel at one o'clock in the afternoon. I was to drive past him slowly. He was to make a sign, stop me. He was to pass me and I was to follow him. The sign was a gesture of a hand.

"The next day I went to Pontchartrain. . . . I did what had been agreed upon and I followed him. We went into the forest of Rambouilet, after having crossed Montfort Lamary and I believe Les Mosmues, after which we entered into the forest, turning left, right, left, in order to come out onto a forest path which was isolated and on a small clearing.

"There he got out of his car and so did I. I found in front of me a man approximately forty to forty-five years of age, short, very definite features, dark-complected, sloppily dressed, speaking with a slight Parigot accent, grouchy looking and not speaking—that is to say, speaking very little.

"I tried to engage him in conversation and he did not carry on with it. Very quickly, he opened the trunk of his car, took out two suitcases—black, as I recall, of poor quality and new. That is to say, they were cheap suitcases, but they were new—and a tool kit.

"Very quickly, he began to remove certain panels of the truck, beginning with the front—without hesitation, which made me think that it was not the first time that he did this. . . .

"We were not able to conceal the total quantity of fifty kilos. He didn't know any more than I did about what to do. He told me it did not matter and took back eleven packages. He took back the two suitcases, placed them in his car along with the tool kit and, by the way, not all of his tools, because a screwdriver was found on arrival here.

"We left together for a few meters. He asked me before to split up so that he left his way. I didn't know in what direction. I returned to Paris."

The following day—March 17—DeLouette drove to Le Havre and consigned the camper to Pacific Intermountain Express for shipment on the freighter *Atlantic Cognac* to Port Elizabeth. On Sunday, April 4, he boarded a TWA jet in Paris, flew to New York, shared a taxi into Manhattan and checked into the Park Sheraton Hotel off Times Square. He was arrested the next morning.

After the initial examination, one of the French policemen, Commissaire Daniel Hartwig, called DeLouette aside and whispered "that I should have never said this to the Americans."

DeLouette was brought back to his hotel room to wait for the call from his "contact." It never came, which is understandable, since all indications point to someone at the French consulate.

According to DeLouette, during one of their last telephone conversations, Fournier had told him "that if in the United States I had any kind of a problem at all . . . I could always address myself to the man whom we [the SDECE] had at the consulate.

"And he told me, 'You know who?'

"I said, 'Yes.' "

The man was later identified as Donald McNab. When called to testify in the case, he claimed diplomatic immunity.

DeLouette was finally turned over to the American authorities for prosecution. Unable to raise the $500,000 bail Judge Frederick B. Lacey set, he was lodged in the Somerset County Jail where he delighted both his fellow inmates and his warders with his culinary talents. As the jail's chef for the following year, he came up with haute cuisine menus the likes of which it had never seen before—or since. On Fridays, sheriff's deputies from miles around found excuses to visit the jail just so they could savor DeLouette's specialty, clam chowder. Croutons and garlic dip were another favorite.

DeLouette was also unable to afford counsel. Judge Lacey picked Donald Robinson, a bouncy bantam who had once worked at Shanley & Fisher, his old law firm. "I thought it was just another garden-variety dope case," Robinson says. He quickly learned. The DeLouette case was to occupy him for the better part of a year, take him to Paris and force him to retain both a Parisian attorney and the Manhattan law firm of Royall, Koegel & Wells—of which Secretary of State William G. Rogers had once been senior partner—to handle the international aspects. For representing John J. Kenny, Robinson received a fee of $50,000. His remuneration in the DeLouette case, set by the court, was $5000.

Under Robinson's guidance, DeLouette continued to cooperate with the authorities. Meanwhile, Stern pondered a way to proceed against Colonel Fournier. He got scant cooperation from the French government, which, after a four-day investigation, decided that DeLouette was lying.

As one government spokesman later put it: "This is merely the word of a smuggler who has been caught red-handed. DeLouette has everything to gain by trying to implicate French authorities." Claude Chaminadas, the French narcotics agent at the New York consulate, said: "He's been lying all along."

The progress of the case can be seen in two letters Stern

sent in September. The first went to Gabriel Roussel, the French examining magistrate:

DWM:jam

September 27, 1971

Monsieur G. Roussel
Juge d'Instruction
   au Pribunal [sic] de Grand Instance,
1, Boulevard du Palais
75 Paris 1ᵉ
France

Dear Juge Roussel:

   I am the United States Attorney for the District of New Jersey and as such am responsible for the prosecution of violations of Federal Law which occur in this District. As you are aware, Roger Xavier Leon DeLouette, a French citizen, has been charged with the importing and concealing of 96 pounds of pure heroin, which heroin was shipped from Le Havre arriving at the United States on April 5, 1971. The indictment which contains 2 charges carries a sentence of a mandatory minimum of 5 years in prison and a maximum of 20 years for each of the 2 charges.

   My office, through one of my assistants, Donald W. Merkelbach, received a request from your honor for the execution of Letters Rogatory upon the defendant DeLouette. A Commissioner was thereafter appointed by a United States District Court Judge to supervise the Rogatory proceeding and arrangements were made through Mr. DeLouette's attorney, Donald A. Robinson, to submit DeLouette on August 4, 1971 to the Rogatory Proceeding. Before the questioning in the Rogatory Proceeding, Mr. Robinson stated that he would not permit DeLouette to answer the questions of the Rogatory Commissioner until he, Mr. Robinson, was assured by the

Government of France that any information or answers
DeLouette gives in response to the Letters Rogatory
Proceeding would not be used against him in any pro-
ceedings in France.

On September 14, 1971 I attended a meeting with
Assistant U.S. Attorney Donald W. Merkelbach at the
office of George Belk, Chief of Criminal Investigation,
Bureau of Narcotics and Dangerous Drugs. Present at
the meeting were Mr. Belk; Philip R. Smith, Chief of
Tactical Intelligence Branch, Bureau of Narcotics and
Dangerous Drugs; Honare Gevaudan, Assistant Director
of the Police Judiciaire, France; Claude Shaminadas [sic],
Police Judiciaire, France. The purpose of this meeting
was to discus˙ the various aspects and problems of the
DeLouette   ˌtter. Mr. Gevaudan explained that the
French could not proceed to bring charges against Colonel Fournier until DeLouette submitted to the Letters
Rogatory. I then repeated to him that DeLouette's attorney would not allow DeLouette to testify until he was
granted immunity by the French Government. I then was
requested by Mr. Gevaudan to request you to grant immunity to Mr. DeLouette in order to aid the French in
their investigation in this matter.

Pursuant to Mr. Gevaudan's request and the concern
shared by your Government and my Government over
the international trafficking of narcotics, I request that
you grant immunity to Mr. DeLouette from prosecution
in any French proceeding which concerns the importa-
tion of the 96 pounds of heroin into the United States on
April 5, 1971. Should your honor grant this immunity to
Mr. DeLouette, I have been assured by Mr. DeLouette's
attorney, Mr. Robinson, that he will answer any and all
questions put to him in the Letters Rogatory proceeding. This then would allow the Police Judiciaire to conduct their investigation of this matter. Please be assured
that this grant of immunity is not only in the interest of

your Government and mine, but in the interest of Justice as well. This grant of immunity will now [sic] free De-Louette from his criminal responsibility because he will receive, at the least, a five year sentence in prison by our Courts for his role in the conspiracy, irrespective of the immunity grant, the purpose of which is primarily directed towards enabling the French authorities to proceed against the "higher-ups" in a criminal organization which is operating between our two countries.

Very truly yours,

s/Herbert J. Stern
Herbert J. Stern
United States Attorney

The second letter went to Max Fernet of the French Sûreté:

DWM:jam

September 28, 1971

Mr. Max Fernet
Central Direction
French Criminal Police
12 Rue Des Saussaies,
Paris, France

Dear Mr. Fernet:

On September 14, 1971 I attended a meeting at the office of George Belk, Chief of Criminal Investigation, Bureau of Narcotics and Dangerous Drugs. I had hoped, as you know, to have an opportunity at that time to discuss the DeLouette matter with you. Present at that time were . . .

We discussed the allegations made by Mr. DeLouette and the pending investigation of Colonel Fournier. The representative of the French Government made it clear to me that it was their belief that DeLouette's allegations were without basis and in fact, DeLouette was lying.

This judgement was made based upon an investigation which apparently lasted four days, April 6, 1971 through April 9, 1971. I expressed my belief that no man can be considered above suspicion because of the position which that person may hold or the reputation which he may enjoy. I then suggested that it was imperative that we be satisfied as to whether or not DeLouette was telling the truth. For this reason I proposed that the defendant DeLouette be subjected to a polygraph examination with the understanding that should DeLouette either refuse to submit to such an examination or submit to and fail to pass such an examination the United States Attorneys [sic] Office would then prosecute the indictment against him and recommend the maximum sentence. On the other hand, I proposed that should DeLouette submit to the examination and pass, the French would agree to reexamine their position regarding Colonel Fournier and proceed with an appropriate prosecution against him. Mr. Gevaudan and the other representatives of the French Government agreed to this proposal.

Pursuant to this agreement, Roger DeLouette was subjected to a polygraph test on September 21, 1971. Present while the polygraph test was being conducted were Michel Nocquet, Chief Commissioner, Headquarters Direction Central of the Police Judiciaire, France; Claude Shaminadas [sic], Police Officer, Office Central of Drugs, Police Judiciaire, France; Special Agent Marion Hambrick, Bureau of Narcotics and Dangerous Drugs, New York; Special Agent Paul Boulad, Custom Agency Service [sic], New York; Donald Robinson, Attorney for DeLouette; Donald W. Merkelbach, Assistant U.S. Attorney; and Phillip Berbereich, Essex County Prosecutor's Office, Essex County, New Jersey. The following questions were asked of Mr. DeLouette:

1. Are you now in the United States?
2. Are you going to lie to any of my questions?
3. Were you recruited by S.D.E.C.E. to work for them?
4. Were you directed by Fournier to received [sic] $17,000 in counterfeit U.S. currency?
5. Was Fournier of S.D.E.C.E. the same Fournier who gave you the instructions?
6. Is your name Roger?
7. Was the smuggling of the heroin done according to instructions of the man sent by Fournier?
8. Did Fournier give you a contact in the French Consolate [sic] in New York?

DeLouette's answer to question number 2 was no. De-Louette's answer to the other seven questions was yes. The results of the test were positive indicating that De-Louette was telling the truth.

Pursuant to our direction of Tuesday, September 14, 1971, your representatives were given an opportunity to submit questions to be asked of DeLouette in the polygraph examination. These questions were to be submitted to Mr. Merkelbach by Friday, September 17, 1971. Because of the limitation of the number of questions which may be asked during one polygraph examination and because of the fact that the questions by the French representatives were not given to Mr. Merkelbach, until 12:00 noon Tuesday, September 21, 1971, one-half hour after the scheduled beginning of the test, none of the French questions were [sic] included in the test of Mr. DeLouette.

In order to accommodate your wishes and in accordance with the agreement of September 4, 1971, I have scheduled a supplementary polygraph examination with the consent of Mr. DeLouette on Monday, October 4, 1971, at which time questions presented by Mr. Nocquet will be asked of Mr. DeLouette.

In the meantime based upon the results of todays [sic] polygraph test and of our mutual desire to curb the international trafficking of heroin, I have written to the Honorable Judge Roussel and requested that he grant immunity from prosecution to Mr. DeLouette, in order that Mr. DeLouette submit to Letters Rogatory, thereby enabling the French Police Judicicaire [sic] to formally commence their investigation.

Very truly yours,

s/Herbert J. Stern
Herbert J. Stern
United States Attorney

DeLouette was submitted to the second lie-detector test, which he again passed, with the exception of one question. When asked if Mlle. Robert was involved in the smuggling operation, he answered "no."

The French reneged on the deal. Judge Roussel replied that it was impossible under French law to grant DeLouette immunity; without immunity DeLouette wouldn't testify; and without his testimony the French wouldn't proceed against Fournier. For his part, Fernet continued to insist that his four-day "investigation" exonerated Fournier, regardless of the lie-detector tests.

On November 5, Stern flew to Paris and attempted to see Fournier. The French authorities refused permission. Balked at every turn by the French government, the prosecutor returned to Newark and on November 14 announced a superseding indictment in the case—one naming both DeLouette and Fournier. It was the first public disclosure of Fournier's role. Needless to say, the indictment of the head of the French Secret Service as a dope smuggler created an international scandal.

Two days later, DeLouette was arraigned on the new indictment, pleaded guilty and publicly named Fournier as his superior in the operation.

When—if ever—Fournier would be brought before the bar remained open. Stern passed the buck to Paris: "It is now up to the French authorities to elect whether they will proceed against Fournier in France or make him available for prosecution here."

The French did neither. According to one report from Paris, the French government "closed ranks" behind Fournier. Defense Minister Michel Debré, Fournier's immediate superior, dismissed DeLouette's story as "a serialized novel."

Fournier's only comment on the case was a two-sentence statement released by Debré: "If I am guilty, Mr. Stern, prove it. Justice will take its course."

Stern replied: "If you are innocent, Mr. Fournier, come to this country and stand trial. If you are innocent, you have nothing to fear. You are assured a fair trial by our own system of justice. Do not hide behind an anonymous service and an international border."

"Anonymous" was truly the right word. Fournier's face and features were unknown outside the upper reaches of the French government and, as it turned out, "Fournier" wasn't even his real name. Like "M" in the James Bond novels, the head of the French Secret Service was a mystery man, unknown to the general public.

A few days after the indictment was handed up, "Colonel Fournier" visited the Hall of Justice in Paris and conferred with the chief magistrate—about what has never been disclosed. On his way out, a newspaper photographer snapped his picture. Gendarmes confiscated the film.

Within a week, though, his "cover" was blown. Colonel Roger Barberot, the head of the French Bureau for Agricultural Production Development—the cover name for a rival intelligence agency to the SDECE—appeared on a Radio Luxembourg broadcast. He disclosed that "Fournier" was really Paul Ferrer and rather than a colonel, he was a former air-force master sergeant. He reportedly was 52 years old and had joined the Free French in 1941.

Barberot's broadcast apparently was part of the bureaucratic infighting between Gaullists and neo-Gaullists in the new Pompidou government. It marked the first break in the official French "line" on the case. According to Barberot, DeLouette had been set up for arrest by his superiors in the SDECE:

"We know that the secret services have been deeply penetrated by American and Soviet agents for ten years. When it was decided to clean house, the old leadership was kicked out, but the infrastructure remained. Thus, Mr. DeLouette belonged to SDECE and a certain number of officers will tell you so.

"My conviction is—and some will tell you so officially—that the operation was mounted by a certain number of SDECE agents in Paris itself. DeLouette had to be got rid of in the United States to get rid of a very heavy past. It is the sequel of that operation that is coming out now."

Judge Roussel ordered the tape of Barberot's broadcast impounded. Needless to say, that did not end the speculation on the case. Others argued that it was all a CIA plot. And some that the heroin was used to finance clandestine operations the SDECE kept secret even from the French government. Only on one thing did all observers agree: The French government was doing nothing to get at the truth.

Even more ominous than the French intransigence was the Nixon administration's. The State Department never moved to have Fournier-Ferrer extradited. Strangely, the man in charge of the matter was Nelson Gross, the old antagonist of

Lacey's and Stern's, having been rewarded with the post of assistant secretary of state for narcotics after his defeat in the New Jersey Senate race. His official line was: "We had an agreement with France and the DeLouette case imperils it."

On November 19, Stern—this time accompanied by defense attorney Robinson—flew to Paris again. Three weeks before he had slipped into town a relative unknown; this time he was an international celebrity. *France-Soir* said he "looked like an inquisitor right off the stage." The inquisitor was suffering from a bout of flu that kept his stomach churning— "Fournier's revenge," said one embassy aide.

Stern refuses to discuss the details of his visit—or any other aspect of the case. Ostensibly, it's because the charges against "Fournier" are still pending—though the likelihood is he'll never be brought to trial on either side of the Atlantic. More likely, Washington has clamped the lid on the case for fear of embarrassing the French and thus destroying any chance of cooperation in halting the heroin traffic. Approximately 80 percent of the heroin in the United States is processed in France.

Stern and Robinson had another futile go-round with Judge Roussel on the immunity issue. Meanwhile, Stern was also getting a go-slow message from the American authorities. But, according to *France-Soir*, the American ambassador, Arthur Watson—"did not succeed in calming Sherlock Holmes."

Once again, the mission was a failure. Under the cumulative pressure from Paris, Washington and Stern's office, Robinson finally agreed to let DeLouette testify in the French proceeding—without a grant of immunity. Judge Roussel flew to Kennedy Airport and was met by Stern. For three days— March 8, 9 and 10—he presided at an extraordinary judicial session convened in the conference room of the U.S. attorney's office—one of the rare occasions a French court has sat in the United States.

Under French procedure, Judge Roussel was judge, jury, prosecutor and cross-examiner all in one. It was obvious that his questions were designed not to elicit DeLouette's story, but to disprove it. As Robinson said, "He was permitted to ask questions no American court would have ever permitted under the rules of evidence and examination."

The hearing solved nothing. The French still refused to proceed against Fournier-Ferrer. Indeed, by the time of Roussel's examination the Sûreté had arrested a petty criminal named Dominique Mariani, alias Marland, and charged him with supplying the heroin that DeLouette had delivered.

Robinson, who says that DeLouette "passed all my private tests" in addition to two lie-detector tests, pooh-poohed the French claim: "I understand that the French police at various times have taken the position that Colonel Fournier did not exist; next that the smuggling was an American CIA plot; that the man DeLouette called Colonel Fournier was an impostor using a disguised voice; and other implausible theories that have since been proved false. I regard this latest development as equally false."

The French kept up their pressure on DeLouette. His family was questioned and their rooms searched. Mlle. Robert was arrested, for possession of the counterfeit currency Fournier-Ferrer had given DeLouette, and released only in time to bear DeLouette's child. Robinson claimed that she was being held "hostage" to force DeLouette's recantation.

"Instead of proceeding against Colonel Fournier," he said, "[they] are continuing to attempt to either silence M. De-Louette or punish him in the worst possible way . . . punish him in a harsh, really cruel, merciless way."

The tawdry drama ground to a close. On April 17, 1972, DeLouette stood before Judge Lacey for sentencing. To illustrate his client's cooperation and the French government's vengeance, Robinson sought to introduce the three volumes of DeLouette's testimony before Judge Roussel. Stern—apparently under order—opposed it. It was not one of his finest moments. Judge Lacey, however, admitted the transcripts into the record.

Stern told the court that DeLouette had been "extremely helpful" to the government: "Within a few hours of his arrest, he laid bare the entire system, the entire enterprise as he knew it, and gave what was, in my opinion, valuable information to the authorities . . . including names of the ones under whose orders he brought heroin into the United States." He asked that the minimum sentence be imposed.

Judge Lacey agreed and gave DeLouette the minimum term allowable under federal law—five years, with allowance for the year he'd already served behind bars.

Robinson did not fault Stern's handling of DeLouette's side of the case: "He told me that if my man cooperated, he'd stand on his two powerful feet and tell the judge of his cooperation and ask for leniency. He kept his word 105 percent, and in my experience, prosecutors don't always do that."

DeLouette is serving out his five years in a federal prison, presumably delighting the inmates and guards with his cuisine. Fournier-Ferrer has not been brought to justice on either side of the Atlantic. Presumably, he's still in command of the SDECE . . . and possibly still smuggling heroin into the United States. Stern's "French Connection" was bared, but not broken. But Stern notes that since the Fournier-Ferrer indictment, the French authorities have been more cooperative with American "narcs" and more diligent about "busting" the heroin laboratories that flourish around Marseilles.

12
RATTLING REPUBLICAN SKELETONS

All the while, the U.S. attorney's office kept busy on other fronts, pinning down instances of political corruption *not* connected with the Hudson County case. As Governor Cahill and Nelson Gross had feared, many of them involved Republicans.

At the outset, though, one of them did not even involve politics. When Lacey and Stern came into office, FBI agents had been looking into irregularities at the Midland Bank and Trust Company in Paramus, New Jersey. The bank had loaned some $2.4 million in unsecured loans to Greek shipping interests and most of the money had been lost. The U.S. attorney's office took over the case and Jonathan Goldstein took charge of the investigation.

The evidence indicated that John Pensec, the bank's president, and Peter Moraites, one of its directors, had split $66,000 in bribes to arrange the unsecured loans.

Moraites, 47, had been an assistant in the New York attorney general's office and had gone on to become an aide first to New York Senator Jacob Javits, then an admiralty-law specialist with the Manhattan firm of Hill, Betts & Nash. By then a New Jersey resident, he had entered politics in the Garden State. He was a Republican assemblyman from Bergen County and had served a term as speaker.

In March, 1970, Goldstein presented the proposed indictment against Pensec and Moraites to the grand jury.

"The foreman of the grand jury asked as to why Walter Jones was not named as a defendant in this case," he later testified. "I explained to the grand jury that the charges of this indictment, bank misapplication, illegal commissions, did not concern Walter Jones.

"The grand jury—or the foreman of the grand jury—said to me that they had heard certain testimony involving Walter Jones in a merger and recapitalization of the Midland Bank. . . . [He] did request of me—and the United States attorney's office—that we initiate an investigation into the merger of the

Englewood and Midland National Bank and into the subsequent recapitalization—in particular, investigate whether or not one Walter Jones had criminally violated any law for his failure to disclose any of the matters pertaining to the ship loans prior to the merger or the recapitalization."

"We have a runaway grand jury," Goldstein, on another occasion, told an attorney for the bank.

Jones, then 59, had organized the bank in 1958 and had served as its general counsel thereafter. He had a career spanning 30 years in politics and had been the Republican chairman in Bergen County, long the GOP's biggest bastion in New Jersey. He had served both in the Assembly (like Moraites, briefly as speaker) and the Senate. He had been a leading contender for the GOP's gubernatorial nomination in 1961, but lost the bid to Senator Clifford Case's candidate, former Labor Secretary James Mitchell. In the general election, Mitchell was defeated by Democrat Richard Hughes, who subsequently appointed Jones a commissioner of the Port of New York Authority.

Despite the grand jury's order, the investigation of Jones was delayed because Goldstein's manpower had been tapped to handle the investigations and trials of Mayor Addonizio and John V. Kenny.

Meanwhile, the Moraites-Pensec case moved toward trial. Shortly before the scheduled start, Stern asked Moraites's attorney, Walter D. Van Riper, "Are you going to plead him?"

"[He] pointed out," Van Riper said, "that if it went to trial, it was a likelihood there would be a conviction on all counts" —including the felonies, and that would mean Moraites's automatic disbarment. But if he pleaded to the misdemeanor counts, Moraites might be able to salvage his lucrative law practice with only a reprimand or a short suspension.

Moraites conferred with his law partners and agreed to plead guilty to two misdemeanor counts. Judge Leonard Garth sentenced him to 16 months in prison. Pensec, who was found guilty after trial, received a similar term.

On April 19, 1971, Moraites bade farewell to his fellow lawmakers, explaining that he was resigning his assembly seat "not because I did anything wrong, but because I cannot operate effectively from jail." The assembly gave him a standing ovation as he walked off to prison.

Moraites served only eight months of his sentence, but went free only to face new charges. Not until he was behind bars did the investigation of Jones get under full steam, and, as it progressed, it appeared that Moraites was equally culpable of bank fraud. The two former speakers were indicted on a string of securities-law violations.

That case is pending.

The office also pursued its probe of Atlantic City. Once one of the East Coast's plushest resorts, over the years its glamour had faded and its façade—the famed Boardwalk—had become as tawdry as Times Square. Atlantic City is nationally known for its jitney buses, saltwater taffy, Steel Pier and Convention Hall, the Miss America pageant and the game of Monopoly, whose streets—from Baltic and Mediterranean Avenues to Boardwalk and Park Place—are named after the resort's thoroughfares.

Atlantic City's officials had also been playing Monopoly— with real streets and real money.

Stern calls the Atlantic City investigation—conducted by Jonathan Goldstein, who had succeeded him as the office's first assistant—"even more difficult" than the Newark and Hudson County cases.

"We were dealing with public officials situated one hundred or more miles away," he explains, "and many of the firms we had to deal with were one hundred or more miles away. We didn't have the same familiarity with the political setup, the dramatis personae, who was connected with whom. We went in cold.

"But I think the result is the total vindication of the methods we had used so successfully in Newark and Hudson County—dealing with people who were totally unfamiliar and geographically remote and still coming up with the same result."

As soon as the subpoenas went out, Atlantic City and some of the contractors petitioned the federal court in Camden to have the investigation shifted there. The resort was closer to Camden—only a half-hour drive on the Atlantic City Expressway—and federal cases arising there normally were tried in Camden. Stern went to Camden and personally appeared before Judge Mitchell Cohen to argue against the motion.

"I felt it was vital to keep the investigation up here in Newark," he says. "This is where I had most of my manpower; this is where I had most of my investigative power. If we had lost that motion we would have been in difficult straits. It would have meant that I would have had to send a great number of personnel down on a full-time basis to live in Camden. It would have been a tremendous hardship for my staff and a tremendous expense for the government."

But Judge Cohen ruled that the investigation could continue in Newark.

Midway through the investigation, Stern was invited to address the New Jersey Conference of Mayors—several of whose members he had put behind bars—meeting in Atlantic City.

"It's far better to have the U.S. attorney before us than have us go before the U.S. attorney," Elizabeth's mayor, Thomas Dunn, said in introducing Stern.

"It's wonderful to be here," Stern replied. "I've been hearing so much about Atlantic City lately." But he gave the mayors no clue as to the progress of the investigation.

"We had one other impediment," Stern says of the investigation. "The State Commission of Investigation had done an extensive probe of Atlantic City and Atlantic County and had come to the conclusion that there was no large-scale corruption there. So we had to work against that.

"Yet within nine months we had indicted a significant portion of the administration of Atlantic City and Atlantic County."

The first indictment came on May 4, 1972. Its 26 counts charged that six contractors had paid at least $28,421 in kickbacks to seven city officials—Mayor William T. Somers; former Mayor Richard S. Jackson, then executive director of the Atlantic City Expressway Authority; Arthur Ponzio, the city's public-works director; Karlos R. LaSane, its director of parks and public property; Robert Glass, supervisor of airports, parks and recreation; Germaine Fisher, Ponzio's secretary; and Florence Clark, a former assistant purchasing agent.

The indictment came five days before the municipal elections, in which Somers placed ninth in the race for five seats on the city commission. Even earlier, the investigation apparently had taken its toll at the polls. In November, Frank (Hap) Farley, long the "boss" of Atlantic County and the dean of the state legislature, had lost his bid for reelection to the state senate.

Later, Patrick J. Doran, the Atlantic County engineer, and one of his assistants, Francis Southard, were indicted in a $162,000 kickback scheme.

Southard pleaded guilty. Doran went on trial in the fall, prosecuted by Goldstein before Judge Cohen in Camden. The 45-year-old engineer admitted taking the money, but said he'd merely been a channel to the Atlantic County Republican organization. The jury needed less than two hours to find him guilty.

The Atlantic City case opened in January, 1973—again prosecuted by Goldstein before Judge Cohen in Camden—and lasted two months. Although kickbacks of only $28,000 were charged in the indictment, Goldstein was able to prove payoffs of more than $100,000—not only from contractors, but from auto dealers and even from the owner of a "jam joint"—one of the auctioneers' outlets that line the Boardwalk—to get a permit. As the trial progressed, Jackson, Glass and Miss Clark copped pleas. The remaining four defendants were found guilty.

"As a result," says Stern, "we successfully broke the back of the third major area of corruption. What I mean by 'area' is not so much a geographic area as a system of corruption—a network of venal public officials working together to guarantee that there would be a steady flow of income to all of them."

After the verdict, Goldstein treated the assistants who'd worked with him to dinner at the Cherry Hill Inn outside Camden and presented each of them with a souvenir of the trial—a Monopoly set. Garrett Brown suggested that the game get a new "chance" card—"Pass City Hall, pay ten percent, go directly to jail." *

The defendants did. In the Atlantic County case, Doran got five years. In the Atlantic City case, Ponzio got six, LaSane four, Mayor Jackson three, Mayor Somers two and a half, Glass and Miss Fisher two each; the 71-year-old Miss Clark was given a two-year suspended sentence and placed on probation.

But one question remained: Had the underlings merely taken the rap while the boss escaped?

---

* During the course of the trial, Public Works Director Ponzio created a national controversy when he attempted to change the names of Baltic and Mediterranean Avenues—the cheapest properties on the Monopoly board and the resort's least desirable streets—to Fairmont and Melrose. Protests from Monopoly fans—and Parker Brothers, makers of the game—finally forced him to back down.

"We never developed any evidence that implicated Frank Farley," Stern says. "Had we, he would have been indicted. It may just indicate that he was in it for power and not for money.

"There's no doubt in my mind that he knew the system was corrupt. He couldn't be the boss of it and not know that it was corrupt, but that isn't the kind of legal evidence that is required to prove participation in the scheme.

"By the same token, to say that Farley was aware of it is not to single him out, because there hadn't been any governor, any prosecutor, any state senator in this state who didn't know that Atlantic City and Atlantic County were corrupt—and the massive amounts of corruption as revealed in that trial demonstrates it."

The John J. Kenny case had strained relations between the federal prosecutor and the state attorney general. More severe strains were to follow.

One started on April 14, 1972, when David A. Biederman called on Stern's director of special prosecutions, Bruce Goldstein (no relation to Jonathan). Biederman had been a deputy attorney general, serving as chief counsel to New Jersey's transportation commissioner. He had left state employ the previous September to return to private practice. He quickly became embroiled on a conflict-of-interest charge for representing a company that had come under his scrutiny in state service— Mal Brothers, one of the firms that had kicked back in the Addonizio case.

Obviously motivated by revenge against his former superiors who had brought the disciplinary action, Biederman, documents in hand, told his tale to Goldstein:

On September 24, 1970, the Department of Transportation received bids for a highway construction project. Centrum Construction was low bidder with $603,871, followed by

Manzo Contracting with $607,657 and Stamato & Co. with $632,000.

Two weeks later, New Jersey's secretary of state sent a note about the bids to the home of Transportation Commissioner John C. Kohl:

October 8, 1970

Dear John,

I am attaching copy of Notice of Bid for Route U.S. 46 (1953), Sections 19A and 2B (Warren County), Federal Project No. RF-56 (17).

I understand that the budgeted amount for this contract was $580,000, and since all bids were above that amount there is an option on the part of the Transportation Department to review the higher bids and to seek bids once again for the contract work. On the other hand, I am told that you could accept the lowest bid since in this instance it is not too far removed from the maximum amount of $580,000.

In this particular case, I would prefer that you reject the bids and request a rebidding and if you will telephone me on Tuesday, I will be glad to give you the reasons for my request.

Sincerely yours,
s/Paul
Paul J. Sherwin

Mr. John C. Kohl
777 West State Street
Apartment 11-B
Trenton, New Jersey

Enclosure as noted.
PJS; hm

Sherwin, then 53, was the Number 2 man in the state government. A balding man with the mien and manner of a bookkeeper, he had been a close associate of Governor Cahill's for years and was regarded by many as "the power behind the throne." Obviously, a request from him could not be ignored.

What happened next was summarized in a memo Biederman sent to Commissioner Kohl on October 30:

> . . . [I] discussed this matter with you and you advised me that you had been requested by the Secretary of State, Mr. Sherwin, *not* to award the contract and to reject all bids, so that the second bidder, Mr. Manzo represented by John E. Dimon, State Republican Chairman, would have another shot at this contract. . . . After discussion with you, you advised that the award *would* be made to the low bidder—Centrum Construction Company and that Mr. Sherwin's request would be rejected. Later that day I discussed this matter with the Attorney General and advised him that in my view Mr. Sherwin's action was in derogation in policy of the bidding statutes. I further advised the Attorney General to take the matter up with Mr. Sherwin. His reply was that he would not do so, but thought that my Commissioner could do so.
>
> Apparently on Monday, October 26, you reversed your decision to reject Mr. Sherwin's request. In light of circumstances reviewed above I must object to the latter decision. This is to confirm my earlier verbal advice to you that Mr. Sherwin's request could be considered as part of a conspiracy to violate the bidding statutes regardless of the rationale utilized to throw out the bids if the prime motive was simply to get Mr. Manzo another shot at this contract. Action in accordance with that request could be a direct violation of those statutes. . . .

Biederman continued to fire off memos to Commissioner Kohl and Attorney General Kugler about the contract, which, as it turned out, eventually went to Centrum. Kugler finally replied with an interoffice memo to Biederman:

November 4, 1970
Re: Manzo Contracting Company
Neither the Director of Criminal Justice nor I feel there is any further action action [sic] required in the above matter.

GFK

But where the state had declined to act, Stern's office did not.

Goldstein told Stern about the case and prepared a memo outlining what Biederman had told him. Stern called Henry Peterson, the assistant attorney general in charge of the Justice Department's criminal division, and advised him of the pending investigation. He obtained personnel from the FBI. Then he set up an appointment with Kugler.

"The purpose of my meeting with Attorney General Kugler was severalfold," he later explained. ". . . to, number one, find out if these were real documents; number two, find out whether or not . . . the thing had already been explored; and, number three, to give notice in the event that the first two questions were answered in the positive and the negative, respectively, to give notice to the state that we were going to investigate."

Stern showed Kugler the documents Biederman had turned over. The attorney general leafed through them and noted—according to Stern—that "this was the only time they had any difficulty with Sherwin; that Garven [Pierre Garven, counsel to Governor Cahill] had stopped it." Kugler denied making such a statement.

Kugler also informed Stern about the conflict-of-interest charge against Biederman, but agreed with the federal prosecutor that "for whatever reasons or motives he may have had [Stern's] office had a duty to investigate the matter." Stern asked that Kugler hold off any further action, pending the federal investigation. Kugler said he'd think it over and let the U.S. attorney know.

Stern then went across town to the U.S. attorney's office in

Trenton's federal courthouse and conferred with his assistants there on other matters. He was lunching at his desk when Kugler called and said he'd discussed the matter with Governor Cahill. According to Stern, "it was their decision that I should go ahead alone."

Stern returned to Newark and immediately had Goldstein prepare a subpoena for the Manzo company's books and records. The first federal investigation of the Cahill administration was under way.

Meanwhile, on May 30, John Petrucci of Warren Limestone Company testified in a civil suit in Superior Court in Morristown, New Jersey. Manzo had brought the action to recover all or part of a $10,000 contribution Manzo had made to the state Republican party on behalf of a Manzo-Warren joint venture.

At one point, Judge Joseph Stamler took over the questioning: "Did you ever discuss this ten thousand dollars with him, Michael Manzo?"

"Yes, I did."

"Did he tell you to whom he had given the money?"

"He told me he had given it to a man in Monmouth County that was a state Republican—was on the State Republican Committee."

"Did Manzo tell you that it was given to this man in Monmouth County to secure the successful bid on a state job on Route forty-six?"

"He told me he gave it to him to have the job thrown out and he promised the man he would give the state anywhere between twenty-five and fifty thousand dollars if it was bid again."

The following day, Judge Stamler called the attorney general's office to report a possible bribe plot. He spoke with Evan Jahos, Kugler's director of criminal justice, who started a state investigation. Kugler did not inform Jahos of his promise to

Stern to leave a clear track for the federal inquiry, but instead took off for a European vacation. He later explained that he was not aware then that Jahos was investigating the same matter as Stern.

Within a few days, the federal and state investigators started stumbling over each other in their race for witnesses. Stern was upset when he learned of the state inquiry. He felt that Kugler had reneged on his promise.

On June 13, Jahos and two of his aides came to Stern's office to attempt to iron out their differences. It was agreed that the federal and state inquiries would proceed jointly and that the indictments, if any, would be announced simultaneously.

That moment came two weeks later, on June 28—the same day that Sherwin's Democratic predecessor, Robert Burkhardt, was sentenced. Stern and Kugler announced the indictments of Sherwin; Michael Manzo, 45; and William Loughran, 43, a GOP fund-raiser. The federal charge was a violation of the election laws; the state's, bribery. It was agreed that the state would prosecute first.

It was highly embarrassing for Governor Cahill, who had campaigned for office on a pledge to "root out the corruptors and the corrupted." After Sherwin's indictment, he said: "This administration has been since its beginning and is now being conducted on behalf of the citizens of New Jersey with absolute integrity and complete honesty.

"I personally have complete confidence in the integrity and honesty of Paul Sherwin and every cabinet member. I have known Paul Sherwin personally for fifteen years. I know his entire family. I know how he lives, what assets he possesses and the kind of man he is.

"Paul Sherwin's office and his reputation are at stake. Those of us who know him personally trust him; those who do not know him personally should withhold their judgment until all the facts are presented at what I hope will be the earliest possible trial date."

Sherwin took a leave of absence from his post, but he didn't drop out of sight—or politics. Within a few days of his indictment, Sherwin showed up at a GOP fund-raising dinner in Sea Girt with Cahill and Loughran. The governor brushed off questions with, "No, no, this [indictment] doesn't dampen our spirits in any way, because we are all convinced that Mr. Sherwin is innocent and that he did nothing wrong."

Sherwin continued to act like a politician who expected to be around for quite a while. At his federal arraignment, he said a friendly "Hi, Herb!" to the prosecutor and stuck out a politician's glad hand.

Stern refused to shake it. "Oh, no!" he said, "it's not like in the ring, Paul."

By midsummer, reports of Biederman's memos had leaked to the press and there were indications that, despite Cahill's call for a speedy trial, Kugler's office once again was sitting on its hands. Several state legislators called for an investigation of Kugler's handling of the case. To avert a legislative inquiry, on August 1, Kugler asked the State Commission of Investigation to look into the matter. A week later, professing his "deep concern about the possibility of an appearance of conflict of interest," he asked Chief Justice Joseph Weintraub to appoint a special prosecutor in the Sherwin case. Justice Weintraub named Matthew Boylan, a former assistant U.S. attorney who had successfully prosecuted "Tough Tony" Provenzano, a corrupt Teamster's Union official, and who had been named special prosecutor in a sensational murder case that was too hot for the elected officials to handle. Boylan set up shop in Stern's office while he prepared his prosecution.

The bribery trial opened on October 16 in Freehold, New Jersey, before Superior Court Judge Francis X. Crahay. After Boylan presented the evidence of Manzo's political payoff and

Sherwin's interference in the bidding procedure, Sherwin took the stand and professed his innocence.

"Did you ever agree to receive ten thousand dollars to the Republican party as a bribe?" asked his attorney, Adrian Foley.

"Positively not."

But the jury felt otherwise. It needed only four hours and fifteen minutes to find all three defendants guilty. Sherwin took the verdict stoically, but his wife wept and his daughter screamed out, "Daddy, you didn't do it!"

Sherwin and his cronies had been so confident of acquittal that they'd rented a hotel suite nearby and had laid in a stock of champagne for the victory celebration.

After the verdict, one of the defense team was heard to say: "Cancel it. Make it six bottles of Scotch."

Governor Cahill did not show up for the wake. Nor would he comment on the verdict. But Stern had a few words of interpretation: "By the verdict today, the citizens of this state have served a clear warning that they will not tolerate anyone, no matter how highly placed, no matter how powerful or well connected, manipulating public contracts for the benefit of their political party."

Sentencing came on November 22. Foley argued that Sherwin was "a decent, honest, deeply religious man" who "made a terrible mistake in judgment." Judge Crahay suggested that the political system should have been on trial as well. But he added that he could not escape the "hard fact" that the men were guilty. He sentenced Sherwin, Manzo and Loughran each to one to two years in prison and fined them $2000. All remained free without bail pending appeal.

On his way out of court, Sherwin was asked if he was through with politics.

Foley answered for his client: "How's that old song go? Nothing is forever."

After the verdict, the State Commission of Investigation got around to its inquiry into Kugler's conduct of the case. Its report came out the following February. "We find no reliable evidence whatever to reasonably justify a conclusion that Attorney General Kugler was derelict in his law enforcement obligations," the panel said. "We find nothing which reflects in any way on his integrity as a public official and, of equal importance, we find no basis for concluding that he engaged in an attempted 'cover-up' of a criminal activity of a fellow state officer."

The SCI's logic seemed as faulty as its grammar. Among those who apparently did not present "reliable evidence" were Stern, both Goldsteins and Biederman. Whenever a matter was disputed, the SCI accepted Kugler's word. The *New York Times* called the report "a whitewash"—and that was one of the milder editorial reactions. The *Trentonian*, for example, called it a "one-sided, occasionally malicious, political-oriented pseudo report."

Another dispute was brewing between the federal prosecutor and the state attorney general. It came to light a few days after the Kervick indictment, when an attorney for Trap Rock Industries asked the New Jersey Supreme Court to let the firm bid on state construction projects. Trap Rock had been barred from doing any state work because its president, Michael Stavola, had been convicted of trying to bribe a state trooper with $5000 to fix an assault charge.

In the course of his argument, the Trap Rock attorney pointed out that Frederick Harris, the engineering firm that had paid off in the Tonti and Kervick cases, was still doing business with the state—nearly $1 million worth since the Tonti indictment was filed a year before. He called it discrimination.

Kugler quickly stepped into the controversy, issuing a statement agreeing with the proposition. He said that contractors who paid off—even those that had cooperated with the federal government and had been given immunity—should be put on the state's blacklist.

To Stern, the issue was simple: "They're trying to destroy our witnesses"—and, indirectly, to coddle the corrupt officials. If contractors who depended on public business couldn't work for the state if they'd paid off, none of them would testify that they had.

As the prosecutor put it in a television interview:

> The fact of the matter is that my office has uncovered all the corruption that you're talking about. These cases that you're all speaking about have not been brought in the state system. . . . I think it ill-behooves the state thereafter to, in effect, put us out of business by putting our witnesses out of business. You must realize that just as we would try to protect a witness against physical reprisal, I think we have to try and protect them against economic reprisal. . . .
>
> In effect, what's happening is this: The federal government moves in and breaks up massive pockets of corruption. We implore the business community to help us. And they do. And then, for the state thereafter to kind of lay back [sic] and sit back and not prosecute initially, but then move against the witnesses which have helped us clean up the situation, I do find anomalous.

When the Atlantic City trial ended and the prosecutor's personnel were released for other duties, the office launched *two* simultaneous "blockbuster" investigations—the first into Republican Bergen County; the second into Democratic Mercer County, which includes the state capital of Trenton.

But both probes were pushed onto a back burner a few days after they started, while Stern was plunged into a new dispute with Attorney General Kugler—and a new investigation of the Cahill administration.

In early March Stern received a call from Lewis Kaden, "an attorney whom I had never heard of before." Kaden said he represented a state trooper who had information he wanted to divulge. "He didn't tell me the name of the trooper or the information that he had," Stern says. Since the trooper was still on duty, he couldn't come during normal business hours. Stern set up an appointment for 4:30 P.M., March 19.

"Unfortunately," he continues, "after I had set up the appointment, the Third Circuit notified my office that the argument in the Ivanov case was going to be held March 20 in Philadelphia and that it would be the first case on the calendar. Since I had been delegated the responsibility of personally arguing that case by the Department of Justice and since it was one of the most important appeals, I realized I would have to stay overnight in Philadelphia." *

So Kaden and the trooper, Detective James Challender, met with Bruce Goldstein and another assistant, Thomas Greelish. Challender said he had been working in the state police's intelligence unit on an investigation into irregularities in Governor Cahill's 1969 campaign funding. But when he started pressing too hard, his superiors transferred him to duty on the New Jersey Turnpike.

Challender's documentation included evidence that corporations had channeled contributions to Cahill's campaign and had written off the cost as "business expenses." Some $100,000 had been converted into cash at the Garden State racetrack.

---

* The case involved a Soviet spy, Igor Ivanov, who had been arrested in 1963 and successfully prosecuted long before Stern came to the Justice Department. In 1969, the Supreme Court, reserving a final ruling, referred the case back to the lower courts for further argument on whether the government has the right to "bug" suspected foreign agents without a court order.

The president and general manager of the track was Joseph H. McCrane, Jr., a lineman on the famous West Point football team that included Glenn Davis and "Doc" Blanchard. Until a few months before, he had been Cahill's state treasurer.

The next day, Goldstein relayed the charges to his boss. "We convened a grand jury and started an investigation," Stern says.

Within a few weeks, word of the inquiry leaked to the press and proved highly embarrassing to Governor Cahill, then in the midst of a reelection campaign. Attorney General Kugler quickly denied that there was any attempt at a cover-up by the state:

> For many months there has been an ongoing investigation by both Federal and State law enforcement authorities into the 1969 gubernatorial fund raising campaign. Federal and State authorities have kept in close contact with one another in connection with this investigation.
>
> There is absolutely no truth to the recently published rumor that any state trooper investigator was removed from this investigation because of a desire to stop the probe. Further, there is absolutely no truth to the published stories that the investigation by the federal officials. was started as a result of a disgruntled state trooper.
>
> As the chief law enforcement officer in New Jersey, I can assure the public that the vicious rumors circulated to the media are unfounded. I now call upon the chief federal law enforcement officer in New Jersey, the United States Attorney Herbert Stern, to issue a statement indicating that these rumors are unfounded and that Federal and State authorities have been cooperating in this investigation.

Stern accepted the challenge, telephoning his statement to the press room at the state capital:

It is against the usual practice of this office to issue any statements concerning grand jury investigations, and this practice should not vary.

However, in light of the demand which has been made upon me by Attorney General George F. Kugler, Jr., I will confirm the existence of the investigation conducted by the United States Grand Jury.

I will also confirm that on Monday evening, March 19, 1973, a state law enforcement officer, accompanied by his attorney, came to my office and met with one of my assistants. He requested that my office conduct an investigation into certain campaign financing practices which allegedly had taken place during the 1969 gubernatorial campaign.

While it would be obviously inappropriate to reveal the substance of his information or the corroboration which he and his attorney brought with them, I can state that this was the first knowledge which had come to the United States Attorney's office concerning these allegations.

I immediately instructed my office to commence a grand jury investigation. . . .

Kugler returned to the attack the following day, telling a capital press conference that he was "literally shocked" by Stern's statement: "For reasons best known to himself—and this is the political season and, some may speculate, the reason for it, I will not—he made it appear in his release of yesterday that he started the investigation as far as the federal authorities were concerned as a result of the complaint of a state investigator. This is simply not accurate."

Kugler said he had spoken with the IRS district director, Elmer Klinsman, who confirmed a joint IRS–state police investigation since June, 1972. He added that departmental charges were "under consideration"—against Detective Challender for going to the feds.

Stern replied in another statement:

It is distressing to note that whenever this office commences an investigation into wrongdoing by public officials, it immediately comes under political attack. This has been repeated, commencing with the Addonizio case, the Hudson County case, the Atlantic City and County cases, the Tonti case and the recent investigation launched in Bergen County.

As recently as one year ago, Mr. Biederman came to my office with a complaint that state crimes committed by high public officials were not being investigated. When I began to investigate, the matter was swiftly culminated in an indictment and subsequent conviction. While I can recognize that this was politically embarrassing in a "political season," this office proceeded without regard to person, party or position.

The situation is no different today. If it were true, as suggested by Mr. Kugler, that the federal government has long been investigating the allegations into certain campaign funding practices of the 1969 gubernatorial campaign, then obviously there would have been no need for Detective Challender to have come to this office with his attorney and to make a complaint which was so strikingly similar to the complaint which David Biederman made just one year ago. . . .

As for Mr. Kugler's "shock" and "amazement" that I would not know of some joint state and Internal Revenue Service investigation, which he claims Mr. Klinsman "freely confirmed"; I can only respond that I was present in the room when Mr. Kugler had a telephone conversation with Mr. Klinsman, asked him to confirm that there had been such a joint investigation, and was told by Mr. Klinsman that he would not confirm any such thing.

In this regard I would like to categorically state that there has been no joint on-going state and Internal Revenue Service investigation in this matter.

Twice now in public statements Mr. Kugler has made reference to the "political season." I can understand why Mr. Kugler would be concerned about that. I, however, have been a professional law enforcement officer for more than eleven continuous years. I have never represented a private client. I have never made a political speech. I have never taken part in a political campaign. I have never been in a political clubhouse in this state in my life.

Perhaps that is why this office is and shall continue to be totally unconcerned with political seasons.

The following day, he issued his final statement on the subject:

Law enforcement is not served by a continuous debate in the press.

One simple fact remains: *Everyone* is talking about possible violations of law which occurred in 1969, and yet, as of today, in 1973, *no one* has done any thorough or complete investigation.

We are going to do one, based on Detective Challender's complaint to this office just three weeks ago and we are going to do it in the Grand Jury, not the newspapers. . . .

McCrane, vacationing in the Caribbean, evaded the grand jury's summons for several weeks. He finally returned, suntanned but silent, invoking the Fifth Amendment to Stern's questions. Meanwhile, the panel had indicted a Bergen County businessman, William Preis, for lying when he told the grand jury that a $5000 contribution to Governor Cahill's 1969 campaign was a business expense. The indictment charged that McCrane had engineered the plot to evade payment of federal taxes.

But Kugler managed to beat Stern to the big blow. On May 19, his office indicted McCrane and two other prominent state Republicans—William Colsey and Bruce Mahon—on an unrelated charge. McCrane was accused of using "the power and influence of his office" to have more than $6 million in state funds illegally deposited in three New Jersey banks and then have the banks, in turn, join with the State Division of Investment to purchase more than $6 million in securities through McCrane's brother, Kevin, a Manhattan stockbroker.

The day before, however, Stern's investigation had taken a startling turn.

Preis, a vice president of the Grand Union supermarket chain, pleaded guilty to the perjury charge. Through his lawyer, Donald Robinson, he told the court that he'd lied because "he had earlier been subjected to and was continuing under unusual pressure by a person occupying great prominence, power and prestige in the community." Although Robinson declined to name him, he was quickly identified as Lacey's old enemy and Stern's onetime rival, Nelson Gross.

As chairman of the Bergen County GOP, in 1969 Gross swung his weight behind Congressman William Cahill and thus secured the gubernatorial nomination for him. He went on to become GOP state chairman and the party's candidate for senator in 1970. After his defeat by Harrison Williams, he was named special assistant for narcotics to Secretary of State William G. Rogers. In 1973 he returned to practice law in Bergen County.

Preis cooperated with the grand jury, which, a week later, handed up an indictment against Gross. The former GOP leader was accused of masterminding a conspiracy to defraud the United States by having contributions to Cahill's campaign written off as business expenses. The contributions were channeled through a Camden public-relations firm connected with

McCrane, Writers Associates, Inc. McCrane was named as a coconspirator. Gross was also charged with perjury and obstruction of justice in the Preis case.

Two days later, the other shoe fell: McCrane was hit with a similar charge. And several companies faced criminal indictments for making the payments.

The indictments came two weeks before the New Jersey gubernatorial primary, June 5. Originally, Cahill had seemed a shoo-in, so much so that no first-rate Democrat had entered the lists against him. But as the scent of scandal developed, the Democratic leaders persuaded Superior Court Judge Brendan Byrne to resign from the bench and make the race; Byrne is a former prosecutor who had been described in the DeCarlo tapes as "a man who can't be bought." Although he steered clear of stating a program, with his aura of sanctity, Byrne walked away with the nomination.

On the Republican side, Governor Cahill was challenged, as he had been four years before, by Charles Sandman, Jr., the ultraconservative congressman from Cape May. Sandman also made corruption his major issue, promising that if elected he'd appoint Byrne as special prosecutor to root it out. In a stunning upset, Sandman won nearly 60 percent of the vote. Herbert Stern had brought down the Cahill administration!

13
A
PROSECUTOR'S
PHILOSOPHY

A prosecutor has little opportunity to state his views in his natural forum—the courtroom. There he's concerned with law and evidence, not social questions. But Herbert Stern, like Lacey before him, has not remained silent on the issues of the day. Although the Hatch Act bars him from discussing partisan politics and propriety prohibits his disputing his superiors in Justice or the Nixon administration, he has not hesitated to speak out on matters affecting his office. He hits the "rubber-chicken circuit" about once a week and boasts that he's always "in" to the press—without the buffer of a press secretary.

What follows is a prosecutor's philosophy, a compendium of Stern's views, compiled and edited from his speeches; his radio, television and published interviews; and from his comments to the author.

On Crime

Crime is the most flourishing and lucrative business in America.

If the financial services were to include the statistics on crime in their surveys, one would find that it is not electronics or motors or banking or oil which plays the heaviest role in the economics of our country; it is crime that does.

I speak now not only of the crime in the streets, the burglaries and the robberies, which represent tens of billions of dollars each year: I speak of the crime which we call "white collar," the crimes committed by the advantaged, not the disadvantaged, the crimes committed with pen and pencil, not with gun or "jimmy," under the bright lights of executive offices, not by stealth in the dark.

Crime in our society is not the exclusive province of the burglar and the robber. Indeed, in terms of criminal economics, they may be the lesser menace. We can insure ourselves against the theft of our cars, but how can be insure the integrity of our banking officials and our business leaders, and what insurance will redeem our society if we continue to systematically corrupt the people who lead us in government?

But perhaps the dearest price of all we pay is with the young people of our country.

As they grow and mature, they gradually discover that the moral code which they have been taught is itself dishonored by those who taught it to them; they also find that the law is violated by those who make and administer it.

When they see men in high public office, men in responsible corporate positions, men with tremendous professional standing violate the law while they, the young, are told by those very same men that the law must be obeyed, they feel betrayed and they rebel against a system which they believe has played them false.

On Corruption

We are not going to be able to eliminate all crime from any walk of life, whether it's the banking field, or the legal field, or the field of public service. And anybody who would proclaim that they're going to be able to accomplish that is either a liar or a fool.

I suppose that there will always be at least the prospect of dishonesty in government as long as there isn't a real fear of apprehension. I do think this state has had serious problems and part of it has been the climate, the feeling of lassitude and do-nothing, a feeling that you could do it and get away with it.

I think that's been materially changed over these past three years. I think today, in the public at large and particularly in officialdom, I think there's a real understanding there's an awfully good chance that if you do it, you're going to get caught; and an even better chance that if you do, you're going to go to jail.

266 / TIGER IN THE COURT

On the Role of a Prosecutor

In my view, a prosecuting attorney has only one question he can legitimately ask: Has there been a violation of the law? If there's a violation of the law, he should prosecute. Our business is not to set the guilty free; our business is not to weed out the laws and statutes of the United States Congress.

No one has given me the right to disregard the acts of Congress, to say which are good laws and which are bad laws. If Congress doesn't want to have those acts, they can repeal them, and I'll stop prosecuting them.

Until that time, it would be the height of arrogance—indeed, I think it would be unconstitutional behavior, indeed, in derogation of my oath of office—to rule by my own fiat.

I don't think it's proper to harass people, any people, merely because somebody has decided that they are undesirable. I haven't got the right to make the decision in this office that A, B or C are undesirable people and that I'm going to harass them until they leave my jurisdiction. That isn't my function. I am supposed to work until I get enough evidence to get an indictment to try them. And if I'm frustrated by it, I'm supposed to work a little harder at it.

On Prosecution and Politics

I will proceed against anybody, regardless of position, power or influence, if he's violated the laws of the United States. And we don't regard political questions in terms of elections, any more than we regard whether the individual is a Republican, Democrat or independent.

I have been a professional law-enforcement officer for more than eleven continuous years. I have never represented a private client. I have never made a political speech. I have never taken part in a political campaign. I have never been in a political clubhouse in this state in my life. Perhaps that is why this office is and shall continue to be totally unconcerned with political seasons.

There is no attempt by this office to influence elections. Once we have enough evidence to indict, we indict. If that period comes shortly before an election, then it comes shortly before an election.

Actually, if we had refrained from indicting because there was an election coming up, that would be a political decision. Then we would be acting out of regard for an election and I'm sure the critics would then have said, "Aha! Stern wanted to hide from the public the fact that he had enough for an indictment until after this fellow ran and was reelected."

Really, we're damned if we do and damned if we don't.

On Political Financing

Private funding of political campaigns, it seems to me, has great potentiality for abuse on almost every level.

The most obvious point about it is it violates the spirit of one-man, one-vote. In the majority of cases, people make large contributions because they expect something in return. When consideration is given to such a large contributor, no matter how slight, it really undercuts not just the theory, but the very principles of our republic. So on that level I think private funding is an evil.

It is also an evil because the system—as has been demonstrated in so many of these cases—degenerates to the point where a public official who begins to collect money for his party, pretty soon begins to collect money for himself. All too frequently, he becomes a partner with his party and it becomes "one-for-the-party and one-for-me"—and sometimes "one-for-the-party and two- or three-for-me."

I think we really ought to give serious consideration as to whether the funding of political campaigns is not a public expense. In the end, whether it's publicly funded or privately funded, the public pays for it anyway. I think they pay more under the private system—not just in terms of honesty in government, but in dollars and cents.

On Narcotics

I have to believe that no subject has been given as much prominence or publicity as the problem of drug abuse. I am forced to believe that the majority of our youngsters, whether they reside in ghettos or suburbia, know that the Establishment, their elders and their parents say that the use of narcotics does yield irreparable physical, mental and psychological damage.

It is equally plain, at least to me, that all of this has been heard, but they simply refuse to believe us. A tremendous chasm has developed between the adult and high-school generations. I sense a feeling of distrust which the young have developed towards us, towards our establishment, towards what we say to them, based at least in part on their feeling that we have been corrupting and abiding by the corruption of the society which we, ourselves, have represented to them as being pure and clean.

The young are not blind to the world around them. When they see their parents participate in illegal gambling, union corruption, political corruption, and outright bribery, from $10 for fixing a ticket to $100,000 to obtain a variance or rezoning, they naturally rebel when these same parents tell them to obey other laws.

If we want to be believed, we must establish our credibility with the young, not by lectures and sermons, but by concrete action of adults who seek a society free from all corruption, not just the corruption of drugs.

On Locking up Pushers and Throwing Away the Key

I have no brief for the nonaddict who sells hard drugs like heroin. I think these people are vermin. I really cannot call up any sympathy for them. But I think a dialogue that focuses on penalty and penalty alone is not the most useful one.

There has to be a severe enough sentence so that others will be deterred. But the most critical moment is before the man commits the crime, in persuading him that there is a substantial likelihood that he will be detected and apprehended. It doesn't matter much what you threaten people with, if you can't persuade them that you're able to deliver. That's the critical area.

If life imprisonment is what the law provides, that doesn't trouble me. But I am concerned that we do not lose track of the fact that just by increasing the penalty we think we're somehow accomplishing something meaningful in the way of deterrence. We're concentrating on the least critical factor. We will not do the job unless we focus on sharpening our techniques for catching these bums to begin with.

On Marijuana

If we could get some kind of guidance from the medical and scientific community, we would have a better idea of which way to go on it. They cannot to this day give us any kind of opinion, in either direction, as to whether or not marijuana is or is not harmful to one either physically and psychologically. The law has no business prohibiting something which is not harmful to one's self or somebody else.

On Wiretapping

To date, my office has never applied for a wiretap. None of the cases that we've discussed involved any wiretapping. We didn't make a single one of them with wiretapping. They were books-and-records cases, made with accountants.

That is not to say I wouldn't make an application, but we haven't had the necessity to do it.

Where you do need it, where it is indispensable, is in the gambling operations. Unless you just want to be satisfied with picking up street runners, the lesser likes who are just collecting, who tend to be poor and insignificant in terms of criminal activity, while letting the higher-ups go free, you have to use eavesdropping.

The very way that a criminal syndicate runs a gambling operation is with the telephone. It is not only the instrumentality of the crime, it is the *sine qua non* of the crime.

On Capital Punishment

I myself do not like to see life taken by government. I don't think it's an especially fine example or one calculated to instill a respect or reverence for human life.

But I am confronted by the situation and by the thought that there are times I could think of where the man's crime is so heinous, so terrible, that people might feel that the only proper, the only just, the only thing that would satisfy their sense of fitness would be the imposition of capital punishment. For example, what would you do with Heinrich Himmler if we had caught him?

I think on balance I'm against capital punishment except where deliberate, premeditated murder is committed by one who has already received the maximum sentence of life imprisonment. And I do think that there ought to be a way to recognize in the law that when a man reached a status of horrors, as Himmler, that there ought to be some way we can do something about that.

On Plea Bargaining

We never indulge in the kind of plea bargaining in which we sit down and promise what the sentence will be, or even discuss it. We won't do it. We will accept a plea only if the scope of punishment afforded under the plea is adequate to meet the crime. But we will never bind the judge's hands in advance.

There's one exception to that rule and that's, of course, if somebody cooperates with the government after he pleads guilty, we'll bring that to the attention of the judge.

On Reportorial Immunity

That's never been a problem to me, because, frankly, newsmen are beating down my door. They want to give me information. In all my years in the business, I've never had to subpoena a newsman.

As a matter of personal taste and speaking for myself alone, I do believe that we ought to encourage the First Amendment right of access to information of the media. And I think that where there is a confidentiality of relationship, I would be opposed to unclothing that as a usual matter of course.

On the ACLU

I'm glad to see that there are people like those in the ACLU who present their views. They are a useful and maybe indispensable watchdog, and within our system perform a very vital function. And I'm not just bestowing an accolade. I mean it. That's a fine thing to have. Now I sometimes grind my teeth that they win and I lose, but I can't lose sight of the fact that the institution is a valuable one, that the service being performed is a necessary one.

On Gambling

[*A proposal was before the New Jersey legislature to legalize casino gambling in Atlantic City.*]

It seems clear to me that the legalization of gambling casinos in Atlantic City would amount to an open invitation to the same underworld interests to do in Atlantic City what they have done in Las Vegas, commencing with Bugsy Siegel in the 1940s.

I do not believe that, in the long run, whatever the monetary "take" to the state may be from its gambling tables, it is going to equal the costs in terms of increased vice, increased ancillary unlawful gambling, increased loan-sharking, car thefts and prostitution.

Measured in terms of money alone, the increased costs of law enforcement would substantially reduce the monetary profit of such gambling. Measured in terms of social policy, the obvious increase in social disorder, attendant to such legalized gambling, it seems to me, makes the establishing of large-scale casino gambling in Atlantic City a most dangerous and imprudent step.

On Ecology

"Ecology" and "environmental concern" have become household words. And yet, their meaning seems lost in rhetoric. The rhetoric must end and we must come to grips with the fact that unless pollution is checked now, our country's water and air will become lost treasures. It is far easier to enshrine these treasures while we have them in our custody than to make the almost impossible attempt to recover them once they are lost. This may well be our last chance to save our precious resources.

On "the System"

I have no patience with those who would change our institutions by force, by shouts or by abject withdrawal. Despite the difficulties in trying to operate within the system, it's impossible to do anything useful if you don't. I'm convinced there's nothing standing in the way of anybody who actually wants to make a change, providing one is willing to work at it.

It isn't the system that's permissive. There's nothing wrong with it. But I see something wrong with people—not just the people who administer the system, but those who tolerate its corruption. We don't have to burn down our courts—all we have to do is use them effectively.

[*He ticks off the indictments and convictions his office has obtained.*]

When you can do that *within* the system, to what purpose do you chuck the system out?

On the Future

I think we'll keep on doing the same kind of investigations. And if we uncover evidence, we'll bring indictments. And if we're right, we'll get convictions. I cannot prophesy what a given public official is going to do in the future. All I can tell you is, my office is going to keep on doing the same thing it's been doing.

APPENDIX HERBERT STERN'S WHO'S WHO OF NEW JERSEY POLITICS

As of June 15, 1973, the following federal, state and local public officials and political leaders had been indicted or prosecuted by federal authorities in New Jersey since Frederick B. Lacey became U.S. attorney on September 3, 1969. (The office listed is that held at the time of indictment.)

Official	Charge	Result
Colonial Case		
1. Walter Zirpolo mayor, Woodbridge Township	conspiracy & bribery —$110,000 from Colonial Pipeline Co.	severed from trial for illness; subsequently convicted (Kiernan), but mistrial declared
2. Robert Jacks council president, Woodbridge Township	"	Convicted (Stern), reversed, reindicted

Zirpolo and Jacks subsequently pleaded guilty to identical charges in state court; 2 to 6 years each |
3. Stanley J. Polack judge, Passaic County Court	IRS	convicted (Lacey); $10,000 fine
Newark Case		
4. Hugh J. Addonizio mayor, Newark	conspiracy & extortion —$253,000+ from various contractors; IRS	convicted (Lacey & Stern); 10 years, $25,000 fine
5. Philip Gordon corporation counsel, Newark	"	convicted (Lacey & Stern); 3 years

Official	Charge	Result
6. Anthony LaMorte former director of public works, Newark	conspiracy & extortion —$253,000+ from various contractors; IRS	convicted (Lacey & Stern); 10 years
7. James Callahan councilman, Newark	"	pleaded guilty to IRS; 1 year
8. Frank Addonizio councilman, Newark	"	awaiting trial
9. Lee Bernstein councilman, Newark	"	awaiting trial
10. Anthony Guiliano judge, Newark municipal court, former councilman, Newark	"	pleaded guilty to conflict-of-interest in state court; died before trial
11. Benjamin Khrush director of public works, Newark	"	awaiting trial
12. Norman Schiff former corporation counsel, Newark	"	awaiting trial

Official	Charge	Result
13. Irvine Turner councilman, Newark	conspiracy & extortion —$253,000+ from various contractors; IRS	too ill to stand trial
14. Calvin West councilman, Newark	"	awaiting trial

Hudson County Case

Official	Charge	Result
15. John V. Kenny "Boss" of Hudson County; former mayor, Jersey City; former Democratic chairman, Hudson County	conspiracy, bribery & extortion—$182,000+ from various contractors; IRS	severed from conspiracy trial for illness; pleaded guilty to IRS; 18 months, paroled after 10 months for ill health
16. Thomas Whelan mayor, Jersey City	"	convicted (Stern); 15 years; pleaded guilty to IRS; 5-year concurrent sentence
17. Thomas Flaherty council president, Jersey City	"	convicted (Stern); 15 years; pleaded guilty to IRS; 5-year concurrent sentence
18. Bernard Murphy purchasing agent, Jersey City	" (except IRS)	convicted (Stern); 15 years

Official	Charge	Result
19. William A. Sternkopf, Jr. commissioner, Port of New York Authority	conspiracy, bribery & extortion—$182,000+ from various contractors	convicted (Stern); 10 years
20. Fred J. Kropke police chief, Hudson County	"	convicted (Stern); 5 years
21. Joseph P. Stapleton treasurer, Hudson County	"	convicted (Stern); 2 years
22. Philip Kunz business administrator, Jersey City	"	convicted (Stern); 2 years
23. Walter Wolfe freeholder, Hudson County; Democratic chairman, Hudson County	"	convicted (Stern); 5 years suspended sentence
24. James R. Corrado secretary, Pollak Hospital, Hudson County	"	pleaded guilty; 5 years suspended sentence (assisted prosecution)
25. Frank Manning county engineer, Hudson County	"	given immunity, testified for prosecution

Official	Charge	Result
26. John J. Kenny former freeholder, Hudson County; former Democratic chairman, Hudson County	conspiracy, bribery & extortion—$182,000+ from various contractors	given immunity, testified for prosecution subsequently convicted of bribery in state court; 6 years

Kearny Post Office Case (Strike Force)

(15) John V. Kenny	conspiracy & extortion —$400,000 from Kearny Associates	awaiting trial
27. Angelo Sarubbi mayor, North Bergen	”	awaiting trial
28. Robert Burkhardt former secretary of state	conspiracy & bribery —$30,000 from J. Rich Steers Construction; perjury	pleaded guilty; 3 years suspended sentence; $5000 fine
29. Willard B. Knowlton former state senator	a. IRS b. conspiracy, bribery & extortion— $106,000 from J. Rich Steers Construction	a. acquitted (Branch) b. awaiting trial
30. D. Louis Tonti former executive director, New Jersey Highway Authority	conspiracy, bribery & exortion—$200,000 from various contractors	pleaded guilty; 3 years, $10,000 fine

Official	Charge	Result
31. Philip May chief engineer, New Jersey Highway Authority	conspiracy, bribery & extortion—$200,000 from various contractors	awaiting trial
32. John A. Kervick former state treasurer	conspiracy & bribery —$113,000 from Frederick Harris engineering	pleaded guilty, awaiting sentence
33. Cornelius Gallagher U.S. congressman	conspiracy, perjury & IRS	pleaded guilty to IRS; 2 years, $10,000 fine
34. Peter Moraites assemblyman, former assem- bly speaker	a. banking law b. securities law	a. pleaded guilty; 16 months b. awaiting trial
35. Walter H. Jones commissioner, Port of New York Authority	"	awaiting trial

Atlantic County Case

36. Patrick J. Doran county engineer, Atlantic County	conspiracy, bribery & extortion—$126,000+ from various contractors	convicted (J. Goldstein); 5 years
37. Francis J. Southard employee, Highway Department, Atlantic County	"	pleaded guilty; awaiting sentence

Official	Charge	Result
Atlantic City Case		
38. William T. Somers mayor, Atlantic City	conspiracy, bribery & extortion—$28,000+ from various contractors	convicted (J. Goldstein); 2½ years
39. Richard S. Jackson executive director, Atlantic City Expressway Authority; former mayor, Atlantic City	"	pleaded guilty; 3 years
40. Arthur W. Ponzio director of public works, Atlantic City	"	convicted (J. Goldstein); 6 years
41. Karlos R. LaSane director, Parks & Public Property, Atlantic City	"	convicted (J. Goldstein); 4 years
42. Robert Glass supervisor, Airports, Parks & Public Property, Atlantic City	"	pleaded guilty; 2 years
43. Germaine Fisher secretary to Ponzio	"	convicted (J. Goldstein); 2 years suspended

Official	Charge	Result
44. Florence Clark assistant pur- chasing agent, Atlantic City	conspiracy, bribery & extortion—$28,000+ from various contractors	pleaded guilty; 2 years
45. Paul Sherwin secretary of state	extortion & election law—$10,000 from Manzo construction	convicted on identical charge in state court, 1 to 2 years
46. Nelson Gross former Republi- can state chairman; Republican Senate candi- date, 1970; former special assistant to the U.S. secretary of state	conspiracy to defraud the U.S., perjury, obstruction of Justice	awaiting trial
47. Joseph M. McCrane Jr. former state treasurer	conspiracy to defraud the U.S.	awaiting trial

Gloucester Township Case

48. John DeRose former mayor, Gloucester Township	a. conspiracy & bribery—$7500 from Thruway Equipment Co. b. conspiracy & bribery—$6000 from various builders c. conspiracy & bribery—$50,000 from various builders	pleaded guilty, awaiting sentence

Official	Charge	Result
49. Joseph Menna former mayor, Gloucester Township	a. conspiracy & bribery—$7500 from Thruway Equipment Co. b. conspiracy & bribery—$6000 from various builders c. conspiracy & bribery—$50,000 from various builders	pleaded nolo contendere; 5 years' probation
50. James Kooistra committeeman, Gloucester Township	" a & b	a. hung jury (Finnegan); acquitted (Tanner) b. acquitted (Finnegan)
51. Donald Mitchell committeeman, Gloucester Township	" a, b & c	a. hung jury (Finnegan); acquitted (Tanner) b. convicted (Finnegan); 1 year c. awaiting trial
52. Joseph Reichart supervisor of roads, Gloucester Township	" a & c	a. hung jury (Finnegan); acquitted (Tanner) c. acquitted (Finnegan)
53. Martin Barrett former member, planning board, Gloucester Township	" c	pleaded guilty; awaiting sentence

Official	Charge	Result
54. Carmen DiLeo member, planning board, Gloucester Township	c. conspiracy & bribery—$50,000 from various builders	pleaded guilty, awaiting sentence
55. Anthony Vittetta former chairman, Utilities Authority, Gloucester Township	" c	acquitted (Finnegan)
56. Daniel Connelly former member, Utilities Authority, Gloucester Township	" c	acquitted (Finnegan)
57. John Giordano former member, Utilities Authority, Gloucester Township	" c	acquitted (Finnegan)
58. D. Vincent Lazzaro former freeholder, Camden County	c. conspiracy & bribery—$50,000 from various builders	acquitted (Finnegan)
59. Edward Carey former freeholder, Camden County	a. conspiracy & bribery—$7500 from Thruway Equipment Co.	hung jury (Finnegan); acquitted (Tanner)

Official	Charge	Result
60. Robert Benson former Democratic committee-man, Camden County	b. conspiracy & bribery—$6000 from various builders & c	b. acquitted (Finnegan) c. acquitted (Finnegan)
61. Edward McDermott tax collector, Fort Lee	IRS	pleaded guilty; awaiting sentence
62. Patrick Parenty former super-intendent, Monmouth Regional High School	conspiracy and bank fraud	pleaded guilty; 2 months, 1-year suspended sentence
63. Martin J. Queenan former prosecutor, Burlington County	IRS	pleaded guilty; 1 year's probation
64. Gotthold Rose mayor, Garfield	bank fraud	awaiting trial
65. Albert Smith manager, General Services Administration store, Federal Building, Newark	fraud	awaiting trial

Official	Charge	Result
66. George J. Sokalski freeholder, Passaic County	conspiracy, FHA fraud	awaiting trial
67. Louis M. Turco council president, Newark	IRS	awaiting trial
68. Martin Tuman former assistant U.S. attorney	IRS	awaiting trial
69. Victor Woodhull director, Morris County freeholders; former mayor, Morristown	IRS	pleaded guilty; 60 days

Union City Board of Ed. Case

70. Patrick Musto president, Board of Education, Union City	conspiracy & extortion —unknown amounts from various contractors	convicted (Brooks); 2½ years, $20,000 fine
71. Joseph D. Lugosch member, Board of Education, Union City	"	convicted (Brooks); 2½ years, $20,000 fine
72. John Powers member, Board of Education, Union City	"	acquitted (Brooks)
73. Nathan Schattell member, Board of Education, Union City	"	too ill to stand trial

Official	Charge	Result
74. Percy Holtje member, Board of Education, Union City	conspiracy & extortion —unknown amounts from various contractors	too ill to stand trial
75. Theodore Bednarz chief appraiser, Federal Housing Agency, Newark	conspiracy, FHA fraud	pleaded guilty; 8 years
76. Peter DelGrande director of recreation, Camden	conspiracy & bribery —$23,000 from Playground Corp. of America	acquitted (Klepp)
77. James DelMauro former chief judge, Newark municipal court	IRS	awaiting trial
78. Francis Kelly former assistant chief, Bureau of Navigation, State Department of Environmental Protection	IRS	pleaded guilty; awaiting sentence
79. Rudolph Kuchta postmaster, Linden	bribery	pleaded guilty; 2-year suspended sentence, $3000 fine

NOTES This is not an authorized account. Although I had the cooperation of Judge Frederick B. Lacey and Herbert J. Stern, there were some things they could not tell me for reasons of security or legal ethics, and other things they would not tell me for reasons of policy or politics. In some instances, I came to conclusions directly opposite to what they said. The opinions expressed are mine, not theirs—and certainly not those of the Department of Justice.

The U.S. attorney's office provided transcripts of the trials. I have not hesitated to repunctuate or reparagraph the texts to my style or to correct obvious typographical or transcribing errors. The office also supplied the texts of Lacey's and Stern's speeches.

I have cited only those cases which were reported—and thus available in most law libraries. The transcripts are on file at the appropriate courts. Newspaper references are too numerous to cite and most Jersey papers can be found only in local libraries. Suffice to say, *New York Times,* Sept. 3, 1969 passim.

In addition to U.S. Attorney Herbert J. Stern, Judge Frederick B. Lacey, Senator Clifford Case and their aides, I would like to thank Robert Aronson, Judge George H. Barlow, John Bartels, Harold Borg, John M. Burns III, Bernard Hellring, John Noonan, Donald Robinson and Patrick Wall for their assistance. Again, my thanks to Congressman Edward I. Koch for his speedy procurement of government documents.

1. The Congressman Cops Out

For other glimpses of Stern, see my "Straight Man in a Crooked World," *True,* September, 1971; Jerome Wilson, "He Threw the Rascals Out," *New York,* Oct. 2, 1972; Dennis Stern, "N.J. Crime-Fighter Makes a Federal Case of It," *Juris Doctor,* April, 1972.

2. The Making of a Prosecutor

For a brief appraisal of Hogan's office, see my "Is It Time for Hogan to Step Down?" *New York,* Dec. 6, 1971. For

Stern's role in the Malcolm X case, see Peter Goldman, *The Life and Death of Malcolm X* (1973).

3. Introduction to Justice . . . and Jersey

For background on Organized Crime, see Victor Navasky, *Kennedy Justice* (1971).

U.S. v. *Zirpolo,* 288 F. Supp. 993 (1968); 450 F.2d 424 (1971); 334 F. Supp. 756 (1971). For another account of the case, see Morton Mintz, "A Colonial Heritage" in Richard L. Heilbroner et al., *In the Name of Profit* (1972).

U.S. v. *Weber,* 437 F.2d 327 (1970); *cert. denied* 402 U.S. 932 (1971).

4. A New Team Takes Over

For another account of Lacey's first days in office, see Fred J. Cook, "The People v. the Mob; or, Who Rules New Jersey?" *New York Times Magazine,* Feb. 1, 1970.

The caseload figures are from U.S. Department of Justice, *United States Attorneys' Offices Statistical Report, Fiscal Year 1971.*

U.S. v. *Polack,* 442 F.2d 446 (1971); *cert. denied* 403 U.S. 931 (1971).

5. A Tale of Two Tapes

The DeCavalcante tapes are excerpted in Henry A. Zieger, *Sam the Plumber* (1970). A volume on the DeCarlo tapes is in preparation.

Rarick's speech is at 116 *Cong. Rec.* H1030 (1970). For another account of the incident, see Fred J. Cook, "New Jersey: State of the Mafia," *Nation,* May 11, 1970.

U.S. v. *DeCarlo,* 397 U.S. 1032 (1970); 445 F.2d 911 (1971) withdrawn by order of court; 458 F.2d 358 (1972).

U.S. v. *DeCavalcante,* 440 F.2d 1264 (1971).

U.S. v. *DeCavalcante,* 449 F.2d 139 (1971); *cert. denied* 404 U.S. 1039 (1972).

6. The Unmaking of Mayor Addonizio
New Jersey, Governor's Select Commission on Civil Disorder, *Report for Action* (1968).

In re Addonizio, 53 N.J. 107 (1969).

U.S. v. *Addonizio,* 313 F. Supp. 486 (1970); 449 F.2d 100 (1971); 451 F.2d (1971); *cert. denied* 405 U.S. 936 (1972). For another account of the case, see John Reddy, "Comeuppance for Newark's Unholy Alliance," *Reader's Digest,* January, 1971.

7. Memoirs of Hudson County
For background on Jersey City, see Thomas J. Fleming, "'I am the Law," *American Heritage,* June, 1969.

U.S. v. *Kenny,* 462 F.2d 1205 (1972); *cert. denied* 409 U.S. 914 (1972).

8. The Senator Advises, The President Consents
Senator Case's office provided copies of his statements.

9. Sons of Hudson County
For background on Gallagher, see "The Congressman and the Hoodlum" and "The Congressman and the Salad Oil Swindler," *Life,* Aug. 9 and Oct. 25, 1968. His remarks are at 118 *Cong. Rec.* H3266 (1972).

U.S. v. *Kenny,* 463 F.2d 1230 (1972).

10. Stranded in the Sludge
U.S. v. *Asbury Park,* 340 F. Supp. 555 (1972).

11. Stern's "French Connection"
For another account of the DeLouette case, see "L'Affaire du S.D.E.C.E.," *Paris Match,* 4 Dec. 1971. For a discussion of

the legal implications of the case, see Henri de Richemont's note, 13 *Harvard International Law Journal* 336 (1972).

12. Rattling Republican Skeletons

U.S. v. *Moraites*, 456 F.2d 435 (1972).

New Jersey, State Commission of Investigation, *Report on Investigation of the Office of the Attorney General of New Jersey* (1973).

U.S. v. *Butenko*, 384 F.2d 554 (1967); 394 U.S. (1969); 318 F. Supp. 66 (1970); *U.S.* v. *Ivanov*, 342 F. Supp. 928 (1972).

13. A Prosecutor's Philosophy

Stern's published works are "Prosecution of Local Political Corruption Under the Hobbs Act: The Unnecessary Distinction between Bribery and Extortion," 3 *Seton Hall Law Review* 1 (1971); and "Pre-Trial Preparation," *Student Lawyer*, October, 1972. For his views on a variety of issues, see the interview, "Herbert J. Stern: Professional Crimefighter," *Newark!*, January/February, 1971.

Appendix. Herbert Stern's Who's Who of New Jersey Politics

The title and format were suggested by Jerome Wilson.

ABOUT THE AUTHOR

PAUL HOFFMAN was born in Chicago, grew up there and received B.A. and M.A. degrees in political science from the University of Chicago. He worked as a reporter for the City News Bureau of Chicago and United Press International in Detroit. While covering the Manhattan criminal courts for the *New York Post,* he first met Herbert J. Stern. He has contributed articles to *New York* magazine, the *New York Times, Washington Monthly, Saturday Review, Village Voice* and other publications. He is the author of *Lions in the Street: The Inside Story of the Great Wall Street Law Firms.*

ABOUT THE AUTHOR